José Carlos Mariátegui
and the Rise of Modern Peru

Mariátegui at the Parque de la Exposición, Lima, 1928

JOSÉ CARLOS MARIÁTEGUI
AND THE
RISE OF MODERN PERU
1890-1930

Jesús Chavarría

UNIVERSITY OF NEW MEXICO PRESS
Albuquerque

Library of Congress Cataloging in Publication Data

Chavarría, Jesús, 1935–
   José Carlos Mariátegui and the rise of modern Peru.

   Bibliography: p. 221.
   Includes Index.
     1. Mariátegui, José Carlos, 1894–1930.   2. Communists—
Peru—Biography.   3. Peru—History.   4. Journalists—
Peru—Biography.   I. Title.
HX222.M38C45   335.43′092′4 [B]   78-21426
ISBN 0-8263-0507-5

Designed by Barbara J. Hoon

To

MY MOTHER AND FATHER

Tu xul ca zatmail ilil zubtalil etlahom tulacal.

("At the end of our loss of vision, and of our shame, everything shall be revealed.")

The Book of Chilam Balam de Chumayel

Preface

This history is a little overdue. I began work on it in the mid 1960s, but along the way I was interrupted by the movement among Chicanos to gain access to institutions of higher education and to create appropriate programs of studies.

By no means were all of those years lost time, however. The experience helped me immeasurably to understand more sympathetically events such as the student strike at San Marcos University in 1919, the anxieties of the Third World intellectuals awakening to a nationalist passion, and so many occurrences in the life of José Carlos Mariátegui.

Throughout those years, before I was able to get back to Mariátegui, many people helped me with locating research materials. It gives me great pleasure to acknowledge my appreciation to them here.

First I would like to mention Dr. Javier Mariátegui, son of the subject of this history, of Lima, who supplied me with countless citations and copies of materials as well as most of the photographic materials included in this work, and Professor Gustavo Beyhaut of Santiago de Chile, who sent me an important *Annales* source.

Another vital piece of evidence came to my attention through Michel Barton, a student at the University of California at Santa Barbara in the late 1960s who, it turned out, knew personally Dr. Jean Otten of Geneva, Switzerland. Dr. Otten had lived as a young man in the Mariátegui household, from December 1925 to July 1928, and had been quite close to the subject of this study.

There were many other people who assisted me in the original research for this project. When I lived in Peru from 1965 to 1967, and during a brief visit in 1968, I met not only Dr. Javier Mariátegui but also his mother Señora Anita Chiappe de Mariátegui, Ricardo Martínez de la Torre, Dr. Hugo Pesce, Humberto del Aguila, Dr. Jorge Basadre, Eudocio Ravines, Luciano Castillo, Héctor Merel, Antonio Navarro Madrid, Esteban Pavletich, and Julio Portocarrero. During long interviews, all remembered their personal contacts with Mariátegui with an uncanny vividness and sharpness. The great use I have made of information they gave me about Mariátegui and his turbulent era is an indication of my large indebtedness to them.

My debt to Dr. Jorge Basadre extends beyond his remembrance of Mariátegui. Anyone working on modern Peru starts with his monumental *Historia de la República del Perú*. But he influenced this study in several other respects as well.

Scattered throughout Basadre's voluminous works are countless Rembrandtesque *semblanzas*, or revealing portraits, of political leaders, businessmen, lawyers, doctors, and, of course, intellectuals of the time. Basadre himself is one of the key figures of the generation of 1919—which included Raúl Porras Barrenechea, Luis Alberto Sánchez, Víctor Raúl Haya de la Torre, César Vallejo, José Carlos Mariátegui, and so many others. Basadre also knew José de la Riva Agüero, Francisco García Calderón, and Víctor Andrés Belaúnde, prominent men of the generation of 1900, which Basadre's own generation displaced as the principal interpreters of Peru's history, culture, and national consciousness. Basadre's works helped me to realize that I should not focus strictly on Mariátegui, but seek to understand him within the context of an entire generation.

Another essential source was Professor Guillermo Rouillón, whose writings continue to appear. Rouillón's works are mentioned in the bibliography, and several interviews with him provided some of the many basic data on which I have relied. I am grateful for his amenable sharing of that information.

At the Departamento de Investigaciones Bibliográficas and the Sala Raúl Porras Barrenechea of the Biblioteca Nacional del Perú, its chief, Ms. Graciela Sanchez Cerro, extended every courtesy and support. In addition, her staff, including Cira Koechling, Lucía Tauro, Isabel Eguren, Irma García, and César Guiven, were at all times generous in their help. For their unfailing courtesy and efficiency I give thanks to them and to the staffs of the UCLA Graduate Library, the UCSB Library, and the University of San Marcos Main Library.

I am also greatly appreciative of the comments made by Professors Jorge Basadre, Eugene D. Genovese, Tulio Halperín-Donghi, Joseph Love, Luis Monguió, and Fredrick B. Pike, who read portions of the manuscript and made invaluable suggestions and corrections. Other readers such as Ms. Carol Crawford,

Russell Schoch, and Ms. Jean White helped edit early drafts of the manuscript and gave me great encouragement.

Finally, it gives me great pleasure to express my appreciation to Ms. Gloria J. Leitner for her outstanding and spirited editorial contribution to all facets of this work.

The Ford Foundation, through the UCLA Latin American Center, extended a one-year fellowship while I worked on this study as a doctoral dissertation. The Senate Committee on Faculty Research and the Graduate Division of the University of California at Santa Barbara made possible a second trip to Peru in the summer of 1968. On the same occasion, a travel grant from the American Philosophical Society supported a trip from Lima to Santiago de Chile, where I obtained copies of the nineteen Samuel Glusberg letters. To those institutions I extend my gratitude for their generous support.

Bonnie Chavarría was spared having to read the manuscript, but that is all she was spared. I hope she enjoys it now.

Contents

Introduction

La idea de la nación . . . es en ciertos períodos históricos
la encarnación del espíritu de libertad.[1]

On the whole historians have shown little interest in the problem of Latin American nationalism. The reader looking for material on the subject will find few studies available.

One result of this state of affairs is that the old stereotypes die hard or not at all. For instance, it is often thought that in Latin America we are not likely to find movements of national liberation or anticolonialist revolutionary struggles so common to twentieth-century experience in the Third World. That assumption is most commonly made because first, the nations of Latin America are considered part of the western world, (even though they are second cousins to the leading Atlantic nations); and second, these countries achieved their political independence from Spain well over a century and a half ago.

The myth of an independent Latin America has come under fire by Latin Americans themselves. Mention of the area's continuing colonialist dependency may be found scattered throughout nineteenth-century history and literature. But they remained rather isolated observations until the first decades of this century, when large numbers of nationalist intellectuals appeared and began to criticize and protest the continent's dependent status. Some of those radical intellectuals went on to organize anticolonialist mass movements.

Our aim here is to get as close as possible to the social perspective of the Latin Americans themselves, and in that way show how they came to understand their similarity with what they called the semicolonial world of Asia and Africa. The goal is to recover from the past a mind-set characteristic of the age: to analyze the social setting that produced the nationalist movement in Peru, describe the generations of intellectuals who nurtured the movement there, and focus primarily on one representative figure of that era.

1

José Carlos Mariátegui (1894–1930) was prominent among those Latin Americans (or Indo-Americans, as some liked to call themselves) who called into question the myth of national independence at the turn of the century.

In his own native Peru, Mariátegui remains recognized as one of the foremost interpreters of his age. Jorge Basadre first proposed in his classic text, *Perú: problema y posibilidad*, that Mariátegui had introduced a new "maturity" to the discussion of "social ideas" in that country. While before there had been "shouting, rhetoric, vagueness, and confusion," Basadre pointed out, Mariátegui brought analysis and interpretation to the nationalist movement. Our own efforts will be to account for how that happened, and to describe the nationalist design shaped so diligently by him.

What was the milieu within which Mariátegui emerged as a leading voice? Between 1870 and 1930, events had transformed Peruvian society to such a degree that we may refer to the era as a time of "the rise of the modern Peruvian nation." During that half-century or so, the accelerated arrival of modern western influences wrought great changes throughout the country. But modernization produced a contradictory result: the more the nation enjoyed progress, the greater became its dependence on the West, evident in the growing presence of foreign capital and the aping styles of the elites in the capital city, Lima.

The young José Carlos grew up during those very tumultuous years. By the time he reached his twenties, all the vital signs revealed just how much this dramatically evolving era had challenged him and shaped him. He had become a journalist, someone who was paid to probe constantly the ever-changing social surroundings.

Mariátegui succeeded as a journalist, but he also went on to become a champion of the cause of national liberation. Indeed, he served the campaign for nationhood with such vehemence that Basadre likened him to "a soul that mortifies itself."

Mariátegui's trial began the moment he identified his own fate with the fate of his country. And he arrived at this crossroads precisely because he lived at a time when the idea of nationhood loomed as the most widely discussed social and cultural question in the country.

Although he remained a frail and sensitive man throughout his lifetime, Mariátegui had a powerful impact on those around him. Even people in faraway places were affected by his work. Despite the fact that he knew Mariátegui only at a distance, Henri Barbusse once remarked, "Don't you know who Mariátegui is? Well . . . he's a new light in America; a new example of the American man."[2]

Not only did Mariátegui live during an era of exceptional dynamism and change, but he was also part of an extraordinary intellectual tradition, rich in other individuals of high talent. His own generation of 1919 and the preceding generation of 1900 are considered the two leading generations of intellectuals during the whole of Peru's national history. As Pablo Macera recently remarked, their ideas still retain their hegemony.[3] Indeed, since the 1920s there have not appeared many works in Peru to match those of the intellectuals who lived the prime of their lives during the years between 1870 and 1930.

For the most part, the works of these men have not yet been fully examined, let alone assimilated. If real understanding comes only after the event, perhaps it is at this point that we can begin to weigh the nature of those figures and events which so profoundly affected the course of twentieth-century Peruvian history.

PART ONE
The Social Setting

1

Birth of the
Modern Peruvian Nation, 1870–1919

No volverán quien sabe hasta cuando los tiempos de vivir
con dulzura.[1]

José Gálvez's *Una Lima que se va*, which evoked sweet remembrances of the vanishing colonial customs and manners of
the Peruvian capital, contributed a nostalgic flavor to the cen-
tennial celebrations of the Republic of Peru in 1921. At the same
time, its quaintly phrased recollections also rendered a general
interpretation of the country's first century of national independence.[2] The little book included an essay entitled "1895," in
which Gálvez proposed that that year marked the beginning of
the modernization of Peru.

Gálvez was not far off the mark in his assessment. The modern
age had not affected Peru to any great degree during the first
two quarters of the nineteenth century. Independence mainly
unleashed conflict; after the decisive Battle of Ayacucho (December 1824) the new republic quickly fell into a prolonged
period of disorder and internal war.

In spite of this violence and disarray, modernization did
gradually come to Peru. By mid century the country had developed some contact with the industrialized countries of the Atlantic, especially England. And by the late 1800s ties with the
industrial world had strengthened to the point that they had, as
Gálvez noted, "totally transformed" the social milieu of the capital.[3]

In this chapter we will trace how modern influences from
abroad affected Peru in the course of the 1800s and particularly
at the turn of the century. Our concern is chiefly to outline how
a dependent relationship unfolded between Peru and western
capitalism, and with the kind of impact this relationship had on
Peruvian society. In turn, the following chapter will trace how

Peruvian intellectuals responded to those very changes, especially from the 1870s onward.

José Carlos Mariátegui, born in 1894, is clearly very much a part of the story, even though he does not appear here as a protagonist. But his generation, and he himself, were clearly shaped, socially and intellectually, by the metamorphosis of which Gálvez wrote; when the "times of living with sweetness," to use Mariátegui's words, were swept away.

Neocolonialism and the Rise of the Bourgeoisie

Two major periods divide the Peruvian nineteenth century. Until the 1860s the country changed little from colonial times, but then followed an epoch of take-off extending into the 1900s. Here we will include only a brief sketch of the years 1820–70.

Peru faced an extraordinary array of social problems after independence, the most pressing one being the problem of economic recovery. It took the new republic several decades to renew its economic vigor, and Great Britain played a crucial part in that process (as it did throughout South America). Indeed, for well over a century before the revolutionary wars, Great Britain had been looking upon Spanish America as a strategic economic area. After the Spanish defeat, England proceeded to extend the sinews of modern economic life to the newly independent states: capital, technology, and markets for Britain's export staples. For instance, by the late 1820s Peru had floated the third largest Spanish American series of loans on the London money market.[4] Overall, however, Great Britain developed its expanding relationship with Peru slowly, although this period has been characterized, perhaps too sharply, as a "conquest" and "domination" of Peruvian commerce and finance.[5]

Actually Anglo-Peruvian commercial relations had begun even before independence. Between 1791 and 1795, already more than half of the 12,937,943 pounds sterling worth of goods arriving at Callao were non-Spanish in origin. By 1818, British vessels could enter Callao "if not with official permission, at least without any notable effort" being made to keep them out.[6] In 1819 the Port of Callao officially opened its doors to British trade for two years, and English traders could even settle in Peru, though they still had to deal through Spanish consignees.

Once the revolutionary wars began in Spanish America, Great Britain astutely exploited the opportunity to establish friendly relations with the potential new states. British diplomats skillfully shaped a foreign policy designed to secure national defense and advance national interests—offering little tangible aid to the revolutionaries but actively supporting the improvement of conditions for English commercial activity in South America.[7] De facto recognition was extended to the revolutionary governments in June 1822 when Britain began to recognize the flags of South American vessels seeking to enter British ports with their goods.[8] During the following years Foreign Secretary George Canning sent commissioners to various Latin American capitals, including Lima, to report on the advisability of de jure recognition.

Conversely, the fortunes of Spain and the Spaniards were collapsing. With the arrival of San Martín's liberation army, Spaniards became subject to severe persecution in Peru. In 1821, unmarried Spaniards were ordered to leave the country and forfeit half of their property, with the same restrictions being placed upon married men soon thereafter. One foreign visitor reported that by July 1822, "the ruin of the old Spaniards was complete."[9]

TABLE 1

Peruvian Government Revenue
(in pesos until 1862, in soles thereafter)

Year	From Guano	Total
1854–1855	4,300,000	9,941,404
1861–1862	16,318,536	20,763,034
1863–1864	18,541,332	23,053,332

Source: Levin, *The Export Economies*, p. 95

TABLE 2

British Imports of Peruvian Guano
(in thousands of tons)

1845	14.1	1848	64.2
1846	25.1	1849	73.6
1847	59.4	1850	95.1

Source: Mathew, "The Imperialism of Free Trade," p. 570

At the same time, Peruvians turned to the British for the essentials of production because they needed technology to repair heavily damaged mines and capital to resume their operation. At first, however, British capitalists invested relatively little in Peruvian mining, with the exception of the Pasco Peruvian Mining Company. In fact, until 1830 British bondholders extended capital primarily to the new Peruvian government.

Anglo-Peruvian trade expanded more rapidly in the early post-independence years. The British imported Peruvian goods, primarily precious metals—which accounted for the greater part of Peru's revenue during this period—but also small quantities of bark, cotton, wool, and hides.

Between 1830 and 1865, however, Peru's financial and commercial relations with Great Britain grew much more rapidly.[10] Expansion of the agrarian export sector and the beginning of steamship navigation on the Pacific Coast contributed to this rise in Anglo-Peruvian trade, but it was the export of guano that resulted in a virtual boom.

Guano was a fertilizer derived from long-accumulated bird droppings on the coastal islands, mainly the Chincha Islands, which contained century-old deposits. Production started out slowly in the 1840s but by the 1850s and 1860s had reached massive proportions. British involvement in the industry was mostly of a mercantile nature, and their purchases rapidly assumed an extraordinary volume: between 1855 and 1865 guano sales reached a higher level than any other South American product imported by Britain.[11]

Instead of revenue from guano sales bolstering the Peruvian government, however, it had a disastrous effect on public finance. Prompted by the illusion of an unending flow of money from the export of guano, the government recklessly increased its foreign borrowing. Between 1861 and 1875 Peru floated government paper in London in the amount of 42.7 million pounds sterling,[12] loans that "amounted to only 1.6 million pounds less than the total for those floated by all the other Latin American countries."[13]

In addition to encouraging foreign loans, guano revenue also led the government to bear the enormous expense of financing a central railroad. Henry Meiggs, a North American adventurer who arrived in Peru in January 1868, cleverly exploited the mystique of the railroad as a symbol of progress and successfully prevailed upon Colonel José Balta, then president, to invest heavily in railroad construction.[14] Eventually Meiggs and his ragged army built the spectacular Andean railroad, a truly fantastic engineering feat.[15] The Meiggs operation, however, also produced gross governmental favoritism, corruption, and rampant patronage, which, together with a primitive accounting system, kept the public treasury in a ruinous state.[16] Guano paid for the railroad and all of the pilfering accompanying its construction, and thereby laid the groundwork for the government's eventual bankruptcy.

The private sector fared much better than the public as a result of the guano trade. Some large fortunes were made at home and abroad, and, as a result, investment capital became available for the development of export agriculture on the coast and service and import businesses in Lima.[17]

In effect, the guano industry, along with the loans and trade that preceded the industry's rise, laid the foundations for the neocolonial relationship that developed between Peru and the outside world between 1820 and 1870. In the course of time Peru had developed

> considerable dependence on British merchants for her overseas trade, on the British market for her sales of guano, wool, nitrate of soda, etc., on British factories for her supplies of textiles and metalware, and on the London money market for the flotation of loans.[18]

At the turn of the century what had been lacking up to 1870 finally occurred—direct "placement of British capital in the agricultural and mining sector," and, increasingly, the infusion of North American capital as well.[19] With the investment of large sums of capital in the export agricultural and mining sectors, Peru reached the take-off stage and the onset of modernization.

The Neocolonial Bourgeoisie and Reformist Nationalism

Parallel to the growth of neocolonial dependence, there emerged new comprador elites who vigorously supported Peru's growing economic ties with Western Europe. Superbly led by

Manuel Pardo, scion of one of Peru's oldest and wealthiest
families, in 1871 the new bourgeoisie came together to organize
the most important political organization of the nineteenth century, El Partido Civil.[20]

Once Pardo and the *civilistas* took office, they proposed a
dynamic program of national development including economic,
administrative, and educational reforms. To be sure, their concern for Peru's progress and the strengthening of the nation was
tied to class interests of the highest order. We are reminded of
Professor Tawney's remark to the effect that "nationalism was an
economic force before nationality was a political fact" in Western
Europe. Certainly this observation seems to apply to Peru in the
last half of the nineteenth century.[21]

The 1870s, initially so promising, soon turned into a decade of
dramatic reversals for the civilistas and the country as a whole.
Pardo was faced with an economic crisis he himself had predicted a decade before in his prophetic *Estudios sobre la Provin-
cia de Jauja*. Guano sales collapsed early in the 1870s, as a result
of economic contraction in Great Britain and elsewhere. In the
past, the government had handled the annual deficits by drawing
advances on guano sales. But Pardo was unable to resort to such
standard practices, and in his first budget of 1872 he faced a
deficit of 8 million pesos. From then on matters only worsened,[22] until in January 1876 he suspended payment on the
foreign debt and the government went into default.[23]

Pardo's administration nevertheless managed some significant
achievements. Modernization of the government's accounting
system and the taking of the first national census since 1791
counted as two definite pluses. Moreover, efforts were made to
secularize San Marcos University in Lima and to establish new
professional institutes, such as the School of Agriculture and the
School of Civil and Mining Engineers. Gripped by Euromania,
the government also tried to entice European immigrants.[24]

Pardo could not, however, stem the overwhelming tide of the
depression. And so an opposition surged, the term oligarchy appeared for the first time in the vernacular of the capital, and the
civilistas were swept out of office.[25]

From then on the situation deteriorated quickly. Pardo's successor, General Mariano I. Prado, proved himself fully incapable
of handling Peru's dual dilemma of the 1870s: the domestic crisis

and the outbreak of war with Chile (the War of the Pacific, 1879–83).[26] The war, in effect, dealt the coup de grâce to the reformist dreams of the civilistas.

After the Chileans' departure, the military strongman General Andrés Avelino Cáceres took over. Upon him fell the task of making peace with the foreign bondholders, involving loans going back to the earliest years of the republic. Finally, the Grace Contract (1889) broke the logjam in the negotiations, and Peru agreed to to turn over the state-owned railroads to British bondholders for sixty-five years, in addition to making other major concessions.[27]

Organizing themselves as the Peruvian Corporation, Ltd. (1891), the bondholders henceforth controlled the principal corporate entity in the country. Soon followed the direct investment of British capital in the agricultural and mining sectors.[28]

Although the economic issue had been seemingly resolved, a political one remained—the presence of Cáceres and his military cronies in government. The perfect foil to remove them from power was none other than the diminutive but persistent adventurer, Nicolás de Piérola. Everyone recognized this, even the civilistas, who had been Piérola's bitter rivals. Civilian groups unanimously rallied around Piérola and supported the mass insurrection, the Revolution of 1895, which rid the national government of military intervention.

Progress and Prosperity in a Neocolonial Regime

Piérola assumed power with the broadest political concensus held by any president since independence.[29] His support derived primarily from the Partido Demócrata of the conservative creole and mestizo middle classes—the not-too-powerful Limeños and provincial folk who took great pride in Hispanic traditions and made their living from small landholdings, modest trade, or the liberal professions. The civilistas also gave Piérola their calculated support.

For the next four years Piérola governed constitutionally and embarked upon a program of modernization consistent with that initiated by Pardo. Setting out to create an *estado técnico*, a nation run by efficient experts, he assigned administrative reform high priority.[30] In 1896 he created the Ministry of Development (Ministerio de Fomento), with departments of planning, industry, welfare, and public works (which concentrated mainly on the modernization and development of the capital).

The currency situation also cried out for reform; defective paper had circulated widely during the war, and, combined with the fall of silver, this precipitated a drop of Peru's currency by some 30 percent on the international market between 1881 and 1892.[31] Prodded by the civilistas, Piérola adopted the gold standard and launched other banking reforms they sought.

Even though Piérola in effect capitulated to the civilistas in terms of policy, politically he was never fully accepted by them. All the while, though supporting him publicly, the civilistas were engineering the return of their own party to power. And in the end, Piérola's organization, or lack of it, and the strength of the *demócratas* could not match the cunning of the civilistas and their new leader, Manuel Candamo. Candamo had acknowledged that only a "man on horseback" could remove the military from power in 1895 and thus committed the party to a rapprochement with Piérola at that time, but this did not imply a permanent reconciliation.[32]

Wealthy, highly talented, and partial to a quiet but effective style, Candamo cultivated *civilismo's* patrician ideal better than most of his peers.[33] To be a civilista during Peru's *belle epoque* meant belonging to the cream of society. Made up of the leading coastal elites, the Partido Civil virtually represented an "official class." If through skill and good fortune an outsider gained access to their ranks, he might or might not gain acceptance in their society. Basadre has described them thusly:

> Generally (though with some notable exceptions) the great urban proprietors belonged to their party; the great hacendados, producers of sugar and cotton; the men of prosperous businesses; the lawyers of the most prestigious firms; the medical doctors with the best clientele; the university professors; in general, the greater part of those people who had done well in life. This ruling class was made up of the gentlemen of the city, some of whom had ties with the countryside—something in the order of a local adaptation of the style of the English gentleman. They had an intense club life, lived in homes opulently furnished in Empire

style, with sumptuous rugs and draperies—signs of a time when fresh air was not considered a desirable good—and they dressed in dark clothing fashioned by the French tailors of the capital. They lived in a world of happiness, integrated through marriage to form a small group of families. The companions of childhood games were later friends in school and the university; and, in the latter, the chairs in jurisprudence, literature, history, and philosophy were theirs with little effort.[34]

Like the best of the civilistas, Candamo worked prudently and did not break abruptly with Piérola. Both agreed on a compromise candidate to succeed to the presidency in 1899. But by wresting control of the cabinet in 1900, during the administration of Eduardo López de Romaña, the civilistas tacitly broke with Piérola. In December of the same year they humiliatingly defeated his harmless bid for a seat on Lima's municipal council. The following year the civilistas gained control of the Senate, and by September 1902, when they took control of the Junta Electoral Nacional, they held Piérola in checkmate.[35]

Piérola, who in the meantime had lost the crucial support of Guillermo E. Billinghurst and of the Huánuco caudillo Augusto Durand because of his dalliance with Candamo, soon found himself in an untenable position. When the 1903 elections rolled around all Piérola could do to save face was "to abstain," and the civilistas, having gained control of the bureaucracy as well, won the presidency without opposition.

Candamo set his government on a firm course of progressive reform, placing young men, such as his proteges José Pardo and Augusto B. Leguía, in positions of leadership. They, along with a small but determined wing of the civilistas, helped him to remain faithful to Manuel Pardo's earlier program of national reform.[36]

Candamo's election represented a great victory, but the triumph came almost too late. Ill when he reached the presidency, he died nine months after coming to office. It was left to Pardo and Leguía to carry on Candamo's legacy as best they could, and the two men presided over Peru's precarious transition from the nineteenth to the twentieth century.

Meanwhile Peru's economy, in response to the sharp rise of foreign investments, had begun to boom after the political rapprochement of 1895. The British were most active, investing in external bonds, Peruvian Corporation, Ltd. bonds and shares (after the War of the Pacific, la Peruvian accounted for 45–90 percent of total British investments), Lima municipal bonds, the Northwestern of Peru Railway, and in sugar estates, mining properties, public utilities, and manufacturing.

American investors also turned to Peruvian opportunities. The first major American acquisition, the Cerro de Pasco Corporation (1901–2), joined la Peruvian as the second giant foreign holding of the country's economy.[37] In a matter of a few years Cerro de Pasco alone accounted for about 90 percent of the total mining production of the country, solely on the basis of its two excavations at Morococha and Cerro de Pasco.[38]

Americans made another major acquisition in 1916. The London & Pacific Petroleum Company (originally incorporated in London in 1889) sold its interests, made up mainly of the oil fields of La Brea and Pariñas in Piura, to the International Petroleum Corporation, a Toronto subsidiary of Standard Oil of New Jersey.[39] In two years' time, Peru nearly overtook Japan as the eighth largest oil-producing country in the world.

In addition, Americans invested in cotton and sugar estates. All told, one estimate placed total British investments at about 121.5 million dollars and the United States total at about 50 million dollars by 1915.[40]

New products, such as copper and petroleum, joined the growing list of Peruvian exports.[41] Not many years after the discovery of vanadium in 1904, Peru produced nearly 70 percent of the world's output. One estimate placed the total value of mining production in 1886 at 423,000 Peruvian pounds. By 1916, the total had climbed to 8,500,000.[42]

Similar developments took place in the agricultural sector. The sugar- and cotton-producing haciendas of the northern departments of La Libertad and Lambayeque recovered fairly rapidly following the War of the Pacific. Within a few years expanding sugar-producing haciendas absorbed not only the lessons of modern technology, but also the land of nearby smaller estates. By the early 1900s, the brothers Larco Herrera, the Cartavio Sugar Company, and the Sociedad Agrícola Casa Grande Ltda., had become, through consolidation, the "big three fiefs" of a northern sugar aristocracy.[43]

TABLE 3
Peruvian Imports and Exports

Year	Imports	Exports	Total	Year	Imports	Exports	Total
1877	Lp. 4,281,714	Lp. 8,601,902	Lp. 12,883,617	1906	Lp. 5,010,496	Lp. 5,695,879	Lp. 10,706,375
1887	1,244,663	1,275,391	2,520,055	1907	5,519,751	5,744,544	11,264,296
1890	1,885,435	1,819,650	3,685,035	1908	5,273,078	5,478,941	10,752,020
1891	2,148,577	1,752,576	3,901,153	1909	4,298,627	6,492,670	10,791,298
1892	1,968,722	2,513,201	4,481,923	1910	4,980,697	7,074,076	12,054,773
1893	1,123,710	1,928,025	3,151,735	1911	5,438,245	7,422,027	12,860,273
1894	943,069	1,100,000	2,043,069	1912	5,140,338	9,438,581	14,578,920
1895	1,040,499	1,406,250	2,446,749	1913	6,088,776	9,137,780	15,226,557
1896	1,677,576	2,095,140	3,772,717	1914	4,827,930	8,767,790	13,595,720
1897	1,612,862	2,779,357	4,392,219	1915	3,095,544	11,521,807	14,617,352
1898	1,929,727	3,027,477	4,957,204	1916	8,683,150	16,541,063	25,224,213
1899	1,873,494	3,072,591	4,946,085	1917	13,502,851	18,643,414	32,146,276
1900	2,317,150	4,497,999	6,815,150	1918	9,705,113	19,972,595	29,677,708
1901	2,717,107	4,318,776	7,035,884	1919	12,203,839	26,899,422	39,103,262
1902	3,428,283	3,703,971	7,132,255	1920	18,358,223	35,304,155	53,662,379
1903	3,783,380	3,857,753	7,641,134	1921	16,669,188	16,660,484	33,329,672
1904	4,357,338	4,066,639	8,423,978	1922	10,592,554	18,692,870	29,285,424
1905	4,357,696	5,757,350	10,115,047	1923	14,132,307	23,950,987	38,083,204

Sources: *Extracto estadístico del Perú* (Lima, 1920) and *Estadística del comercio exterior* for later years

Meanwhile the haciendas in the central and southern highlands were also expanding—the result, explained Chevalier, of
"local history and world conjuncture." Coastal and global demand for agricultural and mining products unleashed an intensely competitive and outright land-grabbing movement in the
sierra.[44] Elaborating on episodes related in José María Ar-
guedas's novel, *Yawar fiesta*, Chevalier focused on Puquio, a
small market town in the southern department of Ayacucho, as
an example of the acquisitive, expansionary trend sweeping
through the Andean highlands in the early twentieth century. As
soon as the *mistis* (whites or mestizos) discovered that huge profits could be made from selling livestock on the coast, they resorted to "fraud, guile or violence" to increase their landholdings, enclosing in the process the hitherto open grazing lands of
the vast *puna*.

Spectacular growth in mining and agriculture was paralleled
by similar developments in finance. Peruvian banking leaped
forward thanks largely to the efforts of José Payán, an enterpris-
ing Cuban emigré. It was Payán who merged the locally owned
Banco del Callao with a branch of the London Bank of Mexico
and South America in 1897, to create the Banco del Perú y
Londrés.[45] With capital of 2 million pounds sterling (the stock
was mostly held by British and French banks), the new institution soon became the most important banking house in Peru and
acted as the government's fiduciary agent.

Industry and trade naturally also felt the impact of the new
changes. The Sociedad Industrial Santa Catalina, organized by
Bartolomé Boggio, Mariano I. Prado y U., and Juan Manuel
Peña Costa in 1890, launched modern textile manufacturing in
Peru. Eventually five factories operated in Lima, one in
Arequipa, and another in Ica. Four other factories produced
woolen goods. Five years later, the Santa Catalina gave Lima's
industry a major push forward by applying electrical power to
production. On July 18, 1895, the Empresa Transmisora de
Fuerza Eléctrica made its first transmission to the Santa Catalina
factory. Subsequently, the Santa Catalina and Empresa Transmisora pooled their resources and, under the direction of
Mariano I. Prado y U., organized the Empresa Eléctrica Santa
Rosa, contracted by the government in 1899 to replace gas lighting in the streets. With the organization of the Empresas Eléc-

TABLE 4
Peruvian Imports by Countries of Origin

Country of Origin	1913	1918	1919	1920	1921	1922	1923	Average per cent of total for seven years
North America:								
United States	1,755,252	5,268,657	7,549,655	10,168,938	8,246,514	4,212,971	5,403,614	49.1
Canada	—	64,790	—	35,849	2,321	474	115,999	.3
Mexico	3,555	10	3,485	6,632	91,145	3,147	—	.2
Central America	12,587	107,395	65,279	116,958	202,245	38,496	32,372	.8
West Indies	33,183	30,351	27,405	59,799	38,491	2,709	9,432	.2
South America:								
Argentina	- 2,729	43,646	70,422	456,921	24,330	414,990	520,085	1.7
Bolivia	273	7,191	5,806	20,801	10,726	6,890	1,597	(1)
Chile	213,077	716,710	- 682,631	1,039,877	1,028,148	407,606	414,628	5.2
Ecuador	17,591	88,433	71,875	126,238	224,609	126,807	128,902	.9
Other	18,532	54,024	58,332	160,785	201,365	98,852	51,332	.7
Europe:								
Great Britain	1,598,606	1,566,387	1,645,947	2,694,196	2,275,110	2,024,903	2,675,690	16.6
France	280,492	134,836	153,018	546,861	633,414	323,394	324,551	2.8
Spain	73,147	203,290	278,139	441,060	370,284	143,032	180,345	1.9
Italy	254,473	138,370	111,616	411,235	491,921	300,945	542,175	2.6
Belgium	384,139	86	—	80,970	180,613	172,415	312,754	1.3
Germany	1,055,975	441	112	312,986	740,980	1,146,166	1,405,871	5.3
Other	27,524	35,229	33,928	297,844	316,155	195,744	201,763	1.3
Asia:								
China	158,368	370,942	365,233	580,052	685,219	373,549	364,383	3.3
Japan	12,938	273,035	316,908	337,596	278,490	190,820	151,780	1.8
India	56,441	472,664	514,975	314,557	13,008	140,443	211,994	1.9
Oceania:								
Australia	129,895	52,580	181,035	88,109	576,982	256,639	38,447	1.5
Not specified	—	76,036	68,039	59,960	37,114	11,562	8,547	.3
Total	6,088,777	9,705,113	12,203,840	18,358,224	16,669,188	10,592,554	13,096,261	—

[1]Negligible

Source: W. E. Dunn, *Peru, A Commercial and Industrial Handbook*, U.S. Dept. of Commerce (Washington, D.C., 1925), p. 283

TABLE 5

Peruvian Exports by Countries of Destination

Exported to—	1913 Thousands of Peruvian pounds	1913 Per cent of total	1917 Thousands of Peruvian pounds	1917 Per cent of total	1918 Thousands of Peruvian pounds	1918 Per cent of total	1919 Thousands of Peruvian pounds	1919 Per cent of total
United States	3,033	33.2	10,942	58.7	9,299	46.6	12,499	46.5
Great Britain	3,403	37.2	3,793	20.3	6,334	31.7	8,441	31.4
Chile	1,203	13.2	2,440	13.1	2,527	12.7	3,232	12.0
Argentina	2	(¹)	108	.6	575	2.9	608	2.3
Germany	610	6.6	—	—	—	—	51	.2
France	322	3.5	87	.5	14	.1	385	1.4
Canada	—	—	157	.8	—	—	414	1.5
Belgium	250	2.7	—	—	—	—	2	(¹)
Bolivia	131	1.4	373	2.0	370	1.8	476	1.8
Japan	2	(¹)	16	.1	69	.3	91	.3
Other countries	182	2.2	727	3.9	785	4.0	700	2.6
Total	9,138	100.0	18,643	100.0	19,973	100.0	26,899	100.0

Exported to—	1920 Thousands of Peruvian pounds	1920 Per cent of total	1921 Thousands of Peruvian pounds	1921 Per cent of total	1922 Thousands of Peruvian pounds	1922 Per cent of total	1923 Thousands of Peruvian pounds	1923 Per cent of total
United States	16,265	46.1	6,539	39.2	6,583	35.2	9,518	39.7
Great Britain	12,682	35.9	5,806	34.8	6,592	35.3	7,950	33.2
Chile	3,214	9.1	1,938	11.6	1,691	9.0	2,098	8.8
Argentina	1	(¹)	803	4.8	1,093	5.8	875	3.7
Germany	15	.2	94	.6	392	2.1	725	3.0
France	840	2.3	49	.3	194	1.0	78	.3
Canada	88	.2	13	.1	347	1.9	716	3.0
Belgium	140	.4	68	.4	201	1.1	293	1.2
Bolivia	413	1.2	242	1.5	221	1.2	278	1.1
Japan	102	.3	115	.1	36	.2	17	.1
Other countries	1,544	4.3	904	6.6	1,343	7.2	1,402	5.9
Total	35,304	100.0	16,661	100.0	18,693	100.0	23,950	100.0

¹Negligible.

Source: Dunn, *Peru, A Commercial and Industrial Handbook*, p. 279

tricas Asociadas on August 1, 1906, Peru decidedly entered the electrical age.[46] Urban commerce also advanced, but, as in most South American countries, businesses remained in foreign hands. Italians dominated food merchandising; the French specialized in retail sales, ready-made clothing, silks, and luxury items; and the English concentrated on the export-import trade.[47]

Insurance companies were an exception to the usual pattern of foreign control—they were financed by national capital.[48] But they, too, including the Internacional de Seguros (1895), Compañía de Seguros "Rimac" (1896), and La Nacional and La Popular (1904), grew and prospered during this period. Leguía had founded the Rimac, and its board of directors included Candamo and Pardo. Between 1913 and 1916 the company paid annual dividends ranging from 30 to 35 percent.

All in all, then, the Peruvian economy underwent a period of great expansion and prosperity during these years between 1895 and 1908, resulting in what has been called the *belle epoque*. For the most part the country enjoyed an uninterrupted favorable balance of trade, and modernization swept the provinces and the capital.[49]

The face of Lima reflected the new spirit of the times. With the opening of the Avenida 9 de diciembre began the progressive transformation of the haciendas ringing the capital into working and middle class barrios.[50] Public electric lighting appeared in 1902, and two years later the first automobiles were seen chugging around. By 1906 a tram line had been built to shuttle city dwellers about. Postal statistics add to the picture: between 1901 and 1905 domestic and foreign mail rose by a total of 7.8 million pieces.[51]

But behind the apparent high times of the *belle epoque*, trouble was brewing. By the time the critical years of 1918–19 rolled around, the era of progress and prosperity had long been displaced from center stage.

The Crisis of Modern Peru

The wave of modernization and progress carried with it seeds of tension and disillusionment. Discontent flourished as the political elites pursued their own interests at the expense of the

Peruvian masses. Mostly, the elites deprecated native customs, imitated foreign styles, and governed aristocratically.[52] On the whole, their nationalist vision was inspired by a foreign model of development: they hoped to make of Peru a modern nation using the same cloth and patterns as the United States, Great Britain, or France.

Mounting unrest among the working and middle classes and the indigenous peoples can be traced directly to several practices common to Peruvian businessmen. As Charles W. Sutton, an American engineer who arrived in Peru in the early 1900s, pointed out, entrepreneurs generally followed three basic principles: applying technology and the factory system to the hacienda for mass production of single crops using cheap labor; selling abroad for gold, but paying labor at home in silver or depreciated paper; and exploiting natural resources for export.[53]

Almost overnight brutalizing modern economic techniques were unleashed upon the inhabitants of the Andes. Long accustomed to traditional production methods and stable, communal social relations, the Indians found their world turned upside down in the wake of the great agrarian and social revolution that had been triggered in the highlands. The prosperity and progress of the early twentieth century did indeed stimulate economic expansion and development in the sierra, but it did so at the expense of the indigenous communities. As a result, a wave of collective rage and rural revolts broke out in the early century.[54]

In the meantime, virtually identical events were taking place on the northern sugar-producing coast. Large-scale recruitment of Indian labor from the sierra increased as the northern plantations expanded and modernized in the late 1890s. Soon enough native rural proletariat emerged expressing dissatisfaction, and violence followed because of the oppressive working conditions prevalent on the plantations. After 1910, widespread labor disturbances increasingly threatened the hitherto untroubled world of the hacendados.

A demographic shift contributed to the unleashing of the newly restive social classes. According to the census of 1876, Peru had a population of 2.67 million, of which 13.7 percent— or 371,195 people—were considered "white," 58 percent were classed as Indian, and 24 percent were counted as mestizos. Comparison of the 1876 figures to those of 1791, the year of the last previous official census, reveals that in the interim "the Indian caste [had] . . . gained members more rapidly than the mestizo caste." The greatest population increase of this period took place in the central highlands from Huaylas to Huancavelica. But after 1876, the trend was reversed; the mestizo world along the coast, reflecting the growth of neocolonial modernization, became the fastest growing sector.[55]

Between 1890 and 1900 the population of Lima rose by 11,803 inhabitants (from 114,733 to 126,536); between 1900 and 1910 by 19,390 (almost double the previous decennial increase); and between 1910 and 1920 by 27,081 (from 145,926 to 173,007).[56] Eventually, the shift of people from country to towns and cities produced an urban, mestizo, working-class movement and growing mestizo middle-class unrest.

Lima's newspapers reflected the impact of modernization on all classes. Beginning around 1900 the city's old newspapers improved their technology, expanded their coverage to carry more national news, and professionalized their reportorial and managerial staffs.[57] As a result, *La Prensa* (demócrata-liberal) and *El Comercio* (civilista-independiente) turned into big-city newspapers. The new middle class claimed its own newspaper, *El Tiempo*, while workers read anarchist *Los Parias* (1904) and *La Protesta* (1902). Growth of these newspapers gave rise to the first public expressions made against the urban ills bred by industrial progress.

The economic situation began to turn very sour by 1913. Sugar, selling at $4.08 per English hundredweight in 1912, dropped in the following year to a low of $2.39. Cotton, the second most important export, held its own in 1913, and copper remained at a satisfactory though by no means "highly prosperous condition."[58]

But World War I had a dramatic impact on the recession. At first the war produced a drastic decrease in customs revenue; between 1913 and 1914 import receipts dropped by 47 percent.[59] But the war's effect on the export sector was more complex. As war-generated demand for Peruvian exports rose, the prosperity of the exporters grew to boom proportions. The working and middle classes, however, suffered from food shortages and rising prices as lands previously used for producing comestibles increasingly shifted over to sugar and cotton production.[60]

In 1913, exports exceeded imports by almost 20 percent, and five years later by almost 100 percent. As the trend continued, food prices skyrocketed throughout the country. The general price index steadily climbed from a base of 100 in 1913 to 225.1 in 1920. In Lima the food price index during that period rose from 100 to 208. Meanwhile, wages remained frozen.

Predictably, as the hardships increased, more and more workers turned to working-class organizations. Anarcho-syndicalists had started organizing in Peru in the late 1890s; by 1915 they claimed two important centers of influence, in Lima and northern Trujillo. Discontent in the north was rife among sugar workers by 1917. After subsiding momentarily, working-class unrest burst forth in 1918–19 with renewed vigor.[61]

As we will see, in view of the changing circumstances, Mariátegui and other intellectuals like him became deeply involved with the pressing social issues of the day and with the national question. Indeed, Mariátegui witnessed and supported a growing alliance of workers and students at San Marcos University. By then, the genteel character of the university student body had undergone a great change as enrollment climbed from 789 in 1907 to 1,331 by 1917, with most of the new students coming from the emerging middle class.[62]

Amidst the growing public unease over economic conditions, the government found itself on the political defensive. The civilistas, who retired Piérola in 1903, had presided over the government, on the whole, until 1919. But they did not enjoy an undisturbed hegemony; in fact, the major threat to their rule appeared within their own ranks.

José Pardo, who succeeded Candamo in 1904, had governed during four prosperous years. But his successor Augusto B. Leguía, bitterly opposed by the most conservative factions, faced a very different situation. Indeed, Leguía found himself confronted by the antagonistic *bloque* within his own party (organized as the Partido Civil Independiente in 1912), which fought him to a draw.

In 1912 the split civilistas threw the national elections to the populist caudillo without a party, Guillermo E. Billinghurst. Billinghurst, however, rather quickly infuriated the powers-that-were, inviting in response the military coup of February 4, 1914.[63] After the coup, *el bloque* brought back José Pardo from

Paris to rule over a Peru vastly different from the one he had left in 1908.

Meanwhile the progressive leaders of civilismo, men like Javier Prado y Ugarteche and Manuel Vicente Villarán, advocated reform. But as circumstances turned politically adverse for their class, they found themselves isolated within their own party. Pardo maintained a semblance of peace and a precarious balance within the party after 1915 by siding with the conservatives while seeking to maintain the face of a progressive leader.[64]

By late 1918 and early 1919, civilismo's fate had been sealed. In effect the party was swallowed up by its own history, and its demise was swift and neat. It was executed by the civilistas' old nemesis Leguía, the black sheep of the party, who had been living abroad (interestingly, Pardo had gone to Paris; Leguía had chosen London). Leguía returned for the 1918 elections to whip the civilistas badly at their own game: first he defeated their lackluster candidate, Antenor Aspíllaga, at the polls (no mean feat in itself), and then assured himself an unchallenged presidency by leading a perfectly carried out, bloodless coup.[65] He then moved to dissolve the Congress and make himself a dictator by shrewdly redistributing power to insure his own longevity (his rule this time lasted eleven years).

Leguía came to power with a broad design for the modernization of Peru. Harboring no illusions about democratic processes or about his people, Leguía insisted that a state's authority must be adapted to "the ethnic, historical, and sociological conditions of a people."[66] Theories and principles were of little import in a society of "Indians and semi-literates"; strong men must rule in such a situation. Leguía therefore promised to lay the groundwork for a dynamic, progressive nation run by *hombres nuevos* from the middle class,[67] who, for the most part, were enthusiastic about such prospects.

He also concentrated his efforts on attracting foreign investors to Peru. Pledging that "foreign capital will be given facilities and opportunities for the development of Peruvian revenues such as have never been accorded before," over the years he lived up to his promise.[68]

Leguía's grand design for national development aspired to nothing less than the creation of a *Patria Nueva,* the building of a new nation. This placed him in the mainstream of the reformist nationalist tradition that had held sway since the 1870s among the country's leading elites. But at the core of this tradition there was the recurrent conflict between Peru's growing dependence, stemming from the manner in which capitalist modernization took place, and a rising demand for national liberation.

TABLE 6

Foreign Investments in Peru
(Public Issues, Nominal Values)

	1900	1913	1925
Great Britain	$110,224,240[1]	$133,292,000	$125,000,000
United States	10,000,000[2]	35,000,000	90,000,000
Italy	...	...	40,000,000
Germany	...[3]	...	22,000,000
France	25,000,000	17,000,000[4]	10,000,000

[1]Rippy's figures, given in pounds sterling, have been converted to dollars at a rate of 5:1.

[2]The best available figures are for 1909, involving mostly railways.

[3]Statistical data on the distribution of Germany's foreign investments for 1900 and 1913 are incomplete. Most were in Europe; those in Latin America mainly in Argentina and to a lesser extent in Brazil, Chile, Venezuela, and Mexico.

[4]The original figure in Rippy has been converted at the rate of 3 francs to the dollar.

Sources: Dunn, *Peru, A Commercial and Industrial Handbook,* p. 261; Cleona Lewis, *America's Stake in International Investments* (Washington, D.C., 1938), p. 609; J. Fred Rippy, "British Investments in Latin America, End of Year 1900," *Inter American Economic Affairs* (1950): 18; J. Fred Rippy, "French Investments in Latin America," *Inter American Economic Affairs* (1948): 62; Max Winkler, *Investments of United States Capital in Latin America* (Boston, 1929), pp. 275, 280; and William Woodruff, *Impact of Western Man* (New York, 1966), p. 152

2

The Intellectuals and the
National Question, 1870–1919

En estos pueblos la idea de la nación no ha cumplido aún
su trayectoria ni ha agotado su misión histórica.[1]

At first the intellectuals of Peru welcomed modernization with
open arms, like everyone else. They looked favorably upon progressive change, especially the promise of science and technology. But the intellectuals were also among the first to sense that
modernization aggravated wounds inherited from the past, and
created new ones.

In their encounter with their country they asked such questions as: What is Modern Peru? Who are the Peruvians? Such
considerations of society and consciousness led to a dialogue
about national identity that was central to the intellectual milieu
at the turn of the century, and out of that concern was produced
an incomparable nationalist literature. They discovered why the
idea of the Peruvian nation, as Mariátegui put it in later years,
had not yet "finished its trajectory or exhausted its historic mission." A member of the intellectual generation of 1919,
Mariátegui inherited his own nationalist perspective as much
from the intellectuals of the generation of 1900 as well as from
those who much earlier had initiated a nationalist revolt.[2]

González Prada and the Revolt of the Seventies

In large part the seeds of modern Peruvian nationalism were
sown by the romantic movement of the nineteenth century.
While the social romanticism of Saint Simon did not reach Peruvian shores, the development of literary romanticism on the continent brought with it a sense of local place and time and an
interest in the past.[3] For instance, Sebastián Lorente, a Spanish
scholar who arrived in Peru in 1842 and became one of the

27

country's leading romantic writers, introduced the study of Peruvian history at San Marcos University in the 1860s.

Literary movements alone, however, did not unleash the nationalist upsurge of the 1870s. It took an event with the intensity of the Chilean occupation during the War of the Pacific (1879)—in Luis Alberto Sánchez's words, "nuestro año terrible"—to do that. And no one better personified the bitter war experience and its effect on Peruvian writers than Manuel González Prada (1848–1918),[4] a blue-eyed creole of aristocratic mien, who rebelled against the traditionalism of the Hispanic legacy with a nationalism that wore the cloak of a succession of philosophies—romanticism, positivism and naturalism, and eventually modernism and anarchism.

González Prada seemed to be born for the role of slayer of convention. While growing up he shattered virtually every canon long held dear by his class and kind.[5] Unlike the majority of his peers, who could not have thought of a more excruciating torture, he enjoyed German and English and their respective literary traditions, along with chemistry and mathematics. He rejected the careers picked out for him by his parents—first the clergy and then law—choosing letters instead.[6]

During his early twenties, while he was living at one of the small family haciendas,[7] González Prada first became aware, through direct observation, of how the country's native poor people lived in rural backwardness. With that experience began his maturity, and his emerging social and political consciousness was sharpened too by the steady stream of books and newspapers (including Marx's *Capital*) that he received from Europe. In all, these were crucial years which inspired him as a radical poet and engendered a love of his country that is so beautifully evident in the *Baladas peruanas*. Only occasionally did he visit Lima during those years of the early 1870s.

But the country's economic crisis and its mishandling in the capital affected Gonzalez Prada more and more—leading to his writing a stinging attack on the politicos, the army, and the church which appeared as a preface to Aureliano Villarán's *Cuartos de hora*. Following that initial blast against the powers-that-were, he began to rally support among a few disenchanted writers and students. When the War of the Pacific broke out, he—like many others—quickly joined the militia.

Peru's ignominious defeat at the hands of the Chileans filled him with bile and nausea. So he retreated to his home, refusing to set foot outside its doors while the Chilean occupation lasted. Eventually his anger gave way to a prolonged depression, and he suffered from a profound indifference "toward things and even toward friends." Gradually his emotions subsided and his head cleared. Feeling that he had become "another man," meant, he said, "that all of my past had died."[8] From then on social criticism and protest became the most important part of his life.

Other writers shared González Prada's feelings of national betrayal and political discontent; so much so that it brought them together to form the Bohemia Literaria, which in 1886 became the Círculo Literario. Usually the group held their discussions at the home of Rey de Castro, one of the heartiest participants, and between 1885 and 1888 they published *La Revista Social,* a journal serving as a sounding board for their social concerns. Well aware of their differences with the more conservative writers such as Ricardo Palma, on the occasion of González Prada's accession to the Círculo's presidency, he referred to the circle as a "group destined to become the radical party of our literature."[9]

The group did just that to a considerable degree. By the late 1880s their interests had shifted away from romanticism to naturalism and positivism. It was a shift reflecting their postwar search for modern alternatives to the archaic colonial notions and old ways which they held to be responsible for defeat at the hands of modernizing Chile.

González Prada led the way, using positivism to fuel his vehement anticlericalism. Against the authoritarian intellectual standards of the Roman Catholic Church, he contrasted "a positive science which in only one century of industrial application produced more benefits for mankind than entire millennia of theology and metaphysics."[10]

But reason does not easily overcome passion. González Prada's lingering romantic and moralistic passions were only partially quenched by the scientific mystique of positivism, for while he may have believed that scientific principles could help Peru solve its great social problems, he never saw social change as anything but the product of a great moral struggle between the weak and the strong, the right and the wrong.

González Prada's famous "Discurso del Politeama," delivered

on the eve of national independence day (July 28, 1888), well illustrates how nationalist emotion co-existed with detached analysis. His rousing speech did not disappoint a house packed with students, writers, and workers: he hammered away mercilessly at the privileged classes and the church and at the end pleaded for the young to commit themselves to the forging of a modern nation. But what was even more significant about this address was the *indigenista* theme fused with his nationalism. He spoke of the unresolved dilemma of the exploitation of the native people, as representing the central problem of the nation. Peru could never achieve nationhood or a national culture, he declared, so long as it continued to exclude from the national patrimony its indigenous heritage and the native population.

Other intellectuals of his circle, too, added a nationalist and indigenista orientation to their interest in positivism and realism. While the politicians of the 1870s and 1880s plodded their way out of the war and toward governmental stability, Juana Manuela Gorriti and Clorinda Matto de Turner hosted the leading literary gatherings where the talk inevitably turned to the new philosophies and the pressing social issues of the day.[11] As a group they were bent on merging social criticism and art, on creating a new nationalist and positivist literature that reflected their indigenista concerns. Thus in a widely read essay appearing in *El Perú Ilustrado* (October 1889), Matto de Turner called for the development of "national writers, writers of the race."

Matto de Turner published her celebrated and highly influential indigenista novel, *Aves sin nido,* in the same year (1889). In it the indigenous masses were depicted as a homeless people; she portrayed the Indian as a victim of the clergy, the *gamonales* ("large property owners"), and the local and national political structure. Only a government espousing a militant nationalism, she wrote, could integrate the Indian into a national community.[12]

Another nationalist writer of the age, Mercedes Cabello de Carbonera, treated in her novels—especially *Blanca sol* (1889) and *El conspirador* (1892)—the corruption and indifference of the authorities in the capital. In the style of Zola and the French naturalists, she artfully traced the scheming lives of a woman and a man blinded by the promise of wielding wealth and power in Lima.

Mindful of the futility of simply pleading for reforms, the Círculo reorganized itself in 1891 as a nationalist political party, taking the name of Unión Nacional. Its program called for the revindication of Indian rights, a federal system to combat the concentration of power in Lima, and greater civil liberties. The party also took a stand against the civilistas and the army. But it was one thing to voice protest, and another to create a movement. Indeed, in the very year of the party's founding, its key member, González Prada, left for Europe.

When he returned to Peru in 1898 after spending nearly a decade in France—well-prepared to resume his former position of number-one public critic—he discovered that many of his former *unionista* companions had drifted away to other groups. Only the few remaining in the fold gathered to hear him espouse a new philosophy and a new tactic. He did not disappoint them; he spoke out in the name of "the greatest liberty," to be acquired through social action and anarchist revolution.[13] This pronouncement had a predictable effect—the small party split over the issue, and finally disintegrated (the new literary wave of modernism, too, had helped erode the party's sense of unity and purpose).

González Prada faced the loss of his intellectual followers not by retreating but by turning instead to Lima's fledgeling working-class movement. Before long he had become the leading radical pamphleteer of the day and a constant flow of workers and students began coming to his house for political discussions. They called him el maestro.[14] Thus he earned the distinction of being the first Peruvian writer of note—and a declassé aristocrat at that—to make contact with the working-class movement.

Some of González Prada's earliest anarchist essays were published in *Los Parias,* one of Lima's first anarchist papers. There he wrote of anarchism as a "new Christianity . . . without Christ," whose goal was "unlimited freedom and the greatest well-being for the individual." An ideal, he added, which could only be achieved through the "abolition of . . . state and private property."[15] But the coming revolutionary struggle was not to involve antagonism between the classes, he insisted, for "the emancipation of the working class must be simultaneous with the emancipation of the other classes." In effect, he rejected both historical materialism and socialism. Socialism, he wrote, is

oppressive and repressive, and very different from anarchism which is wholly free and which rejects any regulating or
submitting of the individual to the laws of the greatest
number.[16]

Though his ethical passions marked him as an idealist, like
most men of strong emotion González Prada also had his contradictions.[17] Despite his rejection of historical materialism, at
times he sounded very much the materialist. For instance, in his
classic indigenous text, *Nuestros indios* (1904), he observed that
nothing "changes faster or more radically the psychology of man
than property."[18] There he also described the Indian question as
essentially "economic and social," rather than "pedagogical," a
view which advanced the national debate over the indigenous
question beyond the liberal stage.

His indigenista concern combined with his anticlerical zeal
and radical politics to produce many a knife-sharp attack on the
social structure. No other Peruvian of his stature ever protested
with such constancy and fervor the sacred icons of a crumbling
neocolonial society.

In Peru there exist two great lies—the Republic and Christianity. We talk about civil rights . . . and most Peruvians
have no security in their freedom or their lives. We talk
about Christian charity . . . and consent to the crucifixion of
a race.[19]

But despite his anarchist passion, or perhaps because of it,
González Prada could never quite shake a nagging skepticism. It
even appears in his most well-known political tract, "El intelectual y el obrero," which was delivered on the memorable May
Day celebration of 1905 to the Federación de Obreros Panade-
ros. In what was to become one of the basic texts of Peruvian
radical politics, he essentially made the simple but startling (for
Peru) proposal that intellectuals and manual workers should join
together to form an intellectual-workers' bloc (this marked the
first time that the term intellectual was introduced to the Peruvian public).[20] But once the concept of revolution was broached,
a note of doubt crept in and he asked, "What will become of the
revolution?" Pessimistically he observed that "every revolution
once it succeeds tends to become a government of force, and
every victorious revolutionary degenerates into a conserva-

tive."[21] He did, however, nurture a continuing hope, the source of which was his vision of a coming apocalypse, a vast millennarian movement of people acting to bring about a revolution. With his heretical and indeed extremist views, González Prada stands as a burning—if solitary—light of radical nationalism in the twilight years of the nineteenth century in Peru.

The Lawyers and the National Question

In the 1870s positivism had begun to excite not only antiestablishment writers but also members of the academic community, who used its principles of progress and evolution to bolster their interest in overturning the traditionalism of Peruvian society and encouraging national development.

Traces of positivism first appeared at San Marcos University in a Law School Inaugural Lecture of 1871.[22] Three years later the dean of the Law School made reference to Herbert Spencer in his annual Faculty Report, and three years after that Manuel Llanos submitted the first positivist student thesis, "Origin, carácteres y tendencias de la civilización contemporánea."

By 1877, the year of the Llanos thesis, the "pernicious concepts" of positivism had attained sufficient notoriety to warrant an attack from Father Manuel Tovar, assistant dean of the School of Theology. Scornfully, Father Tovar excoriated the new ideas for promoting a "terrible force which withers whatever it perceives and kills everything it touches."[23] Father Tovar feared not only the making of San Marcos into an open forum for speculative minds, but also the spread of dangerous positivist ideas emphasizing materialist premises, the scientific inductive method, and the exaltation of change and progress.

Indeed, evidence that Father Tovar's concern was well-founded can be discovered in Professor Adolfo Villagracia's Inaugural Lecture of 1884 to the School of Letters. An idealist as a student, he rejected German idealism and instead expressed a preference for Comte's positivism, which he interpreted as saying, "everything that exists is material or the movement of the material."[24]

By the 1890s an important nucleus of positivist professors was lecturing at San Marcos. Having read Renan, Boutroux, Spencer, and Taine in their own student days, they were now among the most highly regarded intellectuals teaching at the university.

The group included first and foremost Javier Prado y Ugarteche, son of the general and former president, who taught philosophy and history. Another historian, Carlos Wiesse, emphasized the "sociological aspects of historical evolution." Mariano H. Cornejo occupied a new chair in sociology. Manuel Vicente Villarán applied positivist concepts and a comparative method in his law lectures and writings. Also espousing positivist ideas and even toying with socialism was José Matías Manzanilla, a popular lecturer in economics. Other notable figures included Pedro Carlos Olaechea, Víctor Maúrtua, and Mariano I. Prado y U.

With the exception of Wiesse, they were not only men of ideas but also worldly men of influence and power; indeed, they were members of the capital's professional and social elite. In their prestigious law firms they negotiated many of the large financial and commercial contracts between British and American businessmen and Peruvian interests, both public and private.

The positivist lawyers were also the intellectual leaders of the liberal wing of the civilistas. They sought to reinvigorate the party with a dynamic nationalism, just as Manuel Pardo had done earlier, and they appealed to positivism as a source for charting the nation's progress. Positivism, however, also seemed to imply for them not only modernization and change, but also in some respects the maintenance of the status quo. Though viewing themselves as democrats, they had little if any contact with the urban poor and even less with the Indian campesinos. In fact, the wealthy and impeccable Javier Prado could well be viewed as the chief spokesman for the ascending industrial and commercial bourgeoisie of Peru.[25]

One of the premier voices of the new nationalism, Prado established his credentials in 1894 with his superb *El estado social del Perú durante la dominación española*. He even considered the methods of approach that he used—which he termed "scientifically historiographical"—as a kind of "nationalist science."[26] The essay basically argued the thesis that the origins of the national malaise could be found in the structure of colonial society, and leveled some heated criticism against the church. As had other nationalists of his generation, however, Prado also revealed signs of a marked racism. Referring to "inferior races" in the manner of Renan, he urged European immigration to improve the native stock and foster Peru's progressive development (this was written, of course, in the spirit of a high-minded nationalism). In any event, *El estado* fostered a great interest in the Peruvian past and linked historical analysis to a nationalist imagination.

At San Marcos Prado's nationalist vision stirred his students to the core. They thrilled to his dramatic portrayal of the university's mission, calling San Marcos "the center for the formation of the collective soul" of the nation.[27]

Later, as rector of San Marcos, Prado took a step toward carrying out his ideals by establishing the Museo Universitario de Historia Natural y de Arqueología Peruana to exalt the national heritage, including the high art of pre-Hispanic civilizations. Active in politics as well as in university affairs, he initiated his political career in 1904, at the age of thirty-three, by simply asking to join the executive junta of the Partido Civil.[28]

Prado's interests resembled that of another paladin of the civilista liberal cause, Manuel Vicente Villarán. Villarán shared Prado's idea of national progress and his view that the United States should serve as Peru's model of development.[29] Again, like Prado, he attracted attention because of a San Marcos lecture, delivered in his case in 1900. Declaring that educational reform was crucial to the cause of national progress, he castigated those who continued to hold the colonialist idea of viewing education as a "decorative acquisition." Progress, the young scholar reminded his elders, required a citizenry educated in modern science and technology. Yet in Peru, aside from the School of Engineering, "agriculture, commerce, navigation, and the industrial arts" received no attention. Theology, literature, Latin, history, and philosophy still dominated the university curriculum.[30]

Prado had made similar arguments, but Villarán went further by insisting that Peru needed well-educated middle and working classes to forge a modern nation. But he still resorted to Prado's explanation of the cause of Spanish America's low level of development. Invoking the worse racist views of western imperialists, he pointed to the "laziness, the physical and mental inertia" of the native people.[31]

In later years Villarán was to help advance his notion that education was the key to modernization: serving as minister of justice and instruction during Leguía's first administration, he was responsible for bringing to Peru the first American educators. As his ideas became more closely tied to the concrete social reality, he pushed ever harder the notion that economic progress was a "precondition for the greater development of . . . [our] educational capacity."[32]

The Scholars of the Generation of 1900

Villarán, Prado, Cornejo, Manzanilla, and the other lawyer-professors of the turn of the century exerted an enormous impact on many generations of San Marcos students—but most directly and profoundly they influenced a young group of scholars who eventually became known as the generation of 1900.

Members of this generation shared essentially the same early formative experiences. Most were born in the early 1880s, and Felipe Barreda y Laos, one of the youngest of the group, recollected years later how they had all grown up "amid the ruins left by the War of the Pacific . . . and [had spent their] youth assimilating the experiences which came with the bitterness of the national disaster."[33]

They also shared similar creole-bourgeois roots. The three brightest stars of the generation—José de la Riva Agüero y Osma, Víctor Andrés Belaúnde, and Francisco García Calderón[34]—typified the social backgrounds of the generation. Riva Agüero, unquestionably the most outstanding of the trio, came from a powerful civilista family; García Calderón's father had been a distinguished jurist and influential first-generation civilista;[35] and the Belaúndes were among the most prominent families of the Arequipan creole upper class, fervently supporting the church, the demócratas, and Piérola.

For all three, growing up meant coping with an ever-increasing anxiety over how to understand the "historical origins of our calamity."[36] They started out quite early—even as schoolboys they astounded adults with their avid reading habits. Some, like Riva Agüero, read González Prada in their youth, but to them he embodied "the systematic destruction of all Peruvian values."[37] Class forces certainly appear evident here, for just about the time that the working class and more radicalized fringes of the middle class were grouping themselves around González Prada, these sons of the bourgeoisie were rallying around the old literary lion of the *Tradiciones peruanas*, Ricardo Palma.

The first big life-experience of the generation came at San Marcos, where they discovered "Lima was not Peru." At the university they rubbed shoulders with the first batch of mestizo students arriving from the provinces in the early 1900s. The exquisite stylist Ventura García Calderón, the social historian of the generation, recalled those impressions quite delicately. The new arrivals from the sierra, he wrote, had brought to San Marcos an "accent of melancholia" vastly different from the light-heartedness of Lima—which was, he cooed, "so Spanish."[38]

Soon the generation of 1900 began to display their precocious talents at the university, and in their intellectual rigor they seemed to strike "deeper" than the lawyers.[39] Their professors nevertheless had a profound effect on them. Years later Belaúnde described how the "intellectual renovation of Peru" had been started in the School of Letters by the likes of Prado and Wiesse, who lectured to them during their early manhood. Through these teachers they assimilated a much cherished tradition, a deep love for Peru.

The foreign masters of the generation of 1900 were Maurice Barrès, Hippolyte Taine, Ernest Renan, and Herbert Spencer (whose *First Principles* became one of their "essential books"). Such positivist writers reinforced the generation's socially and culturally induced racist and hierarchical values.[40]

Positivism did not initially attract all of them, however. At first Belaúnde resisted positivism's materialist implications, later remarking: "By temperament and intuition I found repugnant the explanation of social phenomena by simple economic factors." Although willing to assign economic forces some causal importance, he could not bring himself to granting them "exclusive or even principal causality" in the social process. And during the university holidays of 1902–3, he fled to his native Arequipa, fearing he might be losing his faith to "the subtle venom of the positivist and lay surroundings of San Marcos"[41]—a feeling that would later, though briefly, give way to an embracing of positivism.

The first of the three to be won over by positivist influences

was Riva Agüero, always the most strong-willed of the group. By
1903 he already had declared scholasticism a "phantom from a
dead world," to which he contrasted the intellectual vibrancy of
biology, sociology, physiology, chemistry, and psychology. As a
San Marcos student he favored a reformist program of industrialization, immigration, and utilitarian education.[42] His important *Carácter de la literatura del Perú independiente*, written in
1905 (at the age of nineteen), revealed traces of the teachings of
González Prada. Like him, Riva Agüero invoked the Black
Legend of Spanish colonial rule; and also agreed with Javier
Prado that "from the colonial period stem all of our misfortunes."

Francisco García Calderón also reflected a strong anticolonial,
positivist, and nationalist strain. He was personally close to Riva
Agüero as well—as schoolboys the two would run home from
class not to play, but to read. They remained fast friends
throughout their lives, though in maturity circumstances separated them as García Calderón, unlike Riva Agüero and Belaúnde, curtailed his studies at San Marcos after a few years and
in 1906 left for France.

Away from his mother country, García Calderón attained a
more objective view of Peruvian society. Two of his major
works—*Le Pérou Contemporain* (1907) and *Les Democraties de
l'Amérique* (1912), both originally written in French—easily established him as a master interpreter of his country and people.

García Calderón searched heroically in *Le Pérou* for the main-
springs of the Peruvian national consciousness, in the manner of
his master Renan, by focusing on the power of religion. Like
Renan, he concentrated on its historical and sociological functions, rather than on purely theological considerations.

The Peruvian saw religion as the central shaper of the Spanish
national character. In peninsular life, the historical conjuncture
of secular law and state religion had produced a theocratic state
and an archetypal, charismatic monarch.[43] As a result, in the
popular mind the charismatic leader embodied the driving force
of history; this belief had the force of law.

Such was the heritage of the newly independent nations of
Spanish America. Thus in the postindependence period they had
quickly discovered they could not easily break with custom. Authoritarian dictators assumed the leadership of the new republics

in order to foster "internal order, develop wealth, and unite in-
imical castes." But tradition, it turned out, was not ironclad after
all. García Calderón wrote that it could be avoided via an en-
lightened oligarchy, organized as a political party standing for
the supremacy of the civil element in government and for "order
as the basis of progress." In a word, only civilismo offered a
realistic alternative to dictatorship in Peru.

The alliance of civilismo and Piérola in 1895 gave García
Calderón even further optimism about the country's future.
While admitting that Piérola's "noble enthusiasm" led many to
overlook the president's faults, the rise of foreign investments
after 1895 convinced him that a "positive economic period" had
begun. Finally the time for "work, order, optimism, and general
wealth" had arrived, he felt;[44] there existed "the elements with
which to shape the destinies of a Peruvian nationality."[45]

And indeed, between 1895 and 1908 most sectors of the Peruvian bourgeoisie joined in expressing similar confidence in Peru's
future. The building of a modern national culture became an
imperative binding on all, and this "spirit of '95" prevailed almost intact until the end of José Pardo's first administration.

Meanwhile, during these years the schools of law, letters, and
medicine at San Marcos University served as the focal point of
nationalist enthusiasm. An intellectual wasteland during most of
the 1800s, the old university had suddenly come alive at the
turn of the century, finding inspiration in the rising nationalist
tide. The university journal *Revista Universitaria* (subsequently
renamed *Anales Universitarios*) frequently carried articles
reflecting the Janus face of Peruvian nationalism—one which expressed both urgent concern with native backwardness and support of unbridled dependence on foreign solutions. At the same
time, a plethora of student theses on anthropological, literary,
and historical themes mirrored and added to the rising nationalist tide.[46]

Closely linked with this new nationalism were stirrings of a
militant university reform movement—and Riva Agüero and Belaúnde were in the top ranks of the student protestors who advocated change inside and outside the institution. Years later
Belaúnde recalled nostalgically that in 1904 there had reigned
"enthusiasm and universal euphoria within San Marcos."[47]

At first this growing wave of nationalist student protest met

with positive response from the men in power. Pardo's government pledged educational reforms and backed up its promises
with fiscal commitments. Further, in 1905 his government came
out in favor of the new emphasis on Peruvian national culture
and history by creating the Consejo Superior de Instrucción
Pública, the Instituto Histórico del Perú, and the *Revista Histórica*. On Pardo's initiative the state also assumed responsibility
for protecting the sites of ancient Indian ruins.

At the same time student activism was erupting in other parts
of the continent, leading to the First Latin American University
Student Congress in Montevideo in 1908. There the *sanmar-
quinos* met with student leaders from all corners of South
America to discuss university reform. Belaúnde, the top orator of
his generation, attended as one of the chief San Marcos delegates, and at the congress he intoned a vigorous progressivism.
He later looked back on the event as having provided the final
touches to the nationalist profile of his generation.

Almost immediately following the Montevideo Congress, San
Marcos students, with Riva Agüero on the organizing committee,
founded the Centro Universitario (September 23, 1908). Oscar
Miró Quesada served as its first president. Under his leadership
the Centro almost immediately undertook the creation of a university extension program for the less privileged classes. By 1915
students were offering classes on national culture, social welfare
legislation, medical care, and civil law to the Confederación de
Artesanos, a government-subsidized labor group.

Meanwhile other students began to call for institutional reform. Invited to lecture at the Centro in 1909, Carlos E. Paz
Soldán, a student from the School of Medicine, proposed a comprehensive plan for academic reform, including the proposal that
students "participate in the directive proceedings of the university."[48] Paz Soldán's utterances are certainly some of the earliest
in Peru calling attention to the student demand for *co-gobierno*
(student participation in university governance).

Soon, student activists were plunged into the national political
arena. Support of the anti-Leguía coup conspirators landed Riva
Agüero in jail, leading to demonstrations on his behalf that eventually succeeded in winning his freedom. These developments,
combined with the widening civilista-demócrata split, and the
bitter memory of the anti-Billinghurst military coup of 1914 that

had shattered the constitutional stability prevailing since 1895, led to a more pessimistic attitude among the student leaders.

Belaúnde expressed this new feeling at an inaugural lecture he delivered at San Marcos, which began with the declaration that the optimism of *Le Pérou* was no longer tenable. He placed the blame on the "personalist politics of the executive," meaning Leguía and Billinghurst—a strange remark coming from one who so admired Piérola. The most striking chord of the entire speech came at the end, though, with the nationalist cry, "¡Queremos Patria!"[49]

After 1915, Riva Agüero's nationalist views also began to change. During a prolonged journey on horseback through the southern sierra in 1912, he visited many historical sites known to him up until then only through books. He was profoundly moved by what he saw, and the notes of his odyssey appeared later as perhaps his finest work, *Paisajes peruanos.* Filled with awe, he wrote that "the sierra is the cradle of our nationality . . . the spinal column of its life . . . the principal region of Peru."[50] He spoke emotionally of the grandeur of the conquistadors, thereby rediscovering the glory of his own aristocratic past, and he also saw that Peru was even more the product of the Incas than the Spaniards.[51]

As Raúl Porras Barrenechea wisely observed, Riva Agüero's journey marked the dividing line between adolescence and adulthood; it was the watershed of his "noonday liberalism."[52] After 1912 he abandoned his former interest in positivism and science. His three classic studies in Peruvian history reflected his new view that history was the work of charismatic men guided by the hand of God—ignoring, however, the historical importance of other social forces.

Eventually, as the working and middle classes increasingly pushed themselves to the forefront of national politics, Riva Agüero found himself in the midst of a social situation he could not bear. Following the Leguía coup of 1919, he hurriedly left Peru and eventually embraced fascism.

Belaúnde's philosophical and political views, too, underwent a transformation. At twenty-three his thesis, "La filosofía del derecho y el método positivo" (1906), had identified him as a positivist. Six years later, when he took a chair at San Marcos, his interests had already begun to shift to Henri Bergson. By

1916 he had totally divorced himself from positivism, ridiculing its dual pillars of "observation and empiricism" as nothing more than intellectual posing. Positivism weighed heavily on the human spirit, he wrote, "because of its fatal connection with intellectualism, materialism, and determinism."[53] And by 1917, a series of essays entitled *La realidad nacional* clearly marked him as a Bergsonian.

His political outlook also turned around, though he did not go as far to the right as had Riva Agüero. Instead he remained a conservative defender of the status quo, pursuing a diplomatic career that gave him an international reputation and level of success denied him by his countrymen. He lived his long life in the shadows of the powers-that-be: his class, the state, and the church.

At this point a new generation begins to eclipse the generation of 1900. It appeared in the welter of the collapse of civilismo and mobilization of a new middle class. Indeed, the generation of 1919 came from this emerging middle class, signifying a new development, for in the past it was primarily the well-to-do who had become artists and intellectuals.[54] (The renegade aristocrat, Manuel González Prada, although not excessively wealthy, lived on inherited income all his life.)

The impact of economic expansion had uprooted a flock of *provincianos* like Víctor Raúl Haya de la Torre, César Vallejo, Eudocio Ravines, and a host of others, and brought them to Lima. Lured to the capital by promises of self-fulfillment and social advancement, they sought educational opportunities and jobs in the bustling and modernizing law offices, schools, and newspapers.

But the promises of progress were double-edged. Recession soon followed the prosperity of the Pardo years. And as the social situation of the country deteriorated after 1915, the intellectuals, suffering from discontent and alienation, decided—like the working class—to take action. Their response was saturated with a nationalism that had much more in common with the González Prada tradition than with the generation of 1900, and José Carlos Mariátegui was one of the members of the generation of 1919 who forged the way.[55]

PART TWO
Of Mariátegui's Trial

3

Adolescence and Manhood

¿Era yo, en mi adolescencia literaria, él que los demás
creían, el que yo mismo creía?[1]

When José Carlos Mariátegui turned thirteen in 1907, Lima was
still flushed with the joyful days of the *belle epoque*. But not
long afterward the era of prosperity and gaiety ended, and a
long, hard period began for the inhabitants of the capital. For
José Carlos, too, those years from 1908 onward got tougher and
tougher.

For a poor boy adulthood comes early. At thirteen José Carlos
already faced the need to start finding a productive place for
himself in not altogether benign surroundings. He did not have
much to go on, objectively speaking. His family was poor, he
was crippled and fatherless, and he had heavy responsibilities to
shoulder. But he was bright, alert, and fiercely industrious,
seemingly driven by a will to get ahead.

As the years wore on and he became a recognized writer and
journalist, he seemed to acquire a certain worldliness of character. But deep inside, his feelings told him otherwise. Much later
he was to wonder, in that confessional style so peculiar to him,
whether in those early days "I was really the person others
thought I was, the person I myself thought I was."

Childhood and Adolescence

José Carlos was born in Moquequa in 1894, not in Lima in
1895 as he apparently thought.[2] His mother, María Amalia
LaChira Ballejos de Mariátegui, came from the small town of
San Jerónimo de Sayán, in the District of Chancay not far from
Lima. A mestiza, her ancestors were from Piura in the north and
of native stock. In 1882 she married a man of the Limeño creole
upper classes. He was a descendant of Dr. Francisco Javier

Mariátegui de Tellería, a hero of the independence era, secretary to the First Congress of Peru, and an anticlerical liberal firebrand. But José Carlos apparently never even knew his father, let alone had any contact with his side of the family.[3] His father left the family, and José Carlos grew up with only his mother for early support.[4]

The question of his father's identity loomed as a troublesome problem in José Carlos's early childhood, and even more during his adolescence. He simply did not know who his father was or why his mother kept it from him. An uncle gave him scattered information but hardly an explanation.[5]

There were other problems confronting José Carlos as well. The family was very poor.[6] His mother had to care for two children aside from José Carlos, an older sister named Guillermina and a younger brother, Julio César (his mother's first four children had died at an early age). His mother worked as a seamstress and her mother and brother helped out some of the time—but basically the burden of caring for and supporting the family fell on her alone.

Health, too, was an early obstacle for José Carlos, for he was born a fragile child. At six he began complaining of "fatigue, fevers, and pains."[7] Then, as if fate wanted to square things all around, in October 1902, while playing at school, he hurt his left leg badly.

Brought to Lima by his mother, he was interned at the Maison de Santé, a hospital run by the Reverend Mothers of Saint Joseph of Cluny. A French physician operated twice on his left knee, but unsuccessfully; and he remained crippled for the rest of his life.[8] José Carlos recuperated in the hospital for three or four months after the operation. Sharing a room with about six European adults, he soon found himself the center of attention; some of the patients pampered him and even taught him his first words of French and German.[9]

At home the eight-year-old remained bedridden for two years, during which time his avid reading habit began. At first stories of the lives of Jesus, Moses, and the heroes Siegfried and El Cid Campeador occupied his imagination. By 1905, at the age of eleven, he was already involved in more serious reading: the literary journal *Prisma* and works by Anatole France, Manuel Beingolea, and Francisco and Ventura García Calderón.

After his long convalescence he virtually had to learn to walk again. But soon enough he was running errands, and on one of his trips to the market, as Guillermo Rouillón tells us, he met Juan Manuel Campos. Campos worked as a linotypist at the newspaper *La Prensa*, and the two became fast friends.[10]

The encounter with Campos was fortuitous; through him José Carlos got a desperately needed job. In 1909 at the age of fifteen he began working at the newspaper, putting in fourteen hours a day, six days a week as a copyboy for three soles (about 75 cents) a week.

One Sunday in April of that year (1909) Campos, who was an anarchist and follower of González Prada, took José Carlos to meet the famous heretic. During the interchange the problem of his father's identity apparently came out in the open for the first time (and it would happen with more frequency from then on). González Prada asked José Carlos if he were related to Francisco Javier Mariátegui, and the boy, to his embarrassment, was unable to answer because he simply did not know.[11] The meeting had an unexpectedly happy outcome, though, for as a result he was introduced to González Prada's son Alfredo, and the two became good friends.

The nagging question of his unknown father, combined with his ill health and then the accident, his family's poverty, and undoubtedly other problems that faced the youth, did not appear to have the effect of bending José Carlos's spirit. On the contrary, to the outside world he had the image of being a quick-minded, creative, promising young man; in fact, at times he even seemed to have an aura of fate about him.

Eventually, his precocious talents and enthusiasm made an impression on his coworkers at *La Prensa*. He continued his prodigious reading habit; an acquaintance remarked that José Carlos always carried "a book with him, at all hours, every day."[12] At the time he was rather awed by the literary world, and he considered writing for publication virtually a sacred act:

The devotion . . . I felt for intelligence since my youth made me attribute to all writers, without exception, qualities of wisdom that were somewhat exaggerated. Any man who could publish what he wrote in a newspaper was to me a sort of superior being.[13]

Soon enough he, too, was writing for publication. In three years' time, with only one year of formal schooling but a lot of inspired, dedicated work, he was promoted from a copy boy to an assistant on the editorial staff, then editor of police reports (1914), and eventually a reporter.

As he rose in the hierarchy he began to have more contact with the star reporters, men like Leonidas Yerovi, Julio Portal, and Ezequiel Balarezo Pinillos—fraternizing with them at the Bar Americano across from *La Prensa* or at the bookstore nearby, La Aurora Literaria.[14] Thus, the adolescent had reached the point of acceptance in the prewar literary world of the capital—having come quite a long way, in many respects, from his obscure and penurious existence as a child.

The Shaping Force of Contemporary History

On the eve of the First World War we find Mariátegui a regular participant in the vanguard literary circle of Abraham Valdelomar, Percy Gibson, Enrique Bustamante y Ballivián, Félix del Valle, César Falcón, and others.

They were a highly introspective group of writers, reflecting the lingering impact of modernism, which had arrived late in Peru and become a highly influential and eclectic school around the turn of the century.[15] Modernism had introduced a greater sense of freedom to Peruvian letters, and although it had essentially spent itself as a literary movement by the war, the "new introspection"[16] it had brought—actually a rather pessimistic, even narcissistic sort of introspection—still pervaded the literary world.

By the prewar years, this ambience had become one of "disorientation and disillusionment," as José Gálvez noted in a 1915 San Marcos doctoral thesis. Valdelomar, the acknowledged leader of the literary circle Mariátegui was involved with, exemplified the mood that had settled over them. Luis Alberto Sánchez has described how between 1911 and 1913 Valdelomar had experienced

> something which destroyed the academic and sophisticated mode of his literature . . . which in turn produced his encounter with himself: what? why?[17]

The alienation Valdelomar and his circle felt paralleled the social anomie of the time—and it is hardly surprising that it
should. For they lived very much in a world of wage labor,
prices, and politics. Valdelomar himself well understood how "a
writer needed, above all, a great popularity, a public that took
an interest in him, a market for his work."[18]

Around 1913–14 the gloom deepened owing to the crises en-
gulfing Billinghurst and Leguía and the global malaise triggered
by the world war. Valdelomar and his circle mirrored this mood
of discontent, and they began to set out, again in the words of
Sánchez, to pursue "new ways of seeing and understanding life
and the world."[19]

The upheaval of the times seems to have stirred young people
outside the capital in a way similar to the Limeño writers.
Around 1915 Trujillo's writers initiated their own efforts to dis-
engage themselves from the old and discover the new.[20] Taking
the name Bohemia of Trujillo, the group inclk José Eulogio Gar-
rido, Antenor Orrego, Alcides Spelucín, Víctor Raúl Haya de la
Torre, and César Vallejo. Likewise, down south in Arequipa
young writers were joining groups such as El Aquelarre and La
Bohemia Andina. Most of these writers later migrated to Lima in
search of fame and fortune: in 1917 and 1918, for example, Haya
de la Torre and César Vallejo arrived in the capital.

Meanwhile, the Limeño circle of Valdelomar and Mariátegui
pursued a high social life, despite the hardships of the times.
They were earning enough now to dress in the dandy fashions of
the day, cultivating the "charming and elegant" Baudelarian decadence style then in vogue.[21] Mariátegui began to sign his articles with the affected pseudonyms of Juan Croniqueur, Jack,
Kandelif, or Monsieur de Camomille. In 1915 he even began
frequenting the racetrack and reporting on the gossip and doings
of high society, coediting, for a while, the journal *El Turf.*[22]

In the evenings the group often retreated to the Palais Concert, a stylish cafe on the Jirón de la Unión, where they enjoyed
the musical entertainment provided by a group of Viennese women. In contrast to the hustle of their working day or their more
formal social affairs, here they could relax and be themselves.
Valdelomar, the self-titled Conde de Lemos, presided at their
ceremonial gatherings. A gifted poet and storyteller, occasionally
he would burst out expansively:

Peru is Lima. Lima is the Jirón de la Unión.
The Jirón de la Unión is the Palais Concert.
Ergo: Peru is the Palais Concert.

But it was in the arena of literary accomplishment, rather than social diversion, that the group stood out. They published a short-lived but influential literary journal, *Colónida* (1916).[23] Like Valdelomar and the others, Mariátegui wrote some poetry and historical plays.[24] His literary production of the period, which he later referred to as his intellectual "stone age," was varied, though some of it of lasting quality.[25]

Literature, however, did not satisfy him completely, and gradually he entered a phase of spiritual seeking. He read the Spanish ideologues Luis Araquistain, Miguel de Unamuno, and Gabriel Alomar and began to write mystical sonnets and other religious pieces. "Eulogy to an Ascetic Cell" celebrated his retreat in 1916 to the Convento de los Descalzos. In early 1917 he wrote the highly emotional "Oration to the Spirit of Leonidas Yerovi" on the occasion of his death (one of the few times he signed hisown name to an article before 1920–21). He also turned out a prizewinning religious essay, "La procesión tradicional,"[26] and in a published open letter to a friend remarked, "I believe in God above everything." Later he summed up his feelings of those years by saying: "At a very early age . . . I set out in search of God."[27]

Some of this was sheer posing, but some not. The fact is, Mariátegui set out to find something to believe in, something to which he could commit his life; and one factor in that quest was the problem of his father's identity, which continued to plague him.[28] In this connection, one day he got up enough courage to ask for an interview with Don Foción Mariátegui, patriarch of the Mariátegui clan and president of the Jockey Club. Many years later Don Foción recalled how Mariátegui had acted with great arrogance and rudeness at the time, seeming to want to give the impression of "one power talking to another power."[29] The meeting turned out to be a completely unsavory and unsatisfactory affair—and afterwards Mariátegui still had no clearer idea of his ancestry.

Despite this preoccupation with the inner questions of his family and spiritual identity, Mariátegui maintained an active interest in social affairs. In 1915 he helped organize the Círculo de

Periodistas, which represented his first practical political experience. The Círculo's goal was to "protect the rights of those who dedicate themselves to the arduous and invaluable tasks of journalism." At the opening ceremony of the new organization, Mariátegui received the title, "First Initiator of the Círculo."[30]

Soon afterward party politics, too, intruded into his formerly apolitical life. Augusto Durand, the political caudillo, bought the pierolista *La Prensa* in 1916, and a revision of editorial policy followed. Not everyone abided the changes and one editor, Pedro Ruiz Bravo, left with a string of writers, including Mariátegui, to establish *El Tiempo*. Serving mainly as a forum for the new middle class, eventually the newspaper became a leguiísta publication, bitterly opposed to the civilistas.

El Tiempo brought important changes into Mariátegui's life. He could now be considered part of the rising middle class, for his new job paid two hundred soles per month.[31] His journalistic personality changed, too. He wrote less about the track, literature, and social gossip, and more about politics, starting a daily column, "Voces," which was modeled after Luis Fernán Cisnero's popular "Ecos."

"Voces" is a primary source for tracing Mariátegui's radicalization between 1915 and 1918. At first he specialized, as did *El Tiempo*, in throwing well-aimed darts at the civilista ruling elites. Often President José Pardo and his Chief Minister, Enrique de la Riva Agüero, served as the targets of his mischievous pen. For example, he ridiculed Pardo for the meticulousness with which he attended to the redecoration of the presidential palace (in French motif) while the people suffered from escalating prices. He also took after Víctor Andrés Belaúnde, a candidate for an Arequipan parliamentary seat, whom he characterized as "Christian, mystic, nationalistic, and rhetorical." Belaúnde, he wrote, was suffering from "the idealism of the Salvation Army."[32]

But after a year of writing "Voces," Mariátegui found himself in a more serious frame of mind (coinciding with the religious phase we have mentioned). He wrote of these years:

> Then we were the same as today, fairly good chaps, part-time priests of joyful nights, squires of unknown knights-errant whose chimeras we never fully understood, half-frivolous and half-serious commentators of the daily

vulgarities, mocking readers of others and of ourselves, and favorite nephews of the delightful national malice, . . . We . . . passed the years in front of an Underwood that was our friend, our confidant, our loved one, our patroness and our interpreter. Typing on it, we laughed many times at men and at life in general, and we imagined that there was in us something of the disciplined Yankee machine, and in the machine something of the creole and of our disordered selves.

But then, he said:

We looked toward the government palace and discovered Señor Pardo was President of the Republic. And then we understood why we were speaking to the country and why we needed to become more serious.

After following Peruvian politics for a year:

[We were] slightly discouraged, fatigued and cudgeled by the realities of this mestizo democracy. A year ago we were more optimistic, gayer, more lively, and more deceived.

With a touch of dramatic excess, he then confessed the "failure and extinction" of his "ideals, aspirations, and chimeras."[33]

Mariátegui's increasingly politicized and disillusioned mood was reflected in his response to being caught in an embarrassing scandal over the visiting ballet dancer, Norka Rouskaya, in October 1917. Answering his critics with unwonted righteousness, he hurled counteraccusations at the "hypocrites" who otherwise passively ignored "gross social and political evils."[34]

At this juncture various elements of the deteriorating socioeconomic milieu converged, as if in anticipation of the 1919 denouement. The objective factors contributing to Mariátegui's political awakening—and that of his generation of 1919—can be reconstructed broadly as follows.

Their generation came of age during the years of increasing class conflict in Peru. As the effects of World War I increasingly aggravated the wage-price squeeze, class lines sharpened and the middle and working classes became more disgruntled and politically restive.

The movement of rural folk into the capital compounded the

situation. The rising demand for housing increasingly pushed up land values, construction costs, and rents in Lima,[35] and soon the first jerry-built shantytowns sprouted up around the city's edge. Scarcity of potable water and adequate sewage disposal produced a shocking jump in the mortality rate because of rampaging diseases such as tuberculosis. In fact, during those years Lima replaced St. Petersburg as the city with the highest incidence of tubercular fatalities in the world.[36]

Meanwhile, as the times worsened, Mariátegui, along with Valdelomar, Federico More, Félix del Valle, Percy Gibson, and others, began dropping in on the political discussions held by González Prada at his home. By 1917, Mariátegui had started to make contact with working-class militants and radical university students attending the gatherings. Still feeling his way politically, he said, it appears, very little at these sessions.[37]

Undoubtedly these sessions at González Prada's house were a contributing factor toward the swaying of Mariátegui's politics to the left. His two close friends, César Falcón and Humberto del Aguila, were also influential. Del Aguila recalled the inseparable trio's talks late at night while riding the tram home to the middle-class suburb of La Victoria. César Falcón, the oldest of the three, invariably dominated the discussions with his more flamboyant radical views. Mariátegui remained cautious and more searching, but by then he definitely saw himself as being on the left.[38]

Soon Mariátegui and his literary friends were being viewed as the radical vanguard of the working press in the capital, reaching a wider and more receptive public as the economic crisis deepened. Years later, Mariátegui reported that in 1918 they began to take a decidedly socialist stand:

There was initiated in the editorial section of . . . of *El Tiempo* . . . an effort to organize a socialist propaganda group. . . . The administration was unsympathetic to this effort, which represented exclusively the socialist orientation of some of the younger reporters who, alienated from . . . [conventional] politics, tended to impress upon the paper's campaign a social orientation. These writers were César Falcón, José Carlos Mariátegui, Humberto del Aguila.[39]

Indeed, by this time Mariátegui had decided to find an outlet for their radical views by publishing his own journal, *Nuestra Época*. Among those working on the first issue in 1918 were Félix del Valle, César Falcón, César Ugarte, Percy Gibson, César Vallejo, and César A. Rodríguez. Vallejo and Rodríguez had arrived in Lima only recently (from Trujillo and Arequipa respectively). Ugarte introduced the socialist influence of Víctor M. Maúrtua, the respected San Marcos professor, to the group. Carlos del Barzo, a worker, also joined them.

Not everyone followed the same path. Valdelomar saw the need for political change, but remained committed to conventional creole politics. He decided to become a leguiísta deputy, which explained his absence from the first issue of *Nuestra Época*. There is an interesting report of an encounter between Valdelomar and César Vallejo in February 1918, just months before Valdelomar's tragic death. Walking together in El Parque de la Exposición, Valdelomar enchanted the younger Vallejo with an eloquent recital of works-in-progress and with his plans for a lecture tour through northern Peru. With great excitement he talked of organizing a "vast intellectual movement" for the enlightenment of a "national conscience," a movement whose goal would be the integration of the masses into a national culture. Yet when Vallejo pressed him for specifics, he would say very little.[40]

Several months later, in mid 1918, *Nuestra Epoca* appeared. Its philosophy was spelled out in an introduction by Mariátegui:

> We bring out this paper and give it the name *Our Epoch* because we believe that there begins with it an epoch of renovation which requires that the energies of youth be placed at the service of the public interest. . . . [We] bring to that task our knowledge of the national reality gained in our work with the press.

But Mariátegui avoided giving the new journal a precise ideological orientation, saying only that "the political program of *Nuestra Epoca* is very simple. Two words could define it: the truth."[41]

In a more personal note, Mariátegui tersely announced that he was giving up the pseudonym of Juan Croniqueur.[42] Referring to his frivolous literary and journalistic past, he asked forgiveness from "God and the public" for the many sins he had committed under that name. (Many years later he talked about his pre-1917 period as his "literary adolescence," a time of "decadentism, modernism, estheticism, individualism, skepticism."[43])

The new journal was born with a bang, not a whimper, for an antimilitarist essay by Mariátegui entitled "The Duty of the Army and the Duty of the State" touched off instant controversy. Its main thesis was based on what is Mariátegui's rudimentary articulation of the problem of national development:

> The country must consider its armed defenses. But it must do so within the limits of its economic resources . . . No state should show greater economy and discretion than the Peruvian state in its military efforts. What we need here is an employment policy and not an armament policy. An employment policy and also a policy of education. Let our territory be developed and our illiteracy eliminated and then we will have the money and soldiers for the defense of Peruvian territory.[44]

Some days later Mariátegui ran into several army officers who, after a brief verbal exchange, shoved and pushed him.[45] Another officer later sought him out at the print shop and challenged him to a duel. Left with no alternative, he went so far as to name seconds, but before the duel could take place a public outcry in his favor arose, for the frail Mariátegui weighed not much over one hundred pounds (his height was about five feet two inches).[46] The incident grew to such proportions that it eventually forced the resignation of the minister of war.

Although only one more issue of *Nuestra Época* was published, the journal was significant as a signpost of Mariátegui's new political consciousness. It was the "point of departure," he would later say, of his "socialist orientation."[47] Indeed, those years when politics began to intrude into the world of the young journalist marked the time when his fate and the country's crossed paths.

The Discovery of Class Politics

The critical year was 1919, the year of reckoning for Mariátegui as well as for his entire generation of young intellectuals. It was the year that Mariátegui turned twenty-five, Víctor Raúl Haya de la Torre turned twenty-four, and most of the other members of the generation were reaching their twenties, having been born in the 1890s.

The generation was studded with an array of exceptional talents. All of them eventually made their mark in the arts, scholarship, or politics, and most of them were deeply concerned with the problem of creating a truly national culture. Among the group figured such outstanding individuals as Raúl Porras Barrenechea, the historian and diplomat; Jorge Guillermo Leguía, the first critical historian of nineteenth-century liberalism; the precocious Jorge Basadre, leading historian of republican Peru; the peripatetic and brilliant Luis Alberto Sánchez, literary historian, essayist, professor, rector of San Marcos University, and Aprista leader; Eudocio Ravines, the able revolutionary tactician and organizer; César Vallejo, the great Peruvian revolutionary poet; and of course, Víctor Raúl Haya de la Torre, the dynamic and charismatic political agitator and founder of the Aprista movement, and Mariátegui himself.

With one or two exceptions, the generation of 1919 was of mestizo and middle-class origin. Thus class and ethnic differences set them apart from the generation of 1900 which, in the words of Luis Alberto Sánchez,

> had everything in its favor: newspapers, money, social position, official favor, a coincidence of values with the governing class, inoffensive theories, vapid idealism, their own university.[48]

Unlike the previous generation, they shared a marked anti-Limeñismo. They all recognized Lima as the social and intellectual center of Peru, but at the same time they extolled the simple virtues of life in the provinces, where many of them had grown up. This gave them a more national outlook.

Another notable difference between the generation of 1919 and the generation of 1900 is that the former were, again with some exceptions, political activists par exellance. In Sánchez's

words, they were "more pragmatic." On the one hand, they, as
the previous generation, looked to the study of history and culture for knowledge about their people and themselves. Thus
they shared some intellectual assumptions and experiences. On
the other hand, neither the nation's leading lawyers nor scholars
exerted a strong effect on Mariátegui and his generation, as they
had on the previous one. Different social worlds shaped them.
González Prada did influence them considerably, though not in
any specific theoretical way. He did draw their attention to the
class basis of society and politics. But the discovery of class politics took place for the generation of 1919 more in the realm of
social action than in theory.

Between 1916 and 1919, a chain of shattering class conflicts
erupted throughout the country. In 1916 farm workers struck in
Huacho and Sayán for an eight-hour day. Talara, Negritos, and
Lobitos petroleum workers also went on strike in that year, as
did smelter workers, telegraph workers, and even employees of
the National Library in Lima. Worker discontent continued un-
abated until 1919. But the events having the greatest resonance
in the country were the December 1918–January 1919 general
strike for the eight-hour day in Lima, followed by the May-June
1919 general strike to lower the cost of living.

The first step toward the general strike was taken on December 12, 1918, when Vitarte textile workers voted to demand
the eight-hour day. Eleven days later, workers from another textile factory, El Inca, joined them. In the days following, so did
the Lima bakers. On December 29 workers established a central committee for an eight-hour strike in Lima, with Manuel
Casabona, president of the Unificación Textil Vitarte, and Julio
Portocarrero and Fausto Nalvarte, also from Vitarte, serving as
members.

On the same day, Héctor Merel, another vitartino, and Nalvarte, went to Lima to set up the Vitarte Propaganda Committee. Its first order of business was to organize support in Lima,
Callao, Huacho, Huarochirí, Junín, and throughout the suburbs
of Lima. They succeeded beyond their dreams. The final step
came when they established the Strike Committee. On January
12 they declared a general strike for the eight-hour day.

Unlike previous strikes, widespread violence and destruction
of private property marked the workers' 1919 campaign. After an

undecided 72-hour struggle for control of the streets of Lima, President Pardo finally agreed to decree, on January 15, an eight-hour work day without a decrease in pay for state employees. Once the proclamation became law, the air cleared, and the private sector negotiated separate agreements. Thus the 1918–19 strike proved a huge success and clearly marked a historic workers' victory.[49]

Mariátegui and his friends actively supported the workers' actions during this period. Eventually, sympathy for the movement brought about an estrangement between the group and the editors of *El Tiempo*, who viewed Leguía as the solution to all of Peru's problems and warned, in editorials, of the "excesses" of the Russian Revolution—a stand that greatly irritated José Carlos and the others. Throughout late 1918 and early 1919, while workers prepared for the general strike, Mariátegui, César Falcon, and Humberto del Aguila argued their differences with Ruiz Bravo, their editor. On January 24 and 25, the two sides exchanged heated letters in the pages of *El Tiempo*. Bravo accused the reporters of subverting his paper, and of offering to buy it with money given to them by Antenor Aspíllaga, the civilista presidential candidate.[50] In the course of disputing this otherwise silly accusation, Luis Ulloa, a fellow reporter, published an open letter in which he observed that because of the controversy, José Carlos and César Falcón were jeopardizing their "ambition to found a socialist newspaper."[51]

Mariátegui's column "Voces" appeared irregularly throughout 1918, and made its last appearance on January 23, 1919. Finally, after securing sufficient financial support for another independent venture, he and his friends broke away from *El Tiempo*.[52]

At first he participated briefly in organizing, along with a small group of intellectuals and workers, the Committee of Socialist Propaganda and Organization. But when the committee announced in April its plans to organize a Socialist Party of Peru, he voiced his opposition.[53] Arguing against the views of Luis Ulloa and Carlos del Barzo, he contended that the committee should first secure working-class support and recognition before organizing as a party. Outvoted within the committee, he left with his inseparable companions of those years, Falcón and del Aguila.

From then on Mariátegui concentrated on launching his new publishing venture, *La Razón*. It finally came out on May 14,

1919, and enjoyed far greater success than *Nuestra Epoca*.[54] Again the opening editorial professed "the paper's commitment to one principle: the truth."[55] The interests of the working class clearly predominated, and the paper articulated a socialist doctrine.

La Razón carried no masthead or editor's name, but Mariátegui guided it. In addition to del Aguila and Falcón, Fausto Posada joined the paper. Posada, a worker, wrote the column, "El Proletariado," covering both national and international working-class activities. The July 10 issue of *La Razón* encouraged proletarian unity, and the July 18 issue carried news about French socialism and Hungarian communism, as did other issues. In terms of local politics, *La Razón* followed a decidedly anti-Leguía line, ignoring the Aspíllaga candidacy and supporting the harmless Isaías Piérola campaign for president.

La Razón played a crucial role in the workers' and students' strikes in the spring and summer of 1919, and in helping to mold a tenuous alliance between manual laborers and intellectuals. The alliance had its beginnings during the eight-hour general strike in December 1918–January 1919. While still with *El Tiempo*, Mariátegui had noted, on January 3, that workers had written to Felipe Chueca, then acting president of the FEP (Federación de Estudiantes del Perú), proposing a student-worker alliance in support of the strike. Chueca, a leguiísta, gave an oblique reply, saying that students had a great interest in helping to better "the socioeconomic conditions of the workers," but he made no commitment. Nevertheless, on January 13, on a motion by Haya de la Torre, the FEP voted for a student delegation to march with the workers, a delegation made up of Bruno Bueno de la Fuente, Valentín Quesada, and Haya de la Torre, all from Trujillo.[56] Later when President Pardo invited a workers' delegation to attend the announcement of his eight-hour-day decree, Haya de la Torre went as a member.[57]

A second general strike in mid 1919, that later spilled over to the university, succeeded eventually in openly bringing the student and worker movements together. On April 13 representatives of about twenty-two labor organizations joined forces to form the Strike Committee. After making preliminary preparations, on April 27 the committee—with Nicolás Gutarra, the fiery anarcho-syndicalist orator and organizer, presiding—agreed on a 24-hour general strike for May 1 unless the government met their demands.

President Pardo refused even to receive the delegation sent to convey the strike demands, and so a general strike was called. After the one-day action, preparations continued for a longer strike, although the May presidential elections slowed down the organizing effort. On May 26, the committee once more resumed its discussions. But at a meeting that night the police arrested the two principal anarcho-syndicalist leaders, Gutarra and Carlos Barba. Adalberto Fonkén then assumed the secretariat of the committee and continued with the meeting; minutes later, however, the police returned and arrested him, too. With three of their leaders in police custody, the Strike Committee decided to call a general strike for the following day, May 27.

Once more rioting and looting gripped the streets of Lima. Red flags appeared and there was rampant destruction of private property. The violence escalated to such a pitch that Pardo surrounded the presidential palace with soldiers and machine guns, and Luis Miró Quesada, the civilista specialist on labor movements, organized an armed citizens militia to help preserve the public order.

Fearful that without their leaders (who were still in jail) the movement might lose sight of its goals, the Strike Committee reluctantly decided on the night of May 31 to end the strike on June 2. Their decision caused much disappointment, especially in Callao, where the strike continued until June 5. In return for the committee's vote to end the strike, the government assumed a conciliatory posture, and suspended martial law, although tense days followed.[58]

Thereafter the center of protest shifted to San Marcos. The visit to Lima of the Argentine socialist Alfredo L. Palacios in May helped catapult the university into the fray. Palacios's brilliant oratory aroused strong support for the Peruvian student movement.

The university protests were also the outcome of previous years of clamoring for reform at San Marcos. Late nineteenth-century positivists initiated the movement, and, as we have seen, others, such as Víctor Andrés Belaúnde, had later championed the cause. Proposals in favor of academic and administrative change had continued right up to 1919, but the generation of 1900 had never taken any direct political action.

A prime mover in the series of events leading to a student strike at San Marcos was *La Razón*. During the second workers' general strike and the student strike of mid June, students and workers met, talked, and planned their tactics at the newspaper's offices.[59] A series of articles appearing in *La Razón*, in fact, triggered the actions. Raúl Porras Barrenechea, then a law student, analyzed the San Marcos student elections for the coming year on June 14, predicting a victory for reform-minded students. Eleven days later the paper launched a series of unsigned articles purporting to expose the dismal and backward state of instruction at the university.

The tone of student politics changed when three students at the Law Faculty—Porras Barrenechea, Humberto del Aguila, and Guillermo Luna Cartland, the actual authors of the *La Razón* articles—initiated a reformist movement in the law school.[60] After the appearance of a June 25 article describing their reform activities, José León y Bueno, a second-year student at the College of Letters, called a meeting at his home to discuss proposals for change, inviting Porras. After a long meeting, they agreed to convene a general assembly of Letters students to demand the resignation of professors Constantino Salazar (second year, History of Modern Civilization) and Flores y Pérez (first year, Spanish literature), and to form a universitywide reform committee.

Two days later, on June 27, *La Razón* reported that students in Professor Salazar's class had suddenly interrupted his lecture and demanded changes. When informed of the incident, the article went on, Faculty Dean Alejandro Deustua had rushed immediately to the classroom, although he did not intervene in the discussion between Professor Salazar and his students. When the interchange ended Deustua spoke, but in a conciliatory manner, whereupon the students had left the classroom "hailing university reform."[61] Two days after this incident, *La Razón* noted, students decided to boycott Flores y Pérez's and Salazar's classes, and declared that "the student movement has begun in the Faculty of Letters."

Shortly thereafter, the activists convened a general assembly of Letters students, which was presided over by Jorge Guillermo

Leguía, a third-year delegate. Among those joining him were Luis Alberto Sánchez, a third-year delegate; Manuel Seoane, a second-year delegate; and Jorge Basadre, a first-year delegate. All the while the official student organization, the FEP, merely observed what was going on and remained committed to a moderate course.

La Razón continued its coverage of the dramatic happenings. Articles reported that other colleges had joined Letters and all college committees had united under a General Committee, with Juan Manuel Calle presiding. On August 2 these groups came together at a tumultuous general assembly in the central patio, where the central committee voted for a general strike against the university. Written by Manuel Abastos, the manifesto began with the words:

> For the first time the students direct themselves to the nation in the name of a cultural ideal.

And so Mariátegui found himself in the center of a political firestorm. Just before the outburst of the San Marcos student strike, still another political front broke out. On July 4, President-elect Leguía assured himself of the kind of government he felt Peru should have by carrying out a perfectly executed coup d'etat against Pardo's administration.

Immediately following the coup, on July 8, all imprisoned strike leaders were released. Once Gutarra, Barba, and Fonkén had been freed, the workers organized a huge march to the presidential palace for a meeting with the new president. Ever the man to seize command of a situation, Leguía stepped out on a balcony and identified himself and his government with the workers' aspirations.

But before reaching the palace the large crowd had passed by the offices of *La Razón*, and Gutarra had invited someone from the paper to speak to the workers, "for the paper had been the only one within the conservative milieu to defend the cause of the people during difficult times."[62] And so it fell on Mariátegui, too, to step onto a balcony and address a multitude of people. He told them, "The people's visit fortified the spirit of the writers of *La Razón* . . . *La Razón* is a newspaper of the people and for the people, and its writers are at the service of noble causes. *La Razón* will always inspire campaigns in the service of high principles out of its profound love for justice. The term 'agitators,' which has been applied to Barba and Gutarra, honors them."

On to Europe

Exhilarated with the spirit of struggle for reform after the tumultuous events of May, June, July, and August, *La Razón's* editors continued their antigovernment criticism, although now it was directed against Leguía. Abandoning the tactical caution that had served them so well under Pardo, Falcón wrote a vituperative antigovernment editorial, which quickly placed the editors under official surveillance and eventually resulted in their exile.

Falcón's editorial never actually appeared on the pages of *La Razón;* the printer refused to set the type. Informed of this action, the editors decided to leave the editorial's space blank, print the editorial as a leaflet, and stuff it into every issue of the paper. When the issue reached the streets it sold out immediately. But it was a short-lived victory; the printer refused to print the paper from then on.

On August 8 Mariátegui announced, through letters in *El Comercio* and *La Prensa,* the demise of *La Razón.* It was the first casualty of *el oncenio,* Leguía's eleven-year dictatorial reign of power. Soon after, intermediaries for one of the leading anti-Leguiísta papers offered the group the use of their presses, but the government got wind of the proposal through Alfredo de la Piedra (Leguía's relative and a friend of Mariátegui, Falcón, and del Aguila). An ultimatum was issued: either they abandon their antigovernment campaign or else they would have to leave the country.[63]

Leguía firmly proposed, and the group accepted, journalists' grants, giving them the titles of "Official Propagandists for Peru." Mariátegui decided to go to Italy; Falcón and del Aguila chose to go to Spain and Germany respectively. They were the first of a growing number of political exiles produced in the ensuing years by el oncenio.

This incident is often cited as a major blemish on Mariátegui's record, for he is charged with having submitted to Leguía.[64] But

he had never either favored or opposed Leguía, and it was Falcón who wrote the editorial that brought the government's wrath
upon them. Furthermore, at the time no one on the Peruvian
left had opposed Leguía, who was enjoying a political rapprochement with all groups after freeing the country's political
prisoners. In any case, Mariátegui had little choice in the matter: on October 8 a government security agent escorted him out
of the country, accompanying him as far as Panama.[65]

Mariátegui left for Europe with an imagination fired by the
events of 1919. Unlike Falcón, he expressed no trepidation or
fear as he set out on this European adventure which would affect
his life so profoundly. Upon his arrival in Europe, he wasted
little time. Almost immediately the intellectuals and the working-class movement became the chief coordinates of his perspective on postwar Europe.

4

Europe and the Rediscovery of Peru

Por los caminos de Europa encontré el país de América
que yo había dejado y en el que había vivido casi extraño
y ausente.[1]

Arriving in La Rochelle, France, on November 10, 1919, Mariátegui headed straight for Paris—the stormy cultural and intellectual center of postwar Europe. Once there he frequented the avant-garde theatre, sat in on the National Assembly, witnessed militant workers' demonstrations in Belleville, and immersed himself in the left-wing political currents of the day.

The vivid impressions of those initial weeks in Europe stirred him so much that he would later say he had found "the signs of . . . [my] destiny" during his short visit in Paris.[2] And not the least responsible for pointing the way was Henri Barbusse and the *Clarté* circle.[3] Reading Barbusse's great antiwar novel, *Le Feu*, he said, was "one of the deepest emotional experiences of my life."[4] The writer himself made an equally strong impact on Mariátegui. Barbusse struck him as a veritable "priest of the downtrodden," a militant activist with a fully committed heart.

In fact, the *Clarté* intellectuals did more than provide a model of political action; they introduced Mariátegui to a set of ideas that were to blossom into an orientation affecting all of his later work. At the time Barbusse and his group had just founded the International of Thought, and were espousing a Bolshevik point of view. In particular, Mariátegui became aware of the psychological dimension of the struggle toward gaining revolutionary awareness through their influence, a problem to which he was to devote much attention in the coming years. At the same time, they also served as Mariátegui's initial bridge to Marxist thought.

These new ideas and new experiences dovetailed with the assumptions Mariátegui brought with him from Peru. He had left

Lima with a host of perplexing questions relating to the country's pressing economic, social, and political problems on his mind. Paradoxically, it was his stay in Europe, his "apprenticeship" as he called it, that served to sharpen his focus on Peru. But Paris alone did not bring forth his new understanding. After several memorable weeks in France he headed south, driven by the winter cold, and settled in Rome. And it was in Italy that he underwent what amounted to, in his own words, a revelation whereby he suddenly began to know truly the country in which he had previously lived "almost like a stranger."

The European Apprenticeship

Mariátegui's departure was spurred by more than a desire to escape the Parisian winter. Earlier he had had some contact with Italian writers such as Gabriele D'Annunzio. This came about in part because of his association with Abraham Valdelomar, who had returned to Peru greatly stimulated by what he had seen, heard, and read during a stay on the peninsula between 1913 and 1914. Undoubtedly some of his enthusiasm had rubbed off on the then adolescent Mariátegui, who used to follow him everywhere.

Indeed, Mariátegui's "Cartas de Italia," which he began sending back to *El Tiempo* shortly after reaching Rome, indicate a ready affinity with Valdelomar's earlier "Crónicas de Roma."[5] We can look at the "Cartas" as a barometer of Mariátegui's changing political temperament during his years in Italy, much as *La Razón* and *Nuestra Epoca* earlier served us the same purpose.

Mariátegui's initial dispatches covered a variety of subjects— "The Problem of the Adriatic" (May 2 1920), "The Entente and the Soviets" (July 9, 1920), the women's question, police chronicles—although most had to do with politics.[6] Rarely did economics enter the picture at first, for he had yet to begin interpreting public affairs from an economic perspective.

The "Cartas" also revealed Mariátegui's maturing skills as a writer and a journalist. His style had always been simple and sparse. Now he refined it further in the direction of a meticulous realism—surgically direct and crystal clear.

The "Cartas" in fact aptly reflected Mariátegui's ambience as he plunged into the thick of Italian left-wing activity and thought. He had arrived on the eve of *il bienno rosso*, the "red two years" that saw the Italian workers' postwar insurgency reaching its peak. When the great Turin general strike broke out in April 1920, he had been in Rome about four months.

The first outward signs of radical changes in Mariátegui's outlook soon came to light. In December his fellow exile, César Falcón, arrived from Spain. With three other young Peruvians—Artemio Ocaña, a sculptor, Carlos Roe, a medical student, and Palmiro Machiavello, the Peruvian consul—they began a study group to analyze conditions in their country and discuss politics. From it evolved what they called a "Peruvian communist cell."[7]

Mariátegui's new communist sympathies came even more strikingly to the fore at the historic Congress of Livorno, which he and Falcón attended soon afterward (January 1921). A heated debate between factions of the Partito Socialista Italiano (PSI) erupted over the Third International's "twenty-one points," which dictated membership requirements. Delegates argued the issue back and forth for days at the Teatro Goldoni, and the deadlock held fast until the radical wing broke ranks and walked out of the meeting. Soon afterward they formed the Partito Comunista Italiano (PCI).

Mariátegui unmistakenly favored the communist group, headed by Antonio Graziadei, Niccolo Bombacci, and Amadeo Bordiga. Impressed especially by their uncompromising militancy, he portrayed them as the vanguard of the Italian left in one of his articles.[8]

The "Carta" on the dramatic events at the Congress of Livorno revealed his own intensifying interest in socialist politics. Thereafter Mariátegui began to follow the Italian Socialist Party closely, then considered by the Russians the most mature revolutionary party in the West, and in a series of three articles explored the organization of the PSI, its relations with the General Confederation of Labor, and the attitude of the moderates toward the fascists.[9] The last article expressed a total lack of sympathy for the Turati reformists, who held that "socialism must prepare within the existing society the bases for the future society."[10]

Curiously, these "Cartas" generally cited Umberto Terracini as
the guiding light of Turin's L'Ordine Nuovo group but neg-
lected, on the whole, to mention the role of Antonio Gramsci.[11]
He had met Gramsci, as well as Palmiro Togliatti, in what he
called a "circumstantial encounter" during the first days of the
Congress of Livorno.[12] But the Gramscian contact appears not to
have affected Mariátegui to any great extent at this time.[13]

As a sign of his more heavily committed political emphasis the
"Cartas" reveal how he began to tag his post-Livorno articles
with his own name or his initials rather than the pseudonym
"Jack" or "Juan Croniqueur," which he had used to by-line his
first seventeen dispatches from Italy.[14]

Indeed, Mariátegui's new journalistic emphasis on the socialist
movement provides us with an insight into his own persona. The
more he immersed himself in his new interests, the more he
found himself favoring the emotional voluntarist Marxism of
L'Ordine Nuovo group. In fact this "conversion" to their brand
of Marxism probably occurred sometime in early 1921, as he related in almost mystical terms to Armando Bazán years later:

> Up to then Marxism had been for me a somewhat confus-
> ing, ponderous, and cold theory; but at that moment I saw
> its inner light and had a revelation.[15]

Yet in the midst of his espousal of the new faith Mariátegui
never was blinded by dogma—which was also characteristic, to
some degree, of the youthful Turin communist leadership. They
had a certain openness toward non-Marxist thinkers like Georges
Sorel and Benedetto Croce. Mariátegui also read avidly the
works of writers like Adriano Tilgher, Giuseppe Prezzolini,
Giovanni Papini, and others. But the Italian intellectual who had
the strongest effect of all on him during this period was the
youthful Piero Gobetti, a leading radical-liberal. So much did
Gobetti captivate him that he wrote a three-part series of articles
about him; two more than he devoted to Lenin, Trotsky, or
Croce.[16]

It is likely that Gobetti's magnetic appeal to Mariátegui derived as much from the consonance of their personalities as from
a more theoretical attraction. As Terracini quite correctly observed, Mariátegui did not yet have a "marked" identity,[17] and
was still highly susceptible to personal influences.[18] In this con-

nection the Peruvian himself wrote that Gobetti was "one of the kindred spirits with whom . . . [I have felt] the most fraternal harmony."[19]

Whether or not Mariátegui consciously modeled his own life after Gobetti's, it is nonetheless true that some close parallels can be drawn between the two. Like Gobetti, he later founded a journal and a publishing house to disseminate his own political writings. He also assembled his books in the same manner, first by publishing individual articles on a common theme and subsequently collecting them in book form.[20] And just as Gobetti fixed his critical efforts on explaining the causes of Italy's backwardness in terms of economic development, Mariátegui later attempted the same in relation to Peru.[21]

Gobetti's philosophical contribution to Mariátegui's work was also crucial. Later he acknowledged that Gobetti had been a "constant point of reference" in his most important writings.[22] Moreover, through Gobetti, whom he characterized as a *crociano de sinistra* ("a Crocean of the left"), he made contact with some of the central writings of Croce and the ideas of Gramsci and L'Ordine Nuovo group.

By far, however, the most important of the variety of intellectual forces that sifted through Gobetti and helped shape Mariátegui was historical materialism, with its emphasis on the economic determinants of society.

The Peruvian described his debt to Gobetti in these words:

> Especially because Piero Gobetti was not specifically an economist does it appear to me opportune . . . to refer to the weight which in the final analysis economics had in his moral, political, philosophic, aesthetic and historical judgements. This sagacious and constant preoccupation with the economic appears to me as one of the most important aspects of the modernism and realism of Gobetti, which he owed, not to a hermetic Marxist education, but to the autonomous and unfettered maturation of his thought.[23]

If Mariátegui can be termed a "modern and a realist," that is, one who is aware of the economic canon, it was largely due to Gobetti's example.

Croce himself also loomed as a giant on Mariátegui's intellectual horizon. The young journalist had direct contact with

Croce's work, and it was Croce who confirmed the importance of
Georges Sorel.[24] Mariátegui was immensely affected by Sorel's
attempt to synthesize a Marxist economic interpretation with
Bergsonian voluntarism, an emphasis on the power of myth to
mobilize the consciousness of men, and syndicalist ideas. Yet he
did not explore any of these concepts in depth at this point, but
only caught the first glimmer of what was to become a new understanding of things.

Of equally momentous import was his falling in love. On a trip
to Florence he met Ana Chiappe, from Siena, at the home of the
Condessa de Antici Mattei, on the eve of his twenty-sixth birth-
day (June 14, 1920). When he returned to Rome it was with Ana
as his bride. They settled in Frascatti, where their first son was
later born.[25]

At long last, the day arrived for Mariátegui to start the journey home, back to Peru. He confessed to his wife that these two
and a half years in Italy had been the happiest time of his life;
but the decision to go home could not be avoided.[26]

Leaving Rome with his family in June 1922, he proceeded first
to Paris, where he met Romain Rolland. Then they traveled east
to Munich, Vienna, Berlin, Prague, and as far as Budapest.
Spending several months in Germany, Mariátegui studied German and may have begun to read Marx in the original. One of
the highlights of their visit to Berlin was an encounter with Max
Gorki.

Nearly a year soon slid by, and when Mariátegui and his wife
and child boarded a German ship in Antwerp in February 1923
and headed home, he turned the last page of a decisive chapter
in his life, the years of his European apprenticeship.

The Rediscovery of Peru

During his absence, far-reaching changes had swept across
Peru. Leguía's oncenio, only an abstract proposal when he left,
had become by 1923 a political reality.

Leguía's grand strategy for curtailing the power of the civilistas and establishing his own *Patria Nueva* unfolded in more or
less three stages. The first step involved taking charge of not
only all bureaucratic patronage, but military appointments and
grade promotions as well. At the same time, the caudillo was

gaining control of parliament and the press. Once these levers of power had been secured, he sought to neutralize the strength of the old ruling class by rooting his regime in a countervailing social group, the new middle class. Finally, the president struck against the civilista relationship with the British by turning Peru into a haven for American investments.[27] Thus, through a calculated redistribution of power and shrewd orchestration of government policy, he solidly achieved his objective: a dictatorship that endured eleven extraordinary years. He prevailed not by destroying the old ruling class, but by isolating it.

Innovative and to a degree charismatic, Leguía made an energetic effort to become a "constructive caudillo" by investing vast sums of public monies in huge public-works projects. Part of his plan of action against the civilistas was to break up their extensive property holdings in and around Lima, and as he succeeded, the construction of broad boulevards, public buildings, and new middle-class suburbs perceptibly changed the face of the city.

Such moves helped Leguía garner popularity not only with the middle class, but with working-class elements as well. Reaching out, too, to the indigenous communities, he sponsored both legislation on their behalf and several indigenista congresses in Lima.

But not everyone was happy with his seemingly progressive policies, nor took kindly to his dictatorship. University student discontent continued despite Leguía's support of the student reform proposals of 1919. He had agreed to the passage of Public Laws nos. 4002 and 4004, which actually resolved nothing and in practical terms left the university crisis in the hands of San Marcos Rector Javier Prado y Ugarteche. Prado, in turn, met one of the principal student demands by convening the governing University Council on November 27, 1919, and securing a favorable vote on a controversial motion terminating several professors declared incompetent by the students.[28]

That concession, however, did not entirely curb the momentum of the student dissidents. Intellectual influences from abroad, including Kropotkin, Barbusse, Tolstoy, and particularly Bergson's philosophy of the *élan vital*, mixed with youthful nationalism and fueled student radicalism. (Introduced to Peru in 1917 by Mariano Iberico, by the early 1920s Bergsonian voluntarism, with its glorification of the power of the individual, vibrant will, was widespread.)

Even a cursory review of the FEP's monthly publication, *Studium*, reveals the intense nationalism that fired the student movement. For instance, the very first issue (December 1919) looked to San Marcos as the "crucible for forging a national spirit." Time and again the magazine exhorted its student readers to "confront their nationalistic tasks," to study the urgent problems of "our nationality." Edwin Elmore, one of the most influential and brightest student leaders and a frequent contributor to *Studium*, went so far as to organize the Unión de Labor Nacionalista, dedicated to "social studies and civic orientation" and promising to "offer youth an ample field of action in which to test the worth of . . . their nationalist spirit."[29]

But the national question did not grip the hearts of San Marcos students alone. Delegates from the three provincial universities of Trujillo, Cuzco, and Arequipa met with San Marcos students at the First National Student Congress in Cuzco from March 11 to March 20, 1920, and passed a string of high-powered resolutions dealing with the national question. On March 13, for example, they voted that "the federation must intensify its nationalistic orientation."[30] Another plank directed the FEP to seek implementation of a nationalist university curriculum, and demanded that Peruvian professors, not Spanish or foreign scholars, teach the classes on Peruvian history and geography.[31] The congress also took strong stands on issues relating to student protest, declaring, for instance, the legitimate right of students to strike against the university.

The proposal that stood out most sharply among this radical constellation was the suggestion to link student politics with the working class movement. The delegates called on the FEP to organize *universidades populares* ("popular universities") run by students to provide educational programs and a variety of social services to workers. The idea quickly gained the backing of the militant factions at the congress, for it offered a concrete opportunity for direct social action.[32]

The original author and strongest supporter of this proposal was Víctor Raúl Haya de la Torre, who had been elected FEP president in October 1919. Haya de la Torre was also the driving force behind the entire Cuzco congress. In the early 1920s he stood out as the only leader with sufficient authority, ability, and fervor to mobilize the student masses. After the congress he continued to preach the gospel of student activism, traveling to Chile, Argentina, and Uruguay. Everywhere he went the students reacted to his dynamic appeal with tremendous enthusiasm. Some of the contacts he made on this tour would last a lifetime, such as his friendship with Gabriel del Mazo, then president of the Federación Universitaria Argentina (FUA).

Returning to Peru, Haya de la Torre settled into his new role as rector of the Universidad Popular (UP). As the first order of business he set out to organize a faculty for the school, recruiting student leaders like Luis Heysen, Oscar Herrera, Enrique Cornejo Koster, and Luis F. Bustamante. Later others like Carlos Manuel Cox, Esteban Pavletich, and Eudocio Ravines joined them.

In late 1922, Haya de la Torre unveiled his "United Front of Intellectual and Manual Workers" while on an organizing trip to Trujillo. When he returned he renamed the Lima UP the Universidad Popular González Prada (UPGP).[33] With these developments, the student movement progressively embarked upon a path of direct involvement in national politics.

In March 1923 Mariátegui returned to this politically charged situation. He came back with his own "declared and vehement ambition: to participate in the creation of Peruvian socialism" and to work "for the organization of a class party."[34] In contrast to Haya de la Torre's activism, he proceeded more cautiously, concentrating at first on renewing old acquaintances. Somewhere along the line Fausto Posada, a worker Mariátegui had known through *La Razón*, introduced him to Haya de la Torre, who immediately invited him to give a series of lectures at the UPGP.[35]

In the meantime the conflict between the students and Leguía had reached the boiling point over the caudillo's decision to consecrate the nation to the Sacred Heart of Jesus. Wholly secular motives prompted Leguía to agree to the consecration. The move had been sought by church groups since about 1917,[36] and Leguía in turn expected to assure himself of church support for the upcoming presidential elections of 1924.

For a variety of reasons, a host of groups quickly seized the opportunity to turn the issue into a great liberal cause in opposition to the regime. To Haya de la Torre, Leguía's gambit became just the spark he needed around which to galvanize mass support.[37] In contrast Mariátegui chose to remain on the sidelines, saying the protest lacked concrete revolutionary ends.[38]

Haya de la Torre triggered the May 23 Sacred Heart of Jesus protest by organizing a rousing student-worker demonstration at San Marcos. The throng soon took to the streets, where a fierce confrontation with the police ensued. In the midst of the clash, a student and a worker were killed (there were three fatalities on the other side). Instantly Haya de la Torre made the incident a dramatic symbol of the worker-student alliance. That evening he moved furtively about the streets of the capital, exhorting the public to attend a vigil at San Marcos and a massive public funeral the following day.[39]

Such events catapulted Haya de la Torre into national prominence, and after the Sacred Heart of Jesus demonstrations his notoriety soon forced him into hiding. Four months later the police arrested him and sent him to the Isla de San Lorenzo. From there he went into exile, passing through Central America, Mexico, and Europe.

Before leaving Lima, Haya de la Torre asked Mariátegui to assume the direction of *Claridad,* the UPGP's official publication. As a result Mariátegui found himself working hand-in-hand with an alliance of students and workers.

All the while, Mariátegui had been discussing publicly the views he had formulated abroad. The first thing he set out to explain was how in Europe he had made a "discovery of America" and of Peru.[40] In other words, he had begun to see with the eyes of one who knew that the future depended on the outcome of the crucial revolutionary struggle between capitalism and socialism.

Since Mariátegui at this time clearly posed no threat to the government, he enjoyed almost complete freedom to publish in Lima's two principal weeklies, *Variedades* and *Mundial.* Leguía apparently even thought the pieces on world revolution were very intelligent. They introduced Peruvians to a treatment of world events they had never before experienced. For example, his article on the Russo-Japanese War of 1904 described the conflict as the harbinger of a vast wave of anticolonialist movements.[41]

Expanding on this radical perspective in a March 1923 interview, Mariátegui answered the rather Spenglerian question posed by an interviewer of whether he considered "the old continent in decline" affirmatively—quickly adding, however, that he meant *capitalist* Europe. A socialist Europe, he predicted, was rising from the old shell of a dying capitalist society, though not without a fierce struggle. In fact, the entire globe was locked in a similar conflict, though America had only "a secondary role to play in this stage of human history."[42]

Mariátegui sketched in the details of his interpretation of the dynamics of world history—and Peru's part in the swiftly-moving drama—in his UPGP lecture series, which began after the May 23 campaign. A large audience of workers and students showed up for the talks, usually on Friday evenings, and as a result he gained his first popular following.

The series opened right with the subject of social revolution in Europe. But he wove his theme around the specifics of the Peruvian perspective, as he seemed to do in all of the succeeding lectures, and stressed that the workers should seek to understand world issues from the point of view of their own class interests and culture.

The initial lectures exhorted the workers to feel that they were more than merely spectators of the world crisis, but were actively and inextricably involved. How? In the same way that Peru was tied to the world economy. Although Peru had gained its independence long ago, the country remained economically dependent on western capitalism, an economic structure now in the throes of crisis precipitated by the world war, the Russian Revolution, and the ongoing struggle with socialism.[43]

The tremors created by the ongoing struggle between capitalism and socialism had split the international left into reformist and revolutionary camps, each with its own ideologies and political strategies. But the Peruvian left did not have to follow this broken path. Instead of dividing, in Peru syndicalists and socialists should unite and fight a common cause, Mariátegui urged. Here Mariátegui was seeking to present his Marxist interpretation conciliatorily, for syndicalism still predominated in the labor movement. He even appealed to the example of Georges Sorel, "the greatest and most illustrious theorist of syndicalism" (which he had never really been), who had fervently endorsed revolutionary Russia.[44]

Striking a similar note in the following lecture, Mariátegui identified himself as "more than anything . . . a partisan of a proletarian united front"—the tactic sanctioned by the Third Congress of 1921—and in succeeding lectures continued to hit home the point that only an alliance of syndicalists and socialists could create a "popular culture" in Peru.[45]

Soon enough he won over most of the workers in the audience. The tension of the initial meetings dissipated, the attendance grew, and the series was extended, demonstrating the degree of responsiveness to the novel interpretation of history and current affairs that Mariátegui had brought back with him from Europe.

Throughout the remainder of the series he highlighted revolutionary figures and movements like a jeweler appraising the shining facets of social history. In particular he emphasized the drive of the voluntarist radicals, which explains his special regard for the German Spartacus movement led by Karl Liebknecht, Rosa Luxemburg, Franz Mehring, and Carla Zetkin. Not surprisingly, he attributed the defeat of their 1918–19 Berlin insurrection to betrayal by the Social Democrats.

Mariátegui also concentrated on the role of the proletariat, remarking, with regard to the German labor movement and the working-class movement in general, that "the instrument of the socialist revolution will always be the industrial proletariat, the proletariat of the cities."[46] In this important respect, however, his ideas would eventually become more flexible.

In the twelfth lecture he zeroed in on the "crisis of democracy." From a short-term point of view, the crisis could be traced to the postwar period. In the clash between workers and the bourgeoisie following the war, he said, the middle class, heterogeneous and lacking in class consciousness, had sided with the bourgeoisie and the rightist reaction. The result in some instances, as in the case of Italy, had been the emergence of the fascist state and the crisis of liberal demcy.[47]

Indeed the war had so intensified the class struggle in Europe, he related, that western capitalists had been forced to turn to Asia, Africa, and South America for a solution to their problems. It was an old remedy that they sought: the "developed peoples of occidental civilization" enslaving the "backward peoples." He bitingly characterized the attitude of the capitalists of the developed world:

> What matters is that the manual labor of Oceania, America, Asia, and Africa pay for the greater ease of the European or American worker. What matters is that the colonized manual worker produce a low-priced raw material that the European worker may turn into a manufactured commodity, and which in turn he will consume in abundance. What matters is that that part of humanity which is less civilized work for those who are more civilized.[48]

Mariátegui did not always interpret western capitalism in such negative terms. Capitalism might introduce social havoc in colonized areas, he noted, but it also eventually introduced revolutionary principles and politics. Thus,

> Asia and Africa want their emancipation from Europe in the name of the ideology, in the name of the doctrine that Europe taught and preached to them.[49]

But special problems were bound to arise in applying western revolutionary socialist principles to the colonized, underdeveloped world. In the colonial world there did not exist, strictly speaking, capitalist economies. Consequently those areas lacked authentic nationalist bourgeoisies. Mariátegui did not elaborate further on this point in his lectures; he simply concluded that "the problems of the people of the West are different from the problems of the Asian people,"and that, therefore, European socialists ought to analyze the problems and formulate the programs solely for their own countries rather than assume they were in a position to do the same for colonial peoples as well.[50]

Mariátegui criticized western socialists, especially those of the Second International, for their stand against the Third International's support of anticolonialist movements in the Third World. Leaders of the Second International were convinced that anticolonialist wars would only result in bringing to power the native bourgeoisies, not the proletariat. These socialists therefore claimed there was an absence of "social struggle in the Orient," declaring:

Socialism must only support socialist movements. And the rebellion of oriental .people is a nationalist rebellion. Their immediate question is not a question of proletariat insurrection, but of a bourgeois insurrection.[51]

Such an analysis, however, rested on a false foundation. Leaders of the Second International were lacking in a global perspective of the struggle between capitalism and socialism, and remained captives of a narrow European point of view. In contrast, he said, Zinoviev had summed up the colonial question quite correctly at the Congress of Halle when he remarked:

The Second International was limited to white men; the Third does not divide men according to color. If you want a world revolution, if you want to liberate the proletariat from the chains of capitalism, you must stop thinking solely of Europe.[52]

Bidding his audience to harken to the call of anticolonialist revolution in the semicolonial world, socialist revolution in Europe, and the need for a similar anticapitalist struggle in Peru, Mariátegui's lectures served as a kind of introduction to a radical interpretation of the national question. We find in his talks—which began in March 1923 when he returned from Europe and concluded in January 1924 with his seventeenth installment—as well as in his published articles and interviews of the period, that he presented the conceptual makings of what Basadre would call "a new way of treating Peruvian history."[53] Mariátegui was beginning to transmit his "rediscovery" of Peru, his new understanding of the country's role in world economics and politics, to the workers, students, and intellectuals of the Peruvian left.

Mariátegui Becomes a Leader

According to Eudocio Ravines, a professor at the Popular University, Mariátegui's lectures introduced "a systematic discussion of radical ideology" to the UPGP student and worker cadres. Armando Bazán, another member of the faculty, reported that "all of us UPGP professors had the same cultural formation as Haya de la Torre: the books of Tolstoy, Kropotkin, Victor Hugo,

Henri Barbusse, Emile Zola, José Ingenieros, and González Prada." And Esteban Pavletich, who arrived in Lima from Huánuco about the same time that Mariátegui returned from Europe, commented that the most talked about "political tract of the day" among San Marcos students was Spengler's *The Decline of the West*.[54]

In other words, up to the moment of Mariátegui's return, none of Peru's student intellectuals were acquainted with revolutionary politics or even, as one said, with "the art of dealing with people."[55] The dissemination of his economic and global interpretation through his UPGP lectures was like throwing a rock in a pond—the ripples spread far and wide.

Mariátegui's innovative approach created waves, too, among the readers of his published works. As Basadre observed:

> There was no one else dedicated then to that type of journalism. At the time the articles of Luis Varela y Orbegoso ("Clovis") in the aftevn edition of *El Comercio* were known; articles which were charming and cleanly written, although bland, superficial, and removed from any attempt at interpretation or orientation.[56]

As his reputation among sectors of the working class and the intelligentsia spread, Mariátegui in effect succeeded Haya de la Torre as the leader of Lima's miniscule left. And almost immediately, differences in personal style and political orientation between the two became apparent. As soon as he took over the UPGP's *Claridad* (which had been originally founded in May 1923), Mariátegui changed its subtitle from *Periodical of the Free Youth of Peru* to *Periodical of the Workers' Federation of Lima and the Free Youth of Peru*.

Moreover, *Claridad's* first issue under Mariátegui's direction carried a front-page article on Lenin, accompanied by a large photograph of the revolutionary. It was a salute to "the memory of the great Russian teacher and agitator" in the name of the "organized vanguard of the proletariat, youth, and revolutionary intellectuals of Peru."[57]

Mariátegui's association with *Claridad* produced his first conflict with Leguía's administration: in January 1924 he was arrested with several students and a few workers for voicing antigovernment criticism. The incident did not inhibit his left-wing activities, but served only to thrust him further into public view.

The following April, *El Obrero Textil,* Lima's principal working-class newspaper (published by the Federation of Textile Workers), asked Mariátegui to write an article for their issue commemorating "The First of May and the Proletarian United Front." He took this opportunity to present an analysis of the labor movement in Peru, which had fallen into disarray for lack of effective leadership. Organizers like Gutarra and Barba were long gone; they had joined either Leguía or other caudillos. As a result the Federación Obrera de Lima (FOL) had fallen prey to rampant factionalism, though it was still dominated by the anarcho-syndicalists, and there were stirrings of sssion by some members of the organization.

Mariátegui's remarks addressed specifically this lack of unity:

This international date invites many reflections. But for Peruvian workers the most pressing, the most opportune, is the one that concerns the need and feasibility of a united front. Lately some secessionist attempts have taken place. Therefore it is urgent that we understand each other. . . . My attitude since becoming part of this vanguard has always been that of a convinced supporter, that of a fervent propagandist of the united front. I remember having declared so in one of the initial lectures [the third] of my course on the history of the world crisis. . . . At that time I said from the tribunal of the Universidad Popular: "We are still too few to divide ourselves. Let us not make issues out of labels or titles." Subsequently I have repeated similar or analogous words. . . . It behooves us, for example, to awaken in the majority of the Peruvian proletariat a class consciousness. . . . This task belongs as much to the socialists as to the syndicalists, the communists, and the libertarians. All of us have the duty to plant the seeds of change and to spread class concepts. Within the united front each person must maintain his individual affiliation and his personal ideas. Everyone must work for his own creed. But we must all feel united by class solidarity, bind ourselves through our common struggle against our common enemy, tie ourselves together by the same revolutionary volition and the same passion for change.[58]

Mariátegui's own passion for change proved contagious. Workers now began seeking him out, and his influence spread.

He turned thirty in 1924, and his history now began to catch up with him. Since his childhood crippling accident, he had suffered periodic infirmities but nothing serious. Throughout the years in Europe he had enjoyed excellent health. But quite suddenly, in mid 1924, he was struck with a near-death trauma. An infection in his right leg caused by a malignant tumor began to spread, and the doctors found no other alternative but to amputate in order to save his life. The illness and the operation took him to the brink. When he came to and discovered he had lost his leg, he went into shock. After the terrible experience he convalesced for months in a clinic in Chosica.[59]

Much like the accident of early childhood, the amputation sealed his fate in many ways.[60] It confirmed in a remarkably strength-giving way his choice to live according to certain principles. Immobile in a wheelchair, from then on he faced ever-increasing responsibilities with a calm that truly astonished his friends.

Because of this "interruption," as he henceforth termed his illness, Mariátegui settled into a more routine way of life. He began to work in a study and to adhere to a rigorous daily schedule. Expanding his literary activities, he cofounded with his younger brother Julio César the publishing house, Editorial Minerva. In this connection they also published a review bulletin entitled *Libros y Revistas*.

The major focus of Mariátegui's attention at this time went to the publication of his first book. Assembled from the many articles he had written for *Mundial* and *Variedades*, it appeared in 1925 as *La escena contemporánea*.

In the *Escena* the basic themes of the UPGP lectures remained unchanged, though they were presented more coherently and comprehensively. The postwar world provided the broad canvas on which he projected, in the fashion of a world news cinematographic report, a biology of Italian fascism, a long analysis of the liberals' caving in to reaction, and discussions of the Russian Revolution, the crisis of social democracy, and revolution and the superstructure. Mariátegui concluded with superb impressions of Tagore and the colonial world, and a critique of the religious zeal of Mahatma Gandhi and the rising fortunes of

Zionist nationalism. Prophetically, this catholic portrait of the age closed with a devastating criticism of the spread of anti-Semitism.

The tour de force was tightly and effectively put together. Throughout, its focus was on the dynamics of class relations among the fascists and the liberals and in general the impact of class forces on culture. The book revealed an acutely perceptive and mature intelligence and a growing sophistication in world affairs.

A great success, the *Escena* catapulted Mariátegui to the forefront of the ranks of the Peruvian and international intelligentsia. "None of us who were companions and friends of José Carlos Mariátegui . . . ever doubted the complete success that life had in store for the then almost adolescent chronicler," wrote one Peruvian reviewer of the *Escena*. [61]

By 1925, then, Mariátegui had concluded his years of apprenticeship, become more knowledgeable about the history of Peru and the world setting, and had progressed far along the path of rounding out his personality. Now began the process of the radical Peruvianization of the self.

5

Amauta, A Journal for Revolutionaries

Yo vine de Europa con el propósito de fundar una revista
. . . producirá o precipitará un fenómeno de polarización
y concentración. . . . Esta revista vinculará a los
hombres nuevos del Perú.[1]

All of Mariátegui's works are autobiographical in the sense that
they can be read as the unfolding stages of an expanding nationalist consciousness. And this is what *Amauta* (September 1926)
was also all about.

What was unique about the journal, what differentiated it
from his UPGP lectures or the *Escena,* for example, was that
here Mariátegui's politics became firmly rooted in the cause of
the nation and the native race. A radical *indigenismo* pervaded
Amauta, linking him directly with the previous generation of
left-wing nationalists, especially the radicals.

Amauta served a dual function—as a platform for Mariátegui's
indigenista revolutionary nationalism, and as an instrument of
"polarization and concentration" of social forces designed to
shape an entire generation of revolutionary nationalists, the
"new men of Peru."

By the time of *Amauta's* appearance, then, Mariátegui had
come to terms with some basic questions. He had identified a
core of basic beliefs, and was now prepared to act on them.

His evolution was, in fact, pointedly mirrored in a series of
luminous essays written between October 1924 and November
1925 called *El alma matinal (The Dawning Spirit).*[2] *Alma* tells us
much about the state of Mariátegui's mind in the two years that
passed between his traumatic illness and the publication of
Amauta. Indeed, so much in *Alma* serves as a prelude to the
process by which Mariátegui himself starts to become a new
man, that our discussion of *Amauta* ought to begin there.

El alma matinal: Prelude to *Amauta*

El alma matinal did not present a panoramic sweep of the external world as did the *Escena*. Rather, in what sounded at times almost like an internal monologue, Mariátegui hammered out some of the basic philosophical assumptions of his politics.

These assumptions bore the dynamic imprint of voluntarism, the Bergsonian, Nietzschean, Sorelian belief in will and action. Through the writings of Sorel, particularly his 1907 introduction to *Reflections on Violence*, Mariátegui had acquired the notion that while science and history followed rational laws, individual action was open to the impulse of the human will.[3] Man reached his highest fulfillment as a creator, as a consciousness with purpose and direction.

Mariátegui applied these ideas to the problem of revolutionary consciousness and action in a way that reminds us immediately of the views of the postwar *Clarté* group he had encountered in Europe. But his preoccupation with the question of belief and will did not stem solely from a study of the psychological aspects of social change; it was also a need that derived from deep inside himself. In fact, the lead article in *Alma*, "Two Conceptions of Life," posed essentially the same choice that Mariátegui must have faced during his recovery from the near-fatal illness: the choice between a life of reason and reflection or polemical faith and commitment to action.

Mariátegui saw these two sharply opposing concepts of life interacting on the broader stage of history. In his view, the rationalist ideal of progress, the crowning achievement of the nineteenth-century bourgeoisie, had dominated the prewar culture so thoroughly that even the socialist and syndicalist masses had been tamed into accepting its reformist precepts. As a result an era of relative peace and prosperity reigned, reaching its height in the *belle epoque*. Enjoying the apparent security of "a world which seemed consolidated forever and insured against any possibility of change,"[4] the socialists fell prey to the same sort of decadence (conceived in the manner of Sorel) infecting the upper classes.

The war, however, shattered the bubble of bourgeois complacence. The shock waves of the ensuing "spiritual and psychological" crisis shook the whole culture. And from out of the debris arose a new combative spirit, an almost mystical affirmation best exemplified by the Bolsheviks, but also evident among the fascists. Only these groups dared to believe in the postwar years that men and women could still create their own history. Not everyone heeded their call; in fact, said Mariátegui, what separated people after the war, more so than doctrinal or material differences, was how they stood in relation to the new assertive spirit.

In "Spirit of the Times" Mariátegui left no doubt about his personal choice between the conflicting prewar and postwar world views. Rejecting bourgeois decadence and rationalism, he cast his lot wholeheartedly in the direction of action and struggle, will and faith. In other words, he saw himself as one of the "new men" of intuitionist commitment.

"Man and Myth," which Mariátegui wrote soon afterward, probed more deeply the meaning of the postwar malaise afflicting bourgeois society. Here relying on the ideas of Adriano Tilgher, he saw the bourgeoisie continuing to believe in the rationalist assumptions implicit in their prewar idea of progress. And therein lay the heart of the crisis created by a society based on science and reason: neither could ever satisfy man's need for a sense of infinity and the unknown. Man was essentially a "metaphysical animal," unable to live without a transcendent concept of life—without "myth, faith, and hope."[5]

These three elements were precisely what nurtured the revolutionary consciousness of the masses. And the mainspring of such basic emotions could be found deep in the collective subconscious, in the region in fact where religious attitudes were formed. Myth, faith, and hope were the foundations of both religious belief and political commitment, for as Sorel had pointed out:

> An analogy . . . [can be drawn] between religion and revolutionary socialism. . . . Bergson has taught us that religion is not the only thing that occupies the profound regions of our mental life; revolutionary myths have their place there equally with religion.[6]

In other words, wrote Mariátegui, the revolutionary zeal of the proletariat did not emanate from "their science," from rational analysis, but from "their faith . . . [from their] religious, mystical, spiritual strength."[7] Reason was a pale, feeble instrument when compared to the vivid motivating power of the suprarational, subconscious will.

Bourgeois intellectuals could not commit themselves to social revolution as did the proletariat because they did not believe in myth, in the idea that social revolution embodied an absolute, eternal truth. Nor did they see, in the manner of contemporary philosophers (meaning Bergson and the pragmatists), that although the truth is relative and "the truth today will prove invalid tomorrow," nevertheless, each man must decide what is useful to believe in and then act on that belief.

Exploring the myth of social revolution in other essays, Mariátegui identified it with the myth of a "final struggle" whose battle cry could be heard in the streets of Moscow, Rome, Milan, Paris, and even Lima. This myth was both real and illusion. It was real in the sense that it was actually believed by the working class (a view akin to William James's pragmatic notion that "we have the right to believe at our own risk any hypothesis that is live enough to tempt our will"). But historically speaking, the "finality" of the struggle was an illusion. For human progress evolves in stages, said Mariátegui, stages that are not entirely linear in their development. Some aspects of evolution are cyclical or repetitive (as in the manner of Nietzsche's or Vico's cycles of history), and thus, as history unfolds, man continually "arrives [at a point in time] only to depart anew."[8]

The impetus to "depart anew," to become engaged once again, body and soul, in the wearisome struggle, could only come from faith in the ultimate cause to be won. The anticolonialist movements in modern China, India, and Turkey were propelled by such a millennial vision. Why did the realization that similar battles had been waged and probably would continue to be fought throughout history not act as ice water on their revolutionary fire? Because man's "vital impulses" respond to the elemental questions of life before considering the intellectual questions, Mariátegui answered; because an unschooled man does not think about the relativism of his myths or even recognize that they are relative. Given that he must act, he acts; given that he must struggle, he struggles.[9]

Throughout all of the essays in *Alma* there nevertheless ran the unmistakeable current of Marxism, but it is a voluntarist current. Mariátegui's was not a mechanistic, deterministic Marxism, as can be seen by his assertion that "no revolution can foresee the revolution to come after it, even if it carries within itself the seeds of the new revolution."[10] Marxist orthodoxy also flew out the window in one of the few specific references made to Marx during this time—not in the *Alma* series but in a review published a year later with the title, "*The Agony of Christianity* by don Miguel de Unamuno." Here he pointedly refuted the claim that Marx believed "things made men."[11] Marx's true image, he argued, was not that of the "monotonous materialist" portrayed by his disciples, but closer to the picture painted by Sorel, Croce, and Tilgher.[12] He believed that only those who felt Marxism in their spirit could truly claim the mantle of Marxist revolutionaries.[13]

"*The Agony of Christianity*" was only one of a myriad of articles that Mariátegui turned out while he was working on *Alma* and shortly thereafter. *Alma*, however, seems to have held a vital key to the transformation of his inner being, for upon the book's completion, Mariátegui assumed the serenity of a person of deep faith. The experience heartily strengthened the resolve acquired in the wake of his illness, and thereafter Mariátegui confronted all obstacles with a determination and self-discipline that was unshakeable.

He began an even more rigorous work schedule, entering his study each morning at eight and remaining there until noon. After lunch and the rest period prescribed by his physician, he returned to his study at three and worked until six. During working hours he was unapproachable, except for appointments on publishing and political matters.[14]

A great deal of the day was taken up with reading the many publications he received from abroad.[15] He also continued to write, and out of force of habit kept up his old journalistic style of waiting until the last minute to put things down on paper— though by the time he went to his typewriter he knew exactly what he was going to say.[16] Several new projects were in the making: a "journal of criticism" he then called *Vanguardia*, which later emerged as *Amauta;* a work-in-progress on Peru (possibly his earliest reference to the *Siete ensayos de interpretación de la realidad peruana*);[17] and plans for a center of social, economic, and educational studies.

Every evening friends dropped by the *rincón rojo*, the "red corner," where Mariátegui lived on Washington eet. A steady stream of students, artists, writers, and workers came and went. Among the most regular visitors were Armando Bazán, María Wiesse, César Miró Quesada, Angela Ramos, Hugo Pesce, José Sabogal, Estuardo Núñez, José María Eguren, Lucas Oyague, Julio del Prado, Xavier Abril, Clodoaldo Alberto Espinosa Bravo, Eugenio Garro, and Ricardo Martínez de la Torre. Some were political associates—Pesce, Bazán, and rtínez de la Torre, for example. But art and literary movements, not politics, were the main topics of these lively discussions. Basadre, who attended a few of the gatherings, has drawn in his inimitable style a vivid portrayal:

> He received his friends at the end of the day, for he zeal-ously guarded, at times even brusquely, the working day for his own tasks or special appointments. When the people arrived they found him sitting on a sofa with the lower part of his body covered. He received his visitors simply, smil-ing not conventionally or in a histrionic way, but only slightly. Always his black and brilliant eyes attracted your attention immediately, as well as his aquiline profile, his thin and tan face, the thick black hair without grey and always neatly cut, though often a forelock fell on his fore-head in a bohemian manner. His dress was always simple and very neat, and he always used a loose bow tie. His conversation was wholly without vanity, without autobio-graphic expansiveness or rhetoric, without conversational vacuousness. On the contrary, he was always ready to listen and question, evasive only when a personal allusion was made, and seldom given to small talk. His wit, reminiscent of his days as the humorous writer of *Voces* and *El Ti-empo*—the wit of the Peruvian *costeño* privy to the bizarre happenings of the day—sometimes suddenly flashed in asides to men and their doings.[18]

The diversity of social contacts and reading of this period en-riched Mariátegui's still-evolving political and intellectual educa-tion. Gradually he integrated two additional strands of thought into the weave of his new consciousness: indigenismo and van-guardismo. The first theme derived from South American and particularly Peruvian sources; the second was linked with the European cultural vanguard. Together with Mariátegui's Marxist and non-Marxist influences, they formed an eclectic, heterogeneous ancestry for the birth of his new journal in 1926, *Amauta*.

Genesis and Overview of *Amauta*

The vanguardista movements were new in Peru, having made their debut in 1917 when Alberto Hidalgo introduced Marinetti's futurist manifesto in, of all places, Arequipa. Four years later *Mundial*, the popular Limeño weekly, published a lengthy essay on dadaism, and other articles followed on creacionismo, futurismo, ultraísmo, and sincronismo, all variants of vanguardismo.

Flecha, the first vanguardista literary journal in Peru, appeared in 1924. Welcoming to its pages "every manifesto of audacity, of creative courage," the magazine championed the cause of social and cultural "radical change" in order to "bring about a new ERA: free, revolutionary, iconoclastic, and creative."[19]

The use of the term revolutionary suggested a significant aspect of vanguardismo in Peru. In assimilating the new theology of cubism, dadaism, futurism, and other avant-garde trends from abroad, most Peruvian vanguardistas retained their concern with the country's national problems. In Peru, therefore, literary vanguardismo included a social revolutionary content.[20] *Flecha* blazed this intellectual trail, followed by other vanguard journals in 1926 and 1927, such as *Poliedro*, the serial *Trampolín-Hangar-Rascacielos-Tímonel*, *Guerrilla Hurra*, and *Jarana*.

In contrast to the relatively new vanguardista movement, indigenismo had roots going back to the previous century. González Prada, Clorinda Matto de Turner, and other writers of their generation in the 1870s and 1880s had pioneered the way, creating an indigenista literature with social content. Later, members of the civilista intellectual establishment contributed to an awakening interest at San Marcos University in doing research on Indian communities. Manuel Vicente Villarán wrote a thesis on *"Condiciones legales de las comunidades indígenas."*[21] Conservative members of the generation of 1900, like Riva Agüero and José Gálvez, were among the early writers to call

attention to the problem of how to treat nativist topics in literature.

By the 1920s, indigenismo had become one of the major concerns of almost all intellectual and artistic circles, regardless of
race or class. Even politicians endorsed the movement; Leguía,
as we have mentioned, sponsored several indigenista congresses.
But obviously it was in the hands of the progressive political
elements that indigenismo acquired its more radical cast.

Perhaps the first member of the generation of 1919 to em-
brace indigenismo was the youthful Luis Alberto Sánchez. In
1920, he wrote a thesis entitled "Nosotros" ("We") for his
bachelor's degree at San Marcos, in which he proposed a fundamental reconsideration of the importance of nativist literature to
the national literary tradition.[22] Essentially, he saw the Indian
culture as the "base of Peruvian nationality," proclaiming that
the Quechua tradition "is ours, its origins exclusively ours."[23] In
other words, the core of the Peruvian legacy, including letters,
was indigenous.

In the same year (1920), Enrique López Albujar published his
classic *Cuentos andinos* (Tales of the Andes), which tore away
the idyllic and sentimental veil from traditional indigenismo.
Using data gathered during his many years as a rural judge, he
portrayed the harsh realities of Indian community life along with
its more positive elements.

Soon collections of indigenous poetry began to make their appearance, such as Alejandro Peralta's *Ande* in 1926 and J. Mario
Chávez's *Ccoca*. New indigenista literary journals also mush-
roomed throughout the country between 1926 and 1928: *Atusparia* in Huarás, *Boletín Kuntur* in Sicuani, *Boletín Titicaca* in
Puno, *Chirupa* in Arequipa, *Inti* in Huancayo, and, of course,
Amauta in Lima.

In art, the painter José Sabogal led the way. Ironically,
Sabogal had discovered the Indian as a subject while he was
studying and teaching in Argentina. When he came back to Peru
in 1919, he set to work painting exclusively indigenous themes
in Cuzco. In 1921, he returned to the capital and held his first
exhibition. Soon a circle of artists gathered around him, including Julia Codesido, C. Sánchez Urteada ("Camilo Blas"), Enrique Camino Brent, and others.[24] Sabogal, whom Mariátegui
called the first truly Peruvian painter, in fact was the one who

suggested the name *Amauta* for his new journal—invoking the image of the wise man or keeper of the sacred and secular knowledge of the Incas.[25]

In tracing the roadmap of Mariátegui's own transformation into a revolutionary indigenista, we find that until 1923–24 there does not appear any mention of special concern for the Indian cause in his writings. Until then he was culturally and politically very much tied to a Limeño mestizo style (even the brief *Colónida* interlude of 1915–17 was really mestizo, if not basically creole, in flavor). Nonnative western sources were the major influences on his intellectual development.

But after his return from Europe, Mariátegui discovered that the most radical, creative wing of the artistic and literary intelligentsia in Peru was indigenista—reflecting, in part, a trend throughout Latin America. Eventually he became a close friend of Sabogal and Codesido, and also favored the works of some of the new indigenista writers.

Soon Mariátegui, too, was swept up in the movement. Although his first public cultural statement after his return from abroad was to organize an exhibit of the latest European avant-garde art, by December 1924, with the publication of "The First Problem of Peru," he was ready to take a strong indigenista stand.

In a style characteristic of his later works—factual, sparse, and hard-hitting, and imbued with the inexorable confidence of someone who knows exactly where he wants to go, Mariátegui wrote that the "first problem of Peru" is

> the problem of the Indian. . . . [It] is the problem of four million Peruvians. It is the problem of three quarters of the population of Peru. It is the problem of the majority. It is the problem of the nationality."[26]

The Indian was, he said, "the foundation of our nationality *in formation* . . . without the Indian, Peruvianness is not possible."[27]

These bold words were penned in connection with the meeting of the Fourth National Indigenista Congress in Lima (the congresses were soon discontinued because of their increasing militancy). The event drew campesino leaders from the provinces to the capital, and Mariátegui took the opportunity to make his first contact with them.

Some six months later (July 1925) he wrote another indigenista article, exalting the "new spirit" of nativist awareness[28] expressed by figures such as López Albujar, Luis Valcárcel, Luis Alberto Sánchez, Jorge Basadre, and Haya de la Torre. At the time he traced indigenismo back to Valdelomar and the *Colónida* milieu, ignoring the earlier efforts of González Prada and other nineteenth-century writers.

Mariátegui's passion for the Indian issue was not, however, merely a product of his own exposure to historical and contemporary intellectual influences. Basically, it was an outgrowth of his entire Peruvian experience. After all, the problem of race had been basic to Peruvian culture since the Spanish conquest, and it was an unavoidable question for Mariátegui's generation. He grew up in an atmosphere where racial considerations were handled subtly (though sometimes not), but they were always present. For example, we have already noted how Ventura García Calderón, of the generation of 1900, could still recollect years later the "accent of melancholia" surrounding the first mestizos of the generation of 1919 arriving at San Marcos University—in contrast, that is, to the more "Spanish" lightheartedness of the Lima he had always known. A certain racial tension, difficult to assess but unavoidable to the senses, always marked the interrelations between the generations of 1900 and 1919.

Aside from the fact that Mariátegui must have shared in the racial awareness of his generation, there can be no doubt that this was also a subject of deeply individual importance to him. The uncertainty and obscurity surrounding his own parentage seems to have intensified his interest in the Indian, although this is a difficult area to probe for lack of sources.[29] But we do have one dramatic bit of evidence. In an unedited article dealing with Roman art, not published until long after his death, Mariátegui suddenly digressed to identify himself first as a South American creole, then as being "more Oriental" than "western or Latin." Finally he said: "I, although an Indian, and perhaps because I am an Indian."[30]

This is a rather startling and wholly unexpected confession, especially if we keep in mind that he made it at about the same time that he was publishing his second indigenista essay—that

is, during the period that he wrote two other articles on Roman
art (June-July 1925).[31] And it was during the same year, 1925,
that Mariátegui first mentioned that he was working on his collection of indigenista-oriented essays, *Siete ensayos de interpretación de la realidad peruana.*

By the time *Amauta* appeared the following year, Mariátegui
had become a zealous indigenista. But his approach was unique
in many respects. Thus, while articles in the journal consistently
lauded the achievements of Quechuan history, art, music, language, and folklore, they never espoused a racist or cultural
nationalist viewpoint or harked back to a golden age to be re-
trieved. On the contrary, Mariátegui vehemently took issue with
those indigenistas who rejected the West. He always defended
the view that the Peruvian revolution needed to draw upon
western and international social theory, technology, and political
experience (which brought him the attacks of being an *europei-
zante*).

Other indigenista publications often nurtured a hortatory and
self-righteous tone, railing at the injustices committed against
the natives and moralizing about "what should be done" for
them. *Amauta*, in contrast, set out to study and analyze the Indian question from a deeper perspective, decisively extending
the notion, first proposed by González Prada and carried forth
by other Peruvian leftists, that the issue should be treated in
fundamentally socioeconomic terms.[32] Mariátegui had articulated
this idea in an article in 1925, in which—using the religious language so much a part of his general style—he spoke of the "sin
of the Conquest. . . . the original sin inherited from the republic, that of wanting to organize a Peruvian society and economy
'without the Indian and against the Indian.' "[33] *Amauta's* goal
was to revindicate that sin, to look toward a Peru of the future in
which native people would figure as equal participants in the
process of national development. In that sense the journal
pledged its "adherence to the Race."[34]

Amauta, of course, was not solely an organ of indigenismo. A
richly diverse array of literary, artistic, and political figures of
the vanguardista and other movements joined in contributing to
the pages of the journal. Peruvian and Spanish American authors
predominated, including Jorge Basadre, Luis Alberto Sánchez,
José Antonio Encinas, poet José María Eguren, novelist Martín

Adán, Bergsonian philosopher Mariano Iberico, as well as Franz Tamayo from Bolivia, Jesús Silva Herzog from Mexico, Pablo Neruda and Gabriela Mistral from Chile, and Emilio Pettoruti from Argentina.[35] The journal also usually included writings from international luminaries like André Breton, Jean Cocteau, George Groz, G. B. Shaw, Freud, Gobetti, Trotsky, Lenin, Lunatcharsky, and Plekhanov. Sabogal and other indigenista and vanguardista artists provided graphics that were stark but colorful.

While literary and artistic movements received considerable space, the Peruvian national question served as the major motif. Mariátegui himself wrote many of the articles dealing with this subject (later incorporated in the *Siete ensayos*). Political and social problems were highlighted, with less attention given to economic questions. Mariátegui and Martínez de la Torre generally wrote the economically oriented pieces; occasionally others were written by contributors such as Basadre, who presented an antiimperialist analysis of foreign investments in Peru in one of the issues.[36]

As we have indicated, emphasis on national problems coexisted harmoniously with internationalist themes. Each issue generally spotlighted an anticolonialist revolutionary movement—the struggles in China, Nicaragua, India, and Mexico.

Amauta made quite a splash at home as well as abroad. *Clarté* described the journal as a "Review of Culture and of Revolutionary Literature, oriented toward the Ancient American civilizations, Defender of a Marxist Program, and, above all, of the antiimperialist struggle of the masses in South America."[37]

Despite its obviously socialist orientation, *Amauta* did not propose a specific political program or adopt an explicit political stand at first. An early editorial stated only that the journal would not serve as a liberal tribunal open to all shades of opinion. Several months later Mariátegui described it as a "journal of ideological definition, of leftist concentration." But for a while he remained firmly nonsectarian, pursuing, for example, a policy of "tactical friendliness" and cordial relations with Haya de la Torre and his fellow Apristas. On occasion he had words of praise for the nationalist achievements of such political antagonists as Riva Agüero, García Calderón, and Belaúnde.

Nevertheless, Mariátegui gradually succeeded in identifying

himself and *Amauta* with a certain set of sociopolitical propositions. Tactically, he understood his own times in terms of the
Third International's general position of the 1920s; namely, that
this was the time of preparing cadres, made up of "vanguardistas, socialistas, revolucionarios" and indigenistas. The idea was to
mobilize them for "some future revolutionary assault." Mariátegui also endorsed the tactic of the United Front (1921), which
he had been actively espousing since late 1923.

Part of the groundwork toward building a revolutionary
movement, in Mariátegui's view, required the development of
an analysis of Peru's problems from a global perspective.
Amauta, he felt, would play a key role in this preliminary task,
and out of such efforts would emerge the "voice of a movement
and of a generation."[38] Like Sorel, Lenin, and the Bolsheviks,
he saw an elite minority as serving as the core of the revolutionary movement. As he wrote in a piece entitled "the Problem of
Elites," published in *Variedades* in January 1928, it was the
elites who affected the course of history by "revolutionizing the
consciousness of an age." Thus, the goal *Amauta* set for itself
was nothing less than to create a polarization of intellectuals
along political lines in Peru; and, then to bring about a concentration of followers behind the ideological banner of revolution
and socialism.

Polarization and Concentration

Amauta succeeded eminently in its self-appointed task of po-
larizing the Peruvian left. Surprisingly, Mariátegui's first antagonist in the process turned out to be Luis Alberto Sánchez,
the author of "Nosotros."

Actually the incident began with an article written by José
Ángel Escalante, a deputy from Cuzco and minister of education, who also served as Leguía's factotum on indigenous affairs.
In "Nosotros los indios," published in the progovernment newspaper *La Prensa*, Escalante alleged that under Leguía the "political and judicial situation of the Indians had notably improved
due to a new understanding of national problems."[39]

Mariátegui took exception to this claim, presenting as evi-

dence a manifesto that had been recently issued by the radical
Cuzco Grupo Resurgimiento (Luis E. Valcárcel, then a young
anthropologist, was one of its members). At this point Sánchez,
who was Escalante's secretary, entered the fray.

Other motives than simply defending Escalante may have
prompted Sánchez. Mariátegui's Marxist views and the thrust of
his position on the Indian question had nettled many indigenistas, especially those with more traditional views. It is also possible that Sánchez was reacting out of some personal pique, for he
launched the debate with a mocking attack on Mariátegui. Sánchez charged him with opposing indigenous and Hispanic cultural
and social traditions, indigenismo and colonialism, as if he were
dealing with "pugilists or fighting cocks." On five separate occasions he questioned Mariátegui's nationalism for being "narrow and
exotic," objected to his depiction of the Indian as the dominant
national social type, challenged the appropriateness of applying
"foreign" or socialist ideas to the study of Peru's social and cultural
problems, and finally expressed doubts about the intellectual honesty of *Amauta*.[40]

Mariátegui issued three replies. He started out by objecting to
Sánchez's tactics, saying that he welcomed polemics involving
ideas but saw little to be gained from vituperative personal
barbs. Sánchez was free to challenge his attempts to link vanguardismo and indigenismo, but ought to elaborate a substantive
argument. As for the tone of his writings, Mariátegui noted that
if he found it necessary to adhere strongly to principle, it was
because he did not wish to appear in the debates of his times as
a "reformer in name but a conservative in actions."

Addressing the charge of applying "foreign ideas" to Peru's
situation, he observed that the sixteenth-century Spanish inva-
sion and the colonial economy it imposed on the country had
produced deep-seated economic, social, political, and cultural
conflicts between the conquerors and the conquered, the rulers
and the ruled. Even after a full century of independence, the
urban and rural masses were still suffering from these contradictions. Since the native population made up by far the majority of
the people oppressed by these conditions, it was self-evident—to
socialists at least—that the indigenous people were the pivotal
elements to be considered in any analysis of Peru's problems.
And it was equally obvious that the semifeudal economy of the

sierra had to be dismantled as a prelude to the revolution that would eradicate the perfidious legacy of the conquest. Such ideas could be disputed and perhaps refuted, Mariátegui remarked, but the empty criticism of "applying foreign ideas" would not do.

Mariátegui's reply to Escalante was even more pointed.[41] Escalante had stressed the need for action instead of theory, and characterized all discussions of the indigenous problem as mere "intellectualizing." Mariátegui countered, somewhat starchily, that before problems could be addressed they must first be understood.

One interesting result emerged from this otherwise awkward debate. It gave Mariátegui one of his first opportunities to present in schematic form his unique synthesis of indigenismo, vanguardismo, nationalism, and socialism. As his beliefs became more widely circulated, they set him apart from most of his peers. *Mundial* and *Variedades*, as well as *Amauta*, served as his forums.

At the same time, Mariátegui became more active in the give-and-take of the political arena. As a result, his relations with the Leguía regime began to undergo a change. At first they viewed each other with suspicion and muted hostility. The government placed Mariátegui under surveillance when he returned from Europe, apparently aware that he was coming back a socialist. But he was nevertheless allowed to publish his views, which were clearly colored by a Marxist class interpretation.[42]

Yet Mariátegui did not flaunt his socialist opinions. He went about his business somewhat circumspectly (Víctor Andrés Belaúnde interpreted this in his *La realidad nacional* as some kind of caution or fear of the Leguía regime). Moreover, Mariátegui initially saw some positive results from Leguía's policies, emerging in the long run, as he made clear in discussions with Ricardo Martínez de la Torre, who had joined Mariátegui as a political associate in early 1926.[43] Mariátegui saw the progressive consequences that would result from Leguía's efforts to break up the large estates and open up new lands through massive irrigation projects.[44]

Mariátegui, however, clearly identified himself with a revolutionary workers' opposition. Even so, he generally avoided direct criticism of the government. This prudence saved him some grief, for he managed to sidestep the police—save the January 1924 arrest.

The standoff between the two abruptly ended on June 5, 1927, a few months after the Sánchez debate. Quite suddenly, the government announced they had uncovered a "communist plot" and raided Mariátegui's house and the residences of about forty workers and intellectuals close to him, most of them working-class militants. Everyone was placed under arrest and *Amauta* and the Editorial Minerva were closed indefinitely.[45]

What apparently provoked the crackdown was the Second Workers' Congress, which was meeting in Lima precisely at the moment that the raids took place. Sponsored by the Federación Obrera de Lima (FOL), an organization made up of almost all of Lima's labor groups, the congress hardly posed any danger to the government, so its overreaction clearly suggests plain harrassment. During the mid 1920s, the FOL had become fractured and disorganized, but it managed to survive somehow and hold several congresses.[46] With *Claridad* Mariátegui made his first close ties with the FOL's top leaders and rank and file, and by January 1927 he was recognized as a fellow comrade in the struggle. The workers asked him to write a "Message to the Workers' Congress" for the June meeting.

Mariátegui's message became the basic working paper for the Lima convention. It suggested the need for a united front; admonished against ideological factionalism; reconciled socialism and syndicalism; linked conceptually the urban workers' struggle with that of the rural peasantry; and proposed a series of coordinating activities. Finally, in a move that appears to have been designed as a bid to influence the FOL directly, Mariátegui proposed the establishment of a General Confederation of Labor.[47]

But government officials also heard of the congress, of course, and infiltrated its proceedings.[48] They evidently decided to clamp down on the efforts of Mariátegui and other militants to revitalize the labor movement.

On June 10, a few days after the raids, *La Prensa* charged that documents had been discovered linking Mariátegui with communist centers elsewhere in South America and in Moscow. Further, the police claimed to have found an organization chart of the Second Workers' Congress in Mariátegui's home which proclaimed the dictatorship of the proletariat, and they pointed to this as proof of some undefined imminent threat to the state.[49]

From San Bartolomé military hospital, where he was being detained, Mariátegui managed to send out a reply to the charges. Subsequently published in the Lima press, the letter acknowledged that he was a Marxist *"convicto y confeso"* and reaffirmed the commitment he had expressed in *Amauta's* first issue. But he vehemently denied being involved in any sensationalist "gazettelike subversion plot," which actually had been concocted by the authorities for their own political ends, he said. At the same time, and this is a point of interest, he also denied having had any contact with the Comintern.[50]

Purely a tactic of harrassment, the arrests did not hold and within six days Mariátegui was released. The others, who were being held on the Isla de San Lorenzo, were freed at intervals;[51] and *Amauta*, caught in its first political scrap, was closed for six months.

Stormclouds of opposition to Mariátegui's politics continued to gather, and trouble soon burst forth on still another front—this time on the left, in the form of Haya de la Torre and the apristas.

Haya de la Torre, we will recall, had been forced to leave the country in 1923 because of his anti-Leguía activities. Twenty-eight years old at the time, he quickly mastered the art of survival as a political exile and managed to tour Central America, Mexico, the United States, and Russia within a year.[52] He met some of the leading intellectuals and politicians in each country by first advertising himself as a foreign correspondent for real or imagined wire services and newspapers in order to gain access to key individuals, and then letting one contact lead to another.[53]

Between 1924 and 1928 he moved across the international intellectual and political horizon like a dazzling, if minor, star. He set up home base first in Mexico City, then in London, and later in Berlin, where he lived in relative comfort (although in his initial years of exile he continued to describe himself as a "poor and proscribed student").[54] Gifted and supremely confident, he worked unceasingly to create an "image" of himself,[55] and succeeded brilliantly. Traveling between London, Berlin, Paris, and Mexico City, his verbal artistry, extraordinary improvisations, and irrepressible enthusiasm charmed not only his peers in exile, but even such experienced and mature men as José Vasconcelos, José Ingenieros, and Miguel de Unamuno.[56] In Moscow, not surprisingly, it was Trotsky who most captured his imagination.[57]

Haya de la Torre's accomplishments during these years included founding his own international movement, the Alianza Popular Revolucionaria Americana (APRA); elaborating the structure of his own ideology, known as aprismo; publishing his first book, *Por la emancipación de América Latina* (1927), an anthology of letters and newspaper articles; "breaking" with the international communist movement at the Brussels Congress (February 1927); and declaring himself "founder and supreme chief" of the Peruvian nationalist left in an attempt to establish a national counterpart to APRA called the Partido Nacionalista Libertador del Peru (PNLP).

The significance of many of these efforts appears open to question. While Haya de la Torre insisted vehemently on the originality of his ideas, most of them were actually borrowed from other movements. He claimed, for example, that the "economic conception" of politics had been forged at the Popular University during his student days,[58] and that aprismo was a new type of revolutionary doctrine because it recognized that the essential need of Latin Americans was "to discover [our] reality" and not "invent it" by "borrowing" from Europe.[59] In reality he had derived his political analysis essentially from Marxism-Leninism, his organizational ideas from the Chinese Kuomintang, and his use of symbolic and mass techniques from national socialism and Italian fascism.

The evolution of Haya de la Torre's political philosophy had really begun only after his departure from Peru. Starting out with a vague notion of social justice and the prophecy of a coming "great transformation," he encountered evidence of the antiimperialist struggle for the first time when he visited Panama. His impressions were reinforced by reading Manuel Ugarte's antiimperialist *El destino de un continente.*[60] As soon as he arrived in Mexico City—on November 16, 1923—he sent his first message "from exile" to his followers in Lima, referring to Ugarte's book and confessing: "I must admit that an awareness of the North American imperialist danger is new to me."[61] Eventually antiimperialism would become one of the cornerstones of aprismo.

Quickly finding a job through José Vasconcelos, Haya de la Torre plunged into action and traveled about meeting Mexican intellectuals throughout the country. In Mexico City, which in those days was virtually a mecca for the international left, he met Bertram D. Wolfe, who invited him to the Moscow Youth International Conference.[62]

Before leaving for Moscow, Haya de la Torre presented the University of Mexico student federation with a red flag showing the Spanish American continent emblazoned in gold. He delivered a speech entitled "Nuestra Bandera," in which he first introduced the concept of APRA. The event later became enshrined as the founding date of the organization, May 7, 1924. APRA's ideology was not yet fleshed out, but the original concept put forth by Haya de la Torre was "united action of the Indo-American people for the political and economic unity of our twenty-one states."[63] (The use of the term Indo-American can be traced to his Mexican experiences, and, particularly, the influence of Vasconcelos.)

Crisscrossing the globe in what he called his mission to "discover" the American reality rather than "invent it," Haya de la Torre developed the other four points of APRA's five-point program over the next two and a half years.[64] Essentially it was his quite selective assimilation of Marxism-Leninism that provided aprismo with its basic tenets. His analysis of imperialism, considered his major theoretical contribution, introduced a novel twist to Lenin's notion. While Lenin had stated that imperialism had appeared in industrialized societies as the final stage of capitalism; Haya de la Torre pointed out that imperialism appeared in Spanish America as the first stage of capitalism.

Further, inasmuch as the continent's economic development received its basic thrust from the outside (i.e., through foreign capital), this translated into an economic dependency and a political alliance between foreign interests and the local ruling classes.

Given such peculiar Indo-American conditions, Haya de la Torre held, the antiimperialist struggle must be waged differently in the region than in Europe. Peru's backwardness, resulting from its dependent posture, left the working class and peasantry the least developed and politically experienced in contrast to the middle class. For this reason, and because the middle class in Peru was one of the exploited sectors of society rather than part of the ruling class as in industrialized nations, it was up to the middle class to assume the leadership of a national revolution. In that sense, as Haya de la Torre often repeated, APRA aspired "to be what the Kuomintang is in China."[65] In other respects, too, APRA's political program was strikingly similar to the Kuomintang's. For instance, the plan called for the creation of an "antiimperialist state" following the projected revolutionary seizure of power. Once the reins of power had been taken, the new state's first objective would be to nationalize the means of production. But foreign investments would not be totally cut off, for it was expected that negotiations would lead to terms of investment that would serve the national interests rather than only the upper classes.

A militant indigenismo also pervaded the aprista philosophy, reflecting, obviously, Haya de la Torre's Peruvian roots.[66] Eventually he went so far as to assert flatly that the "revolution in our America will be, in its meaning and human character, an Indian revolution."[67] He never explained, however, how an Indian revolution could be made by the mestizo middle class.

The development of APRA's platform coincided with the organization of an international movement. In July 1925 the "proscribed student" gathered a nucleus of other Peruvian students in Paris and founded the first "European aprista cell."[68] An indefatigable traveler and letter writer, he subsequently set up cells in Mexico City, Buenos Aires, Guatemala, El Salvador, and Cuba. The Paris, Mexico City, and Buenos Aires contingents were the most active. In January 1927 Eudocio Ravines left Buenos Aires to become secretary-general of the Center for Anti-Imperialist Studies in Paris.

The following month (February 1927) Eudocio Ravines accompanied the APRA chief to the World Anti-Imperialist Congress in Brussels. APRA's "ideological discrepancies" with the communists came out into the open at the meeting, and the affair later became known as APRA's "break with communism."

Indeed, after the congress Haya de la Torre began to talk about APRA as not merely an alliance, but a national party. As soon as this idea filtered through the network of travelers and correspondents around him, a dispute arose over the issue, "APRA, alliance or party?"[69]

Up until this time, Haya de la Torre's aprismo apparently had had little effect on Mariátegui. The two men maintained cordial relations, and the Peruvian exile contributed several articles to *Amauta*. The issue of whether APRA was a national party spurred Mariátegui to write to him for a clarification of his views in late November 1927. But the APRA caudillo did not reply (later he claimed never having received the letter). Instead in January 1928, without consulting the Buenos Aires or Paris apristas, the small Mexico City cell issued a manifesto known as the "Plan de México." Announcing the formation of a national party, it declared:

> For the efficacious realization of the liberating revolution of Peru it is established that the only organ that will realize it, strictly in accordance with the postulates of this plan, will be the Partido Nacionalista Libertador del Perú.[70]

The statement went on to describe the PNLP as a political-military organization,[71] although in reality it only existed on paper as yet, and named Haya de la Torre as the "founder and supreme chief" of the party. Some accompanying documents pledging support to the PNLP were made to appear as if they had been issued in Abancay and Juliaca, towns in inaccessible southern Peru. Known as the Juliaca and Abancay Manifestos, they were intended to launch his candidacy for the presidency in the elections of 1928. The "Plan de México" was apparently double-edged, for it also provided for a workers' and army putsch to be organized by the provocateur Captain Felipe Iparraguirre in Talara.

Any possibility of continued amicable relations between Mariátegui and Haya de la Torre was now out of the question. The reaction came swiftly in the form of a long and troubled letter sent by Mariátegui on April 16, 1928, to the Mexico City group,[72] and its content revolved around three major points: that neither the vanguard elements in Lima nor those of the provinces had been consulted prior to the decision to found the PNLP; that Haya de la Torre had not replied to his letter asking what his stand was on the

alliance or party question; and that the Mexico City group's decision that "all creole means" would be employed to gain political
power was completely unacceptable.

The letter, which amounted to Mariátegui's first public as-
sessment of the apristas, drew a furious reply from Haya de la
Torre himself on May 20, 1928. Avoiding any reference to
Mariátegui's letter, he stated that, yes, APRA sought to become
an alliance, a front, and a party, and if that were not possible in
Europe it did not mean that it could not be accomplished in
Latin America. He denied authorship of the "Plan de México"
but admitted that he intended to exploit it politically.

In a scathing attack on Mariátegui himself, he accused him
of having succumbed to "tropicalism," to a "tropical demagoguery." Mariátegui ought to open his eyes to "reality," he remarked, and concern himself with America, not Europe. (The
charge of "Europeanism" eventually became the standard
anti-Mariátegui line of the apristas.) And finally, he claimed
that only APRA had rejected the practice and tradition of
"Europeanizing" American politics and presented a plan for an
American nonsocialist, antiimperialist revolution. But Mariátegui refused to support this revolution, the only revolution
possible at the time, he said.[73]

In response, the Lima group associated with Mariategui sent a
"collective letter" to all Peruvian groups outside the country,
which recommended that APRA be formally considered an alliance or front, but not a party. Moreover, they declared their
intent to organize a socialist party of their own in Peru.[74]

While the Mexico City and Buenos Aires APRA cells remained loyal to Haya de la Torre, in Paris Eudocio Ravines,
César Vallejo, and Armando Bazán decided to break away. In
Amauta's July-August 1928 issue a letter appeared from Bazán
announcing the dissolution of the APRA Center of Anti-Imperialist Studies over the "party or alliance" question, and proposing that like-minded radicals join working-class revolutionary
parties.

In December, Mariátegui wrote a letter to Eudocio Ravines in
which he pointed out that Haya de la Torre had made the argument into a personal, rather than simply a political, disagreement: "To Haya language is not important; to me it is. . . . if we
do not distinguish ourselves from the past in our political lan-

guage . . . then the only differences between us and the past will be those of personalities, of individuals."[75]

Mariátegui did attempt to present his reasons for the disagreement with the apristas in political terms. In May 1929, he pointed out that when *Amauta* first appeared nearly three years earlier, the journal had endorsed APRA because it represented itself as "an alliance or United Front." But in the light of the June 1927 raids, he said he had decided to revise his concepts and tactics and turn away from the weaker political elements around him—especially the "aprista deviations."[76]

He continued to dispute APRA's legitimacy as a party, appending this note to a letter he published in *Amauta* in January 1930 from Luis E. Heysen of the Paris apristas:

> The only too notorious truth is that APRA never was more than a plan, a project, an idea for an "alliance" or a "front" which a group of Peruvian students tried unsuccessfully to organize. . . . Any attempt, therefore, to take advantage of Latin American credulity with somewhat pompous letterheads is pure opportunism.

And in the last issue of *Amauta* under his direction (February-March 1930), there appeared a final denial of the existence of APRA as a party.[77]

Mariátegui's break with the apristas was also seen as part of the process of "polarization and concentration" that *Amauta* had proclaimed as its task when it initially appeared. Mariátegui's appraisal of the progress the journal had made toward this goal was published in a second anniversary assessment in 1928 entitled "Aniversario y balance." He concluded that *Amauta* had succeeded in defining the consciousness of the "new man"; a consciousness imbued, as we have seen, with a revolutionary nationalism distinct from what was advocated by any "petit bourgeois demagogic nationalist party" (an allusion to APRA). This new posture was not built around a perfect idea of the future—one that was abstract, absolute, and indifferent to human events. Rather, it was a "concrete, dialectical, operative" doctrine, flexible and capable of "movement," and geared toward revolutionaries, not purist intellectuals.[78]

Mariátegui felt that *Amauta* had reached the point at which it could no longer be regarded simply as a publication of the "new

generation," "the vanguard," or even simply of "the left." It was
time to state unequivocally where they stood, and their ideology
could be summed up in one single "but grand word: Socialism."
In the face of the current global struggle between the two antagonistic world systems, capitalism and socialism, it did not
occur to them to offer a "third position."

Amauta's goal now, he said, was to redefine the word revolution for an America long accustomed to a tradition of petty revo-
lutions. A socialist revolution would come to grips with the
fundamental division in world politics that grew from the dichot-
omy in the world's economic system—the western capitalist
powers occupied the "positions of primacy" while Spanish America, like the rest of the semicolonial world, found itself relegated
to a secondary position. The only solution for Peru was to join
the movement alternately called antiimperialist, agrarian, or revolutionary—in other words, the socialist struggle.

Admittedly, socialism was not an originally Indo-American
doctrine. But, he argued, in this period of history no doctrine or
system could be "exclusively" Indo-American. Moreover, no region, no society, no tribe could escape the influence of the
socialist movement, just as no one could escape the expanding
influence of capitalism. This did not mean that socialism in
Spanish America had to be a mere copy of European socialism.
On the contrary, it ought to aspire to be a "heroic re-creation."
And in such a transformation a New World socialist order might
emerge, one in which Indo-America could thrive and retain its
own individuality, although total autonomy in its social and cultural development was not possible.

Amauta could lay claim to still another major accomplishment.
For in it (as well as in *Mundial*) had appeared a number of
Mariátegui's writings on economy, land, religion, the Indian,
education, and literature. In 1928 these were published as a
classic statement on the national question: *Siete ensayos de interpretación de la realidad peruana.*

6

Siete Ensayos de Interpretación de la Realidad Peruana:
An Analysis of the National Question

La historia del Perú republicano ha sido escrita
ordinaria y casi invariablemente como historia política,
en la acepción más restrictiva y criolla de este
término.[1]

In tracing the impulse behind *Siete ensayos de interpretación
de la realidad Peruana (Seven Essays of Interpretation of the
Peruvian Reality)*, the evidence takes us back to 1925. That was
the year of the crucial dual resolve: first, in the aftermath of
Mariátegui's close brush with death, his personal commitment to
voluntarism; second, his decision to reach an understanding of
the national question by interpreting the Peruvian past and
present from a radical indigenista perspective.

Mariátegui made his first public reference to the *Siete ensayos*
on June 6, 1925. By then he had already published two of the
articles later used in the collection.[2] Other installments followed
in 1925 and 1926, but the bulk of the material appeared in
Amauta in 1926 and 1927. The book probably reached the public
in early November 1928.

The *Siete ensayos* represents one of the first efforts by a Peruvian to understand the nation's past not only from an indigenista
perspective, but also from a radical materialist point of view.[3]
The first three pieces—on the economy, the Indian, and the
land—outline the material base of Peruvian society. The last
four—covering education, religion, regionalism and centralism,
and literature—detail at times aspects of the superstructure. But
in addition to the materialist base of the *Siete ensayos* there is
the dialectic, although in this case there are two agents of historical change, race and class; and this accounts for much of the
originality of the work.

107

108 CHAPTER 6

Some of the most searching and perceptive readers of the essays have not found them without fault. They have suggested, for instance, that the book suffers from a certain "conceptual ambiguity."[4] Indeed, Mariátegui has eclectically combined a Marxist discussion of the material base of Peruvian society with a voluntarist conception of the superstructure, and there is a marked emphasis on the latter. If the first three essays are consolidated, they account for little more than a quarter of the entire book, whereas the articles comprising the analysis of the superstructure take up two thirds of the whole. Moreover, a Nietzschean epigraph showing Mariategui's continued attachment to the neoromantic influences prevalent at the turn of the century is the first sign to greet the reader.

Among the principal sources cited in the first three essays figured César Antonio Ugarte's *Bosquejo de la historia económica del Perú* (1926), published just at the time Mariátegui was writing his own articles, and Hildebrando Castro Pozo's *Nuestra comunidad indígena* (1924). References mentioned elsewhere included the official *Extracto estadístico del Perú;* José Antonio Encina's *Contribución a una legislación tutelar indígena* (1918); "Nuestros indios" from González Prada's *Horas de lucha;* Luis E. Valcárcel's *Del ayllu al imperio* (1925); Javier Prado's *Estado social del Perú durante la dominación española* (1894); and Francisco García Calderón's *Le Pérou contemporain* (1907). In approaching the Spanish American colonialist experience Mariátegui particularly relied on José Vasconcelos's *La raza cósmica* (1925). Among a host of European authorities, the most often cited were Sorel, Croce, Gobetti, Pareto, Marx, and Engels.

There can be no doubt that this was the book that Mariátegui felt, as he himself said in his introduction, in the blood, even though he also presented it as a "preliminary" contribution to the socialist critique of the "problems and history of Peru." But it was enough, or so he hoped, to provide his countrymen with an alternative to the "political history" invariably written by the ruling elites.

The Economy

The first three essays sought to outline the mode of production in Peru from a historical perspective. The initial essay attempted a chronological periodization of the evolution of the

national economy, while the other two characterized the relations of production in terms of the system of labor and property.
Overall, they outlined the unfolding of the classic Marxist three
stages of economic development (while also making reference to
a fourth in pre-Hispanic times); yet at the same time they
pointed to several novel aspects of the "special character" of
Peruvian historical development.

In fact, the first essay began with a reference to the pre-
Conquest indigenous economy.[5] But it started out in a somewhat
idealized vain. For instance, it proposed that from the interaction
of land and people in ancient times had evolved, "freely and
spontaneously," a "collective organization" and a "collective labor
system." This "formidable machinery of production" had in due
time given rise to a society of "industrious, disciplined, pantheist,
and simple" people living amid material plenty.[6] Here Mariátegui
completely ignored the authoritarian nature of the Inca regime.
Though admitting that individual initiative had been suppressed in
ancient times, the fact that the Empire's production kept pace with
population growth meant the Incas deserved great credit for having
eluded the Malthusian trap.[7]

Some fifty pages later, however, in an extended footnote, the
author presented a more modern and realistic portrait of pre-
Hispanic times. He now described the Incas as "despotic" and
"theocratic." But he still continued to stress what he called the
"admirable aspects" of their rule; in particular, they had nurtured a form of "communism" by allowing basically the con-
tinuity of the *ayllu*. A social formation predating the Incas, the
ayllu basically consisted of a kin group occupying a definite territory and following a collective way of life. Mariátegui noted
that the ayllu had not been "violated" by the Incas, but had
remained the basic "cell" of the Empire. The essay further assumed that the ayllu had carried over into colonial times in the
form of the Indian community (failing to note, however, that
under Spanish colonial rule the ayllu had been transformed into
a group of unrelated extended families occupying a common
area).

But the text also distinguished between the primitive example
of "Incaic communism" of the ayllu and its modern counterpart.
The communism practiced under the Incas corresponded to an
agrarian society, in which man was forced to submit to nature;

the communism of Marx and Sorel applied to an industrial society, where nature was sometimes forced to submit to man. What
mattered, though was that both models of primitive and modern
communism shared one thing in common: their "incorporeal
similar essence," which was in effect the collectivist consciousness of the people.

As for the lack of personal liberty in the ancient regime,
Mariátegui observed that the ideal of individual liberty had
evolved as a juridical concept only in modern times. But though
despotic, the Inca Empire used its awesome machinery of production benevolently, for the creative ends of producing a great
civilization.[8]

We soon grasp Mariátegui's twofold purpose in painting this
picture of Incaic society. It served to provide a contrast with the
economic system imposed by the Spaniards. It also provided a
historic basis for one of the key assumptions of the work, that
the indigenous rural masses had always felt a "natural tendency"
toward socialism and communism.

In Mariátegui's schema, the first stage of economic development, the feudal stage, had appeared as a result of the Spanish
Conquest. Following the Conquest, the Spaniards disrupted and
almost destroyed the indigenous economic structure, but they
ended up building their feudal system "on the remnants of a
socialist economy." Here Mariátegui did not say anything about
economic developments in Spain that could have affected the
Conquest. Nor did he give too many specifics about the type of
economic structure introduced by the Spaniards, except to mention they had brought black slavery to the coast and thus added
the characteristics of a "slave society" to those of a Spanish
feudal economy.

But the essay did seek to establish a general argument, beginning with the criticism that the Spaniards had failed to organize
a "solid and organic" economy such as the one they had found.
Instead, they had disrupted what existed and produced a parasi-
tic society "colonial to its roots."[9] It was an economy based on
the mining of precious metals, and settlements in the sierra centered mainly around the sites of such mines. This mode of production, which gave little importance to agriculture, lacked drive
and momentum, eventually produced the legacy of "Spanish
pauperism." Essentially a society based on the exploitation of

mining and the native race, its most representative portrait was a Lima composed of a small court, a tiny bureaucracy, some convents, merchants, native servants, and slaves. Peru as a colony thus remained more of a "military and ecclesiastical" venture, rather than becoming a progressively developing political and economic entity.

About the only positive statement made about the colonial Hispanic economy appeared in the discussion of the missions organized by the religious orders. The Jesuit missions had succeeded, the essay emphasized, because they wisely made use of the "natural tendency of the indigenous population toward communism."

Little by little a second stage evolved, that of bourgeois economy. The revolutionary wars of independence announced the military and political character of the new phase. But although the heroics of the liberal revolutionary generations could not be disputed, they had not been "anterior or superior" to the economic causes of the independence movement. At the roots of independence, stood the "needs of the development of Western, or more precisely, capitalist civilization."[10] Mariátegui traced the economic causes, and lauded the colonists' demand for freedom from the "rigid authority" of Spanish monopolists. But the basic desire was to trade with the new capitalist markets directly. Basically, the independence struggle had been waged for the moneyed creole population, with complete disregard for the indigenous masses.[11]

After throwing off the yoke of Spanish rule, the new republics welcomed a brisk trade with the capitalist West. To them they exported their primary products receiving, in turn, "cloth, machinery, and a thousand industrial products." Great Britain assumed the role of chief trading partner, and in the process gradually assimilated the South American republics into its sphere of influence. Argentina and Brazil, closer to Europe, were integrated into the "function and structure of the European economy and culture" earlier than Peru. Because of the country's enormous distance from Europe, Peru found it easier to establish relations with Asia in the nineteenth century. In the wake of Asian trade, thousands of Asians arrived to provide cheap labor for coastal haciendas.

So far in this essay we have what have been called incisive "approximations," lacking in some important historical respects but original for their application of a modern socioeconomic form of analysis. This approach prevailed throughout the *Siete ensayos*, giving it a distinctive and realistic character not common to Peruvian letters, especially when compared to the scholarship of the generation of 1900.

The essay went on to explain that Asian trade could not provide Peru with what the country most needed: technology and capital. These factors of production could only come from the capitalist West, the opportunity for which eventually came with the rise of the guano and nitrate industries, giving Peru access to British technology and the British market. Starting out in the 1840s, profits accruing from guano exports led to the concentration of native capital, especially during the two Castilla governments of the 1840s and 1850s. As a result, the "first solid elements of commercial and banking capital" appeared and a sui generis national bourgeoisie emerged. [12]

From the start, Peru's class structure revealed the internal weaknesses of its material foundation. The nineteenth-century bourgeoisie lacked a solid class base, for it remained "related in its origins and structure to the aristocracy." What Mariátegui meant here was that essentially feudal attitudes had continued to coexist alongside the selective assimilation of capitalist ones. From then on, to the Europeans the Peruvian bourgeoisie tried to appear as another bourgeoisie, but within their own milieu they persevered in the pursuit of aristocratic privileges and avoided any changes running contrary to the colonialist status quo.

The bourgeoisie thus adopted the political and economic principles of liberalism, but it was a liberalism that never led to the elimination of aristocratic privileges, which continued to be rooted in the persistence of the feudal large estate. Materially weak vis-à-vis the foreign bourgeoisie, the Peruvian bourgeoisie retained many of the class attitudes of the traditional aristocracy. As a result, in Peru the emergence of a bourgeoisie led to little more than a "mediocre metamorphosis" of society.

Aside from giving rise to the bourgeoisie, the guano and nitrate trade linked the economy of Peru in a new colonial relationship with the West, said Mariátegui. But at the same time, this trade reinforced a fundamental "social dualism and conflict" between the sierra and the coast. It reinforced the old colonial tendency whereby the creole and mestizo coast exploited the more backward sierra, a problem that remained one of the country's chief sources of soil discontent.

In sum, a nineteenth-century, British-dominated imperialism spawned a new colonialism in Peru, according to Mariátegui. But the more dynamic aspects of this development did not become evident until the third stage of the economic evolution of the country had been reached. Historically, this third stage corresponded to the present epoch, which had begun with the almost total collapse of Peru's productive forces following the War of the Pacific with Chile.

Afterwards, the country had entered a much more complex phase of economic development: there appeared the rise of finance capital; the emergence of modern industry; the formation of an industrial proletariat; the intensification of market relations with the West due to the opening of the Panama Canal; the resurgence of foreign loans; the gradual substitution of British hegemony by a North American presence; and the development of a capitalist class no longer dominated by the old aristocracy (a reference, no doubt, to leguiísmo).

Obviously, such developments reinforced the growth of a capitalist economy and society on the coast. But as modern capitalism penetrated agriculture in the sierra and reinvigorated Peruvian mining, it also assimilated many feudal labor practices. Capitalist interests most often reached an accommodation with local interests, and even coexisted in the sierra with remnants of the "communist indigenous economy" residing within or alongside the semifeudal agrarian structure of the large estate. In other words, capitalism, rather than revolutionizing the means of production, in most instances simply adapted to local conditions of production.

Both foreign and coastal bourgeois interests benefitted from this accommodation, so that outside modernizing influences introduced change in Peru only to a degree. And this in turn meant the country's economy would long remain basically agrarian, and dominated by the large estate.

Not only did the Peruvian bourgeoisie fail to revolutionize the mode of production, but they failed to take control over the national economy. As a result, most of the "mining, commerce, and transport remained in the hands of foreign capital."

Thus, concluded Mariátegui, all foreign forms of economic development ultimately worked to the detriment of the native people. Progress in Peru evolved slowly, and even though industry was mobilizing a modern class-conscious proletariat, for a long time in the future the great masses would continue toiling in the fields.

The Indian and the Land

The second and third essays focused upon the Indian and the land question, which were intimately linked in the system of gamonalismo (the gamonal, or large estate proprietor, ruled over a particularly predatory form of private land ownership in the Andes). But gamonalismo was more than an economic system; it also involved social and political processes touching on the entire country, and in fact was the root cause of Peru's backwardness. According to Mariátegui:

> The term "gamonalismo" does not signify solely a social and economic category—that of the latifundistas or large agrarian property-owners. It designates a whole phenomenon. Gamonalismo is not exclusively represented by the gamonales in and of themselves. It encompasses a far-reaching hierarchy of officials, intermediaries, agents, parasites, etc. Even the assimilated Indian is transformed into an exploiter of his own race when he places himself in the service of gamonalismo. The central factor of the phenomenon is the hegemony of the large estate in the politics and mechanism of the state.[13]

Gamonalismo had survived into republican times, camouflaging itself with "liberal and capitalist principles." But in actuality the linking of large landholdings and feudal privilege with republican sanctions represented the chief impediment to the development of an authentic national capitalism. Thus, the process of national development in Peru acquired a "special character" due to the strategic importance of gamonalismo and the agrarian question.[14] Similarly, the Indian problem as a whole could be essentially reduced to the same issue of economic development.[15]

Gamonalismo produced great waste of human and natural resources. It perpetrated itself through two of the most backward
labor devices known on the coast and sierra, the *yanaconazgo*
and the *enganche*. Both rested on varying kinds of sharecropping
arrangements and other means of binding even salaried workers
to the gamonales through debt peonage.[16]

At this point class and race intersected. Mariátegui brought
out how the white hacendado usually justified his way of manag-
ing things on the basis not only of his own superior social status,
but also of racial superiority. On the coast, where most of the
white population resided, the laboring class had always been Indian, Black, or Asiatic.

Compared to gamonalismo, the indigenous community and its
collectivist form of agriculture seemed vigorous and productive.[17] The native population had survived the ravages of the
colonial mita (forced labor drafts), of independence, and even
the liberal attempts to break up their communities in the 1800s.
Mariátegui here relied on Castro Pozo's recently published
Nuestra comunidad indígena to support his argument. Castro
Pozo had found that work among the natives generally tended to
take place among them within an atmosphere of "cordiality,
cooperation, and social harmony," while the gamonales had to
resort to deception and guile in order to hold onto their workers.[18]

In other words, the native communities had retained their
"potentialities for evolution and development,"[19] and had amply
demonstrated their capacity to assimilate modern techniques and
technology. In the central sierra, the village of Muquiyauyo well
illustrated how an indigenous community could transform itself
into a functional modern cooperative. Muquiyauyo even distrib-
uted electrical power to neighboring communities.[20]

The analysis of the social functions of gamonalismo, of course,
extended into further detail than we can present here. It cited
diverse statistics from the *Extracto estadístico,* and made broad
comparisons, for example, with the Russian *mir* (in that connection Eugène Schkaff's *La question agraire en Russie* was mentioned).

Ultimately, the most important conclusion drawn in the first
three essays reduced to this: given the hegemonic functions of
gamonalismo and the fact that the liberal regime governing the

country had become "an instrument for colonizing the country on behalf of foreign imperialist capitalism,"[21] the classical liberal tasks—such as the break-up of feudal property—could in Peru only be accomplished by a socialist revolutionary regime. At this point Mariátegui did not elaborate further on his rather original set of proposals but simply included it in a footnote.

Obviously, this conclusion raised several crucial issues. The main one was perhaps the question that, given the "special character" of Peruvian social development, what role was the rural Indian likely to play in the socialist revolution to come? He did not deal with this question here either, but did stress the vigor of the indigenous masses, particularly when compared to the dependent and flaccid social behavior common to the Europeanized coastal creoles and mestizos, in this manner.

> The people of Asia, who are in no way superior to the Indians, have not needed any transfusion of European blood in order to assimilate the most dynamic and creative aspects of Western culture.[22]

Education

The succeeding essays on education, religion, and the political administration of the country narrowly explained the superstructure as a function of the colonialist semifeudal base outlined in the initial essays.

In describing the evolution of the educational system, the first essay quickly established its three phases, each paralleling the succeeding stages of Spanish, French, and North American influence. According to the established colonialist way of doing things, such foreign influences had been simply superimposed on the country and not selectively adopted. In Peru the ideas of other nations never commingled with the "sentiments and customs" of the native people; they were simply imposed by hegemonic fiat. Indeed, "four-fifths of the population, the indigenous masses," had never participated actively in the formation of national institutions or of a national consciousness.[23] Education in Peru therefore lacked a true "national spirit."

During the colonial era, the Spanish aristocratic view of education prevailed. High culture and class privilege converged,

1. Manuel González Prada

2. José de la Riva Agüero y Osma

3. Francisco García Calderón

4. Conservatorio Universitario in 1921. Seated from left to right: Jorge Basadre, Ricardo Begas García, Raúl Porras Barrenechea, Luis Alberto Sánchez; standing: Manuel Abastos, Carlos Moreya Paz Soldán, Jorge Guillermo Leguía, Guillermo Luna Cartland

5. An early photograph of Mariátegui

6. Mariátegui at the time that he worked at *La Prensa,* 1915-16

7. Mariátegui, Lima, 1917

8. Mariátegui's passport photograph

9. Mariátegui in Nervi, Italy, 1921

10.   Mariátegui in Rome, 1922

11.   Anita Chiappe de Mariátegui

12. Mariátegui after his return from Europe, Lima, 1924

13. Painting by the Peruvian Sérvulo Gutiérrez, done for the jacket of *El alma matinal,* and capturing the essence of Mariátegui's trial

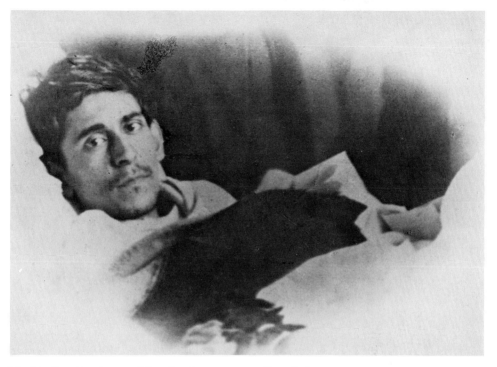

14. Mariátegui on the second day after the amputation of his right leg, Lima, 1924

15. Mariátegui in the late 1920s

16.   Mariátegui, Lima, 1929

17.   Mariátegui, Lima, 1930

with the common people having no right to education. With the coming of independence and the influence of Jacobin ideology, a new egalitarianism had emerged. But it was an egalitarianism that applied mostly to the white creoles. When the government declared education to be free, its main concern was for the plight of creole families whose "notorious depletion of private fortunes" had reduced them to the "bitter situation of not being able to give their sons an elightened education,"[24] as noted in a decree issued by Minister Matías León dated April 19, 1831.

Under the republic, education in Peru continued to be a class privilege—consistent with the survival of feudal privilege. The aristocratic model of education also continued to prevail, with its emphasis on literature, theology, and law.

In criticizing the Spanish educational system, Mariátegui relied particularly on objections voiced by such leading civilista luminaries as Dr. Manuel V. Villarán, who had assailed the "sickness of the old, decadent" educational system in a notable lecture in 1900. Villarán invoked the "black legend" with regard to Spanish rule, linked educational reform to economic development, and advocated inviting North American educational missions to come to Peru to spur the nation's educational modernization.[25] But Mariátegui departed from the assumptions of these critics, insisting that Peru's educational system could never be democratized without the country first democratizing "its economy and political superstructure."

Mariátegui devoted considerable space in this essay to analyzing the student university reform movement. Students received credit for bringing change to Peru's educational institutions, while the contributions of positivists like Javier Prado y Ugarteche or Mariano Cornejo were largely ignored. Inspired in Wilsonian rhetoric and, more specifically, in the struggle launched by Argentine students in Córdoba in 1918—which in Peru actually had exerted little influence—he described the postwar student movement as having given birth to "a new Latin American generation" and a "new spirt."

The student movement had its origin in a specific socioeconomic base, Mariátegui argued, citing in detail the analyses of writers like Julio V. González, José Luis Lanuza, and Mariano Hurtado along these lines. Even the idealist philosopher Ripa Alberdi, another Argentinian, had recognized that the reform was rooted in a specific social reality.[26] It was the mobilization of new class forces at the turn of the century which predetermined the configurations of university reform.

The text then went on to stress the student movement's eventual ties with the proletariat and interest in Marxism. This development was comparable to a similar process in China and Japan, where the universities were the "principal classrooms of socialism." In China, in fact, students had figured as the "vanguard of a revolutionary nationalism."

But in the end, the Peruvian student movement had fizzled out. Not only did it fail to define a lasting program, but it also lost its zeal for basic reform once the university administration assumed a compromising attitude. While Mariátegui did make a complimentary reference to Haya de la Torre here and also to the May 23 campaign, he also concluded the student movement had attained few concrete gains in the area of educational reform by the time it went into decline after 1924. In some respects, this section can be read as a veiled criticism of the APRA project.

In the last few pages of the essay, Mariátegui commented on the notable Deustua-Villarán debate on education that had taken place a few years earlier. While Villarán had posed lofty progressive arguments in favor of enlarging the North American educational influence, Deustua had called for a more careful (and traditional) definition of the education to be given to the "ruling class" of the country.[27] Mariátegui portrayed the debate as an illustration of the tensions and contradictions existing within civilismo, within the ruling bourgeois class.[28]

The real blame for the backward state of education in Peru, however, ought to be laid at the doorstep of gamonalismo, Mariátegui claimed. One crucial consequence of the prevailing educational system, was that the problem of indigenous illiteracy remained untouched. Critical discussion of the problem of education was in the end useless; the real task was to change the social and economic organization of the country.

Religion

The essay on religion began by noting how revolutionary critics no longer denied the social importance of "religion and the church." As support for this assertion, he quoted in the course of the essay from Marx and also from such diverse sources as the right-wing, Spanish, neoscholastic Ramiro de Maeztu; Papini "during his period of pragmatism"; Waldo Frank (who had pointed out the importance of Puritanism to the development of American capitalism); Sorel, of course; but also William James. What interested him most about such thinkers was how they focused on the "social function" of religion and the church and therefore focused their attention and interest not on dogma but on religious practices.[29]

Here again the question of religion is considered from an indigenista perspective. About the most important notion he extracted from his examination of the sources was how the ancient pre-Inca practices of animism, magic, totem, and taboos had not been eradicated by the Incas. Indeed, the secret of their success as imperialists was their policy of not seeking to change subject peoples, but simply extracting from them loyalty and productivity while allowing them to retain their own ways, including their religious practices.

Over the centuries, those ancient practices survived in the popular culture of the people. They did so because they were rooted literally in the soil, in the very nature of the agrarian economy. Wherever the indigenous people still lived close to the old ways, their old religious practices also survived—despite the hegemony of the Incas and the mass religious conversions of the Spanish colonial era. Totemism, for example, lived on in contemporary practice, but also in the very "blood of the Indian" (meaning in the Nietzschean sense, the "collective subconsciousness").[30] Animistic worship had proven more resistant to the Christian missionary effort in the end, than the Inca worship of the sun.

With the Spanish Conquest, there had arisen on the ruins of the indigenous empire a new theocracy, the theocracy of Spanish Catholicism. The Spaniards had tried to superimpose their religion on the Indians, viewing the indigenous practices as demonic and of no social use. But in the end, the conversion effort of the missionaries proved to be not very effective. Christianity impressed the Indians primarily because of its sumptuous liturgy and intense devotion, rather than because of its content.

In another aspect, however, the missionary effort did ultimately produce success. Quite early the church assumed the task of educating the native people and introducing them to modern European culture. Along with their rituals, the religious orders brought a variety of plants, tools, and domesticated animals to America, and these the native people welcomed.

At first the missionaries pursued their task with militant zeal, and their contribution to the development of colonial culture was, as a result, considerable. But eventually their missionary drive waned. Once the great masses succumbed to Catholicism, the clergy lost its heroic sense of mission and fell prey to "pleasure, indolence, and self-indulgence." The church lost its moral force.[31] (In this passage he was following Sorel closely.)

Later, the assimilation of the "fetishistic sensualism and dark superstition" of the black slaves further enervated the spiritual energy of Catholicism, Mariátegui observed. On this rather stark racist note, Mariátegui stood right alongside Javier Prado y Ugarteche.[32] As previously pointed out, there is a racist strain in Mariátegui's writings that is complex. When dealing with the contributions of Blacks and Orientals to the process of national development, he usually interpreted their role in negative terms, whereas on the international level he saw these groups as victims of racist imperialism just as much as the native Indian population in Peru. We will comment further on this aspect later.

Mariátegui went on to argue that parallel to the moral decrepitude befalling the church, there also unfolded an economic feebleness that further weakened Spanish colonial institutions. Catholicism had never inspired any great economic enterprises; in fact, he asserted, "no Catholic country has reached a high level of industrialization."

In contrast to the "sensuousness and wasteful experience" of the Spanish colonists, he opposed the austere social ethic of the Puritans. Capitalism and industrialism had flourished best in Protestant countries, he noted. Indeed, Mariátegui's admiration for Anglo-Saxon progress came through clearly in this part of the text, an unbegrudging kind of admiration he shared with Gobetti.

Independence did not materially affect the church's status in Latin America, Mariátegui went on (here he ignored the great property losses of the church beginning in the mid eighteenth century). The republican constitution proclaimed Catholicism the national religion, and nineteenth-century liberalism, as Jorge Guillermo Leguía had shown, "never denied the church or its dogmas."[33]

Only when the aristocratic landowning class started assimilating bourgeois functions did its progressive factions assume more secular attitudes toward the church. Once again Mariátegui alluded to the "special character" of Peruvian development, pointing out that only in those Spanish American countries where liberal and capitalist developments followed a "freer course" had Protestantism and a national church evolved early in the national period.[34]

Peru lagged behind, and still awaited its democratic-bourgeois revolution. Inasmuch as ecclesiastical forms and religious dogmas followed the main lines of the socioeconomic structure, only when the latter changed could the former be modified.

In bringing about that change, Mariátegui remarked, socialists did not ignore the power of "religious sentiments" and their sway over the masses. In fact, Sorel had demonstrated how social myths could "affect man's deepest consciousness just as much as the ancient religious myths." And the power of myth could produce and reach the intensity required to move the masses politically, to propel them into revolutionary action in order to alter their material conditions.

Regionalism and Centralism

The following essay, organized around the long-standing issue of regionalism versus centralism, was really the only outrightly political chapter in the entire *Siete ensayos*. On another occasion, it appears, Mariátegui made reference to writing a fuller political analysis of the Peruvian situation, but there is controversy on this point.

Mariátegui observed that the issue of regionalism lacked a precise definition and, as a cause, could not claim a concrete program in Peru, despite its widespread significance. As a problem, the issue centered on Lima's preponderant influence in the country and its resulting negative effects on a comprehensive national development.

In the nineteenth century, the regionalism/centralism debate had taken place mainly "within a single class," that of the "regional bosses" and the perpetrators of gamonalismo. To gather support in the provinces, caudillos like Pardo and Piérola would support either the federalist or regional cause, although reforms along such lines usually went no further than being mere administrative gestures. The Partido Radical of González Prada also embraced federalism, though without really elaborating a concrete argument to support its stand.

Not until the 1920s had there appeared an approach less concerned with "politics," and more prone to emphasize the social and economic bases of the long-standing problem.[35] In Mariátegui's own view, "modern Peruvians" (meaning the vanguard intellectuals) now understood the heart of the regionalism versus centralism question to be the problem of the Indian and the agrarian issue. Both Pardo and Piérola had granted greater autonomy to the gamonalista regional bosses, thus allowing them a greater degree of exploitation over the native population. It was in that sense that the regionalist-centralist issue converged with the Indian and agrarian question; the traditional regionalism had always tended to reinforce the most retrograde sector of the national economy.

Historically, the conflict between the capital and the outlying regions began in the early days of the republic, when arbitrary administrative fiat laid down the regional boundaries of the country, as in colonial times. In reality, geography and economics and not government regulation determined Peru's three principal regions: the costa (coast), the sierra (mountains), and the montaña (Trans-Andean forest lands). The sierra was Indian, and the coast creole and mestiza; moreover, the coast (where Lima was located) dominated the sierra. Yet the coast had always lacked the power to integrate the sierra into a creative process of national development. The conflict between the two regions kept the country divided within itself.

To the "new regionalists," or socialist critics, it seemed indisputable that a realistic policy of regionalism must take into account the needs and directions of the national economy. Peru's development should be planned around two chief regions, the southern sierra and the northern coast.[36] In the south, the departments of Cuzco, Arequipa, Puno, and Apurimac made up one of the most integrated areas of Peru. Similarly, the northern coast provided the other example of a dynamic and well-integrated region.

Lima on the central coast evolved as the core area of the country, simply because it had been so designated by the Spanish conquerors.[37] But it was an artificial capital, lacking the geographic and economic characteristics associated with other core urban centers such as Buenos Aires.

For instance, Lima served as the center of the national railway system simply due to political considerations, with the result that instead of the Ferrocarril Central depending on Lima for economic support, the reverse was the case. Furthermore, Lima lacked access to those resources vital to the growth of industry, such as hydroelectric power, iron, and coal.[38]

Mariátegui examined an array of legislative proposals aimed at resolving the regional issue, concluding that the country must first choose between the gamonal or the Indian, for the fate of that question would determine the role Lima would play in the Peru of the future. At the end of the essay, Mariátegui tantalizingly posed the resolution of both the gamonalismo and the regionalism questions as a function of whether the rural masses of the highlands or the coastal proletariat would play the vanguard role in the political transformation to come.[39]

Literature

The essay on literature is without doubt the most uncompromisingly militant of the seven. At the very outset it likened the inquiry to be outlined to a trial, with the author as a partisan witness. And he identified Riva Agüero and the entire generation of 1900 as the opposing party; in effect, the defendants and their respective interpretations of national letters as the point at issue. For the time of "uncontested civilista authority over the intellectual life" of the country had passed, and to Riva Agüero's "civilista and colonialist disposition" he contrasted his own "revolutionary and socialist sympathies."

In the opening section of the essay appeared Mariátegui's famous declaration that for him "politics are philosophy and religion," a claim linking him intimately to the dual influence of Sorel and Croce. But it was Gobetti who in fact provided

Mariátegui with a theory of literary criticism justifying his rejection of the possibility of impartial, objective criticism.

Nevertheless the authority of Croce remained central—especially his *Nuovi saggi de estética*—to sanction the critical approach, one embracing both an aesthetic and a historical line of inquiry. We are hardly surprised to learn that the key issue for Mariátegui in this essay was the problem of a national literature, and, of course, the relation of Peruvian letters to the overall social process of national development.

There is an attempt at novelty in the Peruvian's identification of three literary periods in Peruvian history. Instead of using the traditional categories of feudal, bourgeois, and proletarian he used the terms colonial, cosmopolitan, and national, saying he preferred the latter categories because they were more "modern and literary" rather than "sociological."[40] Despite the alteration of terminology, however, the three categories he used corresponded neatly to the three Marxist stages of historical development.

We next find an interesting comparison made between the development of national literatures in Europe and the process in Peru, which was revealing of his assumption that Peruvian development generally followed along the same lines as that of the western nations (though affected of course by its own "special characteristics"). Relying essentially on the Schlegel brothers (August and Friedrich, paladins of German Romanticism) and Francesco de Sanctis, he outlined how through Latin and Papal authority the unity of European culture had been preserved in medieval times. But the splintering effects of the Reformation and the Renaissance had produced a variety of nationalist movements in more modern times, and with them national literatures written in national languages.

In the case of Peru, it had been relatively easy for Spanish to dominate the national literary tradition inasmuch as the indigenous Quechua culture lacked a written language. Nevertheless, few Quechuan creative works, like the *Tucuipac Manashcan*, existed, as did other writings by bilingualists such as "El Lunarejo" and "Inocencio Mamani." Nevertheless Spanish, "more or less Americanized," remained the essential linguistic tool of Peru's yet "undefined nationality."

The essay further pointed out that although thought, felt, and

written in Spanish, Peruvian letters "in many instances" revealed traces of nativist "intonations," and even Indian "syntax
and pronunciation."[41] In any event, he established that any
theory of criticism applied to Peruvian literature would have to
deal with this Quechuan-Spanish dualism, or so he contended,
which gave further proof of the "special character" of Peru's development.

During the colonial era the Spaniards introduced to Peru an
advanced literary tradition, one that had already evolved from
the epic poem to the novel. But Peruvian literary works of the
colonial era stood out mostly for their dependent and virtually
plagiarized qualities, as had been noted even by such a strong
admirer of the Hispanic colonial tradition as José Gálvez.[42]
Peruvian writers, on the whole, were "servile and inferior im-
itahors of Spanish literature and especially of Góngora," with the
few exceptions being such exalted figures as "El Inca" Garcilaso
de la Vega and Juan del Valle Caviedes.

The survival of colonial economic and social structures after
independence were reflected in the survival of a colonial literature.[43] Until the late nineteenth century and the emergence of
such outstanding exceptions as González Prada and later, José
María Eguren, Peruvian letters generally had continued treating
colonial subjects. On the whole, the common people, the majority of whom were indigenous, were ignored. It was true,
Mariátegui admitted, that in the course of the nineteenth century Peruvian literature had started to become less Spanish and
more creole in character. But even creolization had not produced a homogenization of European colonizer and Indian,
which explained why creole literature was so lacking in popular
appeal.

Riva Agüero and the generation of 1900 had chosen to stay
with the Spanish tradition. They continued to ignore the rele-
vance of indigenous culture in their works. But writers like González Prada had initiated a break with the Hispanic tradition. In
essence, they were the precursors of the cosmopolitan period
launched by the *Colónida* generation in the early 1900s.[44] (We
can easily detect here an intense sense of generational competi-
tion, reflecting in turn any number of imagined or actual racial
and class contradictions.)

Turning to individual authors, Mariátegui's primary concern

remained, as it had been throughout the book, to give an account based on race, class, and politics. For instance, the encomiums showered on Ricardo Palma by the generation of 1900 reflected, he felt, clear-cut class and political interests. The civilista youth had championed Palma's side of the argument in his feud with González Prada, and thenceforth claimed Palma as one of their own. But such a claim could never be justified on a literary basis, for Palma's work could never qualify as colonial literature. The old traditionalist had always portrayed the daily life of the colonists "irreverently, satirically, and with mocking realism," and even Riva Agüero admitted that at times the old master disrupted the reader's "historical sympathy."

Instead of seeing a Palma enamored of Spanish colonial letters, Mariátegui saw him as representative of the capital's middle classes. More democratic in his political views than the civilistas, Palma reflected, he said, the spirit of the people.[45]

Inversely, the generation of 1900 had treated González Prada in a highly critical fashion. Ventura García Calderón even portrayed him as the "least Peruvian" of national writers because of his openness toward non-Hispanic literary influences. In contrast, Mariátegui acknowledged González Prada's important "break" with the colonial literary tradition, and further emphasized his championing of the cause of the native people and recognition of the need for a greater realism in dealing with national problems (by which Mariátegui meant a concern with the economy). And even though González Prada had been more of a harbinger than a builder, the new generation admired his "intellectual honesty, his noble and energetic rebellion."[46]

In discussing other writers, Mariátegui continued to consign aesthetic criticism to a second-place concern. Instead, he stressed the socioeconomic implications of Peruvian letters, and saw literary problems as being representative of the general constellation of problems characteristic of the overall national social process. For instance, he approached José Santos Chocano, a highly popular poet of the turn of the century, mainly in social terms and reviewed the purely literary quality of his work in a highly generalized fashion.[47]

As for the futurista generation of 1900, Mariátegui judged them harshly for having studied the past mainly "to glorify it." Elsewhere he paid tribute to the national accomplishments of the futuristas, but here he appeared as their relentless antagonist.

Oddly, Mariátegui did not claim for his own generation of 1919 the break with the literary biases of the generation of 1900. Rather, he gave credit to the *Colónida* circle for having rejected the tradition of glorifying the past and having taken up a critical outlook toward national problems. Here Mariátegui judged his old friend, Abraham Valdelomar critically, though somewhat sympathetically. El Conde de Lemos, he wrote, had best embodied their youthful contradictions; and having failed to resolve them had died without "finding himself, without attaining self-knowledge."[48]

Mariátegui did not ignore "independent writers," that is, writers without partisan affiliation like José María Eguren and Alberto Hidalgo. But he reserved some of his best lines for the charismatic poet, César Vallejo. He clearly felt a deep spiritual affinity with Vallejo's poetry, identifying especially with its expression of a great alienation, and quest for a revolutionary truth. Though Mariátegui commented on the aesthetic currents affecting Vallejo's poetry, such as French symbolism, it was the "indigenous note" of his work that received the greatest attention.[49] He gave Vallejo the highest accolade possible, that of being the "poet of the race."

Toward the end of the essay all of the strands of the book's argument came together in a discussion of indigenismo. The essay first defined "literary indigenismo" as an "ideological and social current" that daily attracted new adherents. As a movement, he likened it to the "muzikism" of prerevolutionary Russia.

Like the "muzikist" movement of Russia, Peru's indigenismo must also contribute to the development of a revolutionary popular culture and awareness among the masses. This it could do by shaping a core of nationalist beliefs to serve as the driving force of national self-realization. But the roots of this dramatic indigenismo could not be only intellectual and rational in nature; they must also be "instinctual and biological."[50]

What we find in this concluding section, which is more suggestive than conclusive, is an attempt to round out the social argument of the *Ensayos*. The race question practically preempts the final pages of the essay, though without reaching any clear resolution. In fact, the relationship of class and race is not ulti-

mately resolved in the *Siete ensayos*, which in itself contributed
to the "conceptual ambiguity" mentioned earlier.

Take for example the distinction he drew between the native
Peruvian Indians and other races. It is clear he favored racial
and ethnic affirmation as a positive experience mainly for the
Indians, who could use their racial solidarity to mount a struggle
for national liberation: but usually he did not express such interests in the "Negro, mulatto, and Zambo" (a mixture of Indian
and Black) who, as he wrote, constituted "colonial elements" of
the Peruvian past.

When the Black mixed with the Indian, he said, the former
corrupted the latter "with his false servility and exhibitionist and
morbid psychology." He also wrote that the mulatto felt closer
"to Spain than to the Inca." But in another passage he made
clear that he was talking of prevailing but not unalterable modes
of consciousness, for he argued that "socialism can awaken in
[the Black] . . . a class consciousness" that could liberate him
from the past.

Essentially, Mariátegui faulted Blacks, Orientals, and mestizos
for having been contaminated with the white man's ways—that
is, participating in the exploitation of the native race. But he also
acknowledged that even many Indians had been so corrupted,
joining in the oppression of their own people.

Though the section on race remained incomplete, it did reach
some startling and useful intuitions, as for example when he
wrote:

> Although the inferiority of colored races is no longer one of the
> dogmas that sustain a battered white pride, all the relativism of
> today does not suffice to abolish cultural inferiority.[51]

The false consciousness of racism, in other words, might have
been exposed by socialist criticism, but this did not mean that
the colored races could attain their proper place in society and
history without undergoing a radical struggle to transform the
cultural consequences of their oppression.

Mariátegui himself never doubted for a moment, or so it
seems, that this could be done; in fact, the native people revitalized him and charged him with an élan vital. Always he
reached out for contact with their still living culture, finding it in
diverse sources, including Enrique López Albujar's *Cuentos an-*

dinos, a collection of indigenista short stories. Comparing his "Los tres jircas" with Luis Valcárcel's "Los hombres de piedra" (from *De la vida inkaika*), Mariátegui found both stories confirming the fact Indian religious myths had not yielded to Christian missionary efforts. They still lived on. Similarly, in López Albujar's "Ushanam Jampi," he found living traces of the ancient indigenous communistic practices.

But he was the first to admit there still did not exist an authentic indigenous literature. What had been created thus far was much more the product of a radical mestizo culture than Indian, for many mestizos, idealizing the Indian reality, favored indigenismo. That is why, Mariátegui explained, the literary movement was called indigenista, indigenous in style, rather than simply indígena, indigenous.

It was ultimately up to the native people themselves to produce a truly indigenous literature. And perhaps that was not too much to expect, for despite the illusions of the present century, the Indian may not have really changed as much as many believed over the four centuries since the demise of Tahuantinsuyu, the Kingdom of the Incas. Serfdom had depressed him, his psyche and his flesh, but in the obscure depths of his soul he remained Indian.[52]

In a final section called the "Provisional Balance Sheet," Mariátegui finally announced the verdict in this trial of Peruvian letters. He concluded that in literature, at least, the dominance of colonialism had finally waned. And a new generation was bringing about a new nationalist indigenista literature.

Mariátegui nostalgically recalled how in the "precarious flow" of their individual lives the members of this new generation had been affected by different forces and taken different paths. He drew a parallel between his own life and that of the poet Alcides Spelucín, observing that both had initiated their search for meaning in life via letters. Valdelomar had introduced the two when both were pursuing "decadentism, modernism, aestheticism, individualism, and skepticism." Later both had left for Europe in search, not for the truth about the world, but for "the secret to ourselves."[53] Although other members of the generation had led very different lives, ultimately, "through universal and ecumenical paths, for which we are so much reproached, we are coming closer to our true selves."

The *Siete ensayos* were only a "preliminary" contribution to a socialist critique of the problems and history of Peru, or so said Mariátegui. Here we have presented but a gloss of its main configurations, which outlined a radically different interpretation of the Peruvian nation. One contemporary critic hailed the book as a "Bolshevik work," and indeed it contained the germ of the Leninist notion that a bourgeois revolution did not necessarily have to take place before the working masses mobilized and arose against their oppressors.[54] In Peru, due to its "special characteristics," socialism might have to carry out those aspects of social transformation normally associated in the West with liberalism.

Another strong theme of the *Siete ensayos* was its emphasis on the pernicious survival of gamonalismo as the fundamental cause of Peruvian backwardness. In fact, in some respects the book downplayed the overpowering effects of contemporary imperialism by stressing the role of gamonalismo in retarding the nation's development.

Little by little, Mariátegui was beginning to touch on the multifaceted reality of the national experience. In his next major work, *Defensa del Marxismo*, he was to deal with the problem of revolutionary consciousness and practice.

7

Defensa del Marxismo:

Toward a Theory of Revolutionary Practice

¿Quiénes son más idealistas, en la acepción abstracta de
este vocablo, los idealistas del orden burgués o los
materialistas de la revolución socialista?[1]

It is a little ironic that Mariátegui should have said of his *Siete
ensayos* that it employed a Marxian method "insufficiently rigid
for the orthodox," inasmuch as the work insistently repeated the
formula that base determines superstructure.[2]

But the irony disappears, or at least is grasped, if we keep in
mind one of his leading Marxist assumptions; namely that
economics—and we must remember his statement, "Marxism is
the theory that seeks in the movement of the economy the decisive impulse of political and ideological transformations"[3]—
converged diatectically with "emotion, with a revolutionary
pathos."[4]

So the emphasis given the base notwithstanding, emotion,
pathos, the will—indeed the entire voluntarist constellation—
also figured as critical elements in the overall process of revolutionary transformation. Moreover, practice was the vital field
for the interplay of base and superstructure.

When Mariátegui made the above comment about his lack of
Marxist orthodoxy in 1929, he already found himself deeply immersed in a new polemic aimed at making public his voluntarist
beliefs.

Originally, the idea behind writing a *Defensa del Marxismo*
simply obeyed the intent to write a "defense of the West," by
which he meant the socialist West. Unhappy with the, as he put
it, "fascists'" attempt to dissociate Marxism and the Russian
Revolution from its Western sources, he wrote to the Argentine
Samuel Glusberg (publisher of the Argentine journal *Babel*), as

early as January 10, 1927, of his plans to write a revolutionary polemic.[5]

But as things turned out, his original proposal, which appeared initially in the customary form of a series of articles on the European "rightist reaction" of the 1920s, was eventually relegated to the last section of the *Defensa*. *Amauta* published the first installments between October and December of 1927. But the most important essays of the *Defensa* were those written in 1928 and 1929, during a period of intense political struggle; years during which he founded *Labor*, a working-class newspaper, and organized the Partido Socialista del Perú (PSP). In 1929, he also established the Confederación General de Trabajadores del Perú (CGTP), the Peruvian labor confederation.

As in the past, the articles appeared piecemeal, but once he brought them all together they easily fell into place as a book manuscript.[6] But in this case he died shortly after finishing the series, and did not see the work published.

In his letters to Glusberg, Mariátegui expressed himself very clearly as to his purpose in writing the manuscript, which was that his ideas should be disseminated widely. And he confessed himself well aware of their unorthodoxy. He even said that *Vanguardia*, the Buenos Aires communist publication, would have in all probability rejected the manuscript had it been sent to them. And again, on May 10, 1929, he referred to the work as being "unfavorable to Marxism"; on March 11, 1930 (just one month before his death) he wrote that it was "unconcerned" with orthodoxy. After the entire series of essays had appeared in *Amauta*, Ramón Doll, the Argentine critic and one of Mariátegui's most prescient contemporary interpreters (who earlier had referred to the *Siete ensayos* as a "Bolshevik work"), noted that the *Defensa* represented an "abandoning of orthodoxy without abandoning socialism."

Roots of the *Defensa*

Consistent with his style, Mariátegui relied on a variety of Marxist and non-Marxist sources in the *Defensa*. Blended together, the disparate elements formed the core of his own open disposition and style of practice.

Mariátegui seldom commented directly on Marxist texts, though he did have direct familiarity with Marx and Engels.[7] But in one of the few instances where he dealt with Marx directly, he especially stressed Marx's own revolutionary consciousness. Marx's "true image," he wrote, was not that of a "monotonous materialist," but of "an agonized soul, a polemical spirit."[8] The real meaning of Marxism was to be found in "Marx himself," in his inner being. This emphasis on consciousness, incidentally, coincided with the climate of opinion of the early 1900s, and in particular could be traced to Georges Sorel; indirectly, Bergson; Nietzsche; and generally speaking, in Durkheim's phrase, the "renascent mysticism" of the turn of the century.

If Marx's true historical presence was conceived in terms of an agonizing soul, Lenin was presented as the model revolutionary mass leader. The *Defensa* included numerous references to *Materialism and Empirio-Criticism* (a fragment of which had been published in *Amauta*) and *Imperialism, the Highest Stage of Capitalism*. Nikolai Bukharin's *Historical Materialism, A System of Sociology* also served as a useful reference, though on the whole these Bolshevik works did not appear as central sources for Mariátegui's argument here.

Essentially, then, the *Defensa* reflected the charges leveled against orthodox Marxism by the critics of the 1890s, individuals like Georges Sorel and some of his contemporaries such as Antonio Labriola and Benedetto Croce in Italy.[9] It was really from such Marxist and non-Marxist mediators, that he assimilated his understanding of the historical role of violence and of a volitionist class struggle in the bringing about of revolutionary consciousness. Their importance to Mariátegui stemmed from the strategic importance assigned by such figures to the psychological and cultural nature of the superstructure, and to the significance of revolutionary will.

Sorel's *Reflections on Violence* and the *Decomposition of Marxism* served as a principal text for the argument of the *Defensa*'s opening essay. Sorel's combative and moralistic spirit proved irresistible to the young Peruvian. Mariátegui's regard for him was so high that he even put Sorel alongside Marx and Lenin, and dropped Engels altogether. He even mistakenly credited the *Reflections* with having influenced Lenin.[10]

Mariátegui's high esteem for Sorel hinged, in its most basic way, from his belief that it was he who had liberated Marxism from the all-embracing grip of the Social Democrats and the Second International. In the manner of Sorel, Jean Jaurès and Ferdinand Lasalle, the two nineteenth-century social-democratic stalwarts, were singled out in the *Defensa* for having misled the revolutionary movement down the path of parliamentarianism. All of the illusions associated with universal suffrage and electoral politics which so dominated the socialist democratic imagination could be traced to their leadership, or so he wrote.

As a result, a particular outlook toward power had set in among the left. The road to power had become wholly conceived in terms of electoral victories, and the original Marxian idea of violent class struggle had been cast aside. Mariátegui repudiated this historic situation as fervently as had Sorel.

In the postwar period, the limitations of reformist socialism had become self-evident. Confronted with the opportunity for seizing power through violent means, the Social-Democrats had resisted, revealing in the process a psychic conditioning going back to previous generations.

It was Sorel, then, with his attacks against bourgeois historicism and evolutionism, who had inspired the revolt against reformism.[11] Transcending the rationalist and positivist milieu of his times, the Frenchman had found in Bergson and in the pragmatists the means by which to restore to Marxism its original passion, faith, and will.

Therein lies the importance of Sorel to Mariátegui: that he distinguished "what is essential and substantive from what is formal and contingent" in Marx. Sorel was a "true" revisionist according to the text of the *Defensa*—unlike Thomas Masaryk, Charles Andler, and Eduard Bernstein. The "true revisionism" was true in that it contributed to the "renovation and continuation of Marx's work"; Sorel's writings had paved the way for a "return to Marx," in that they revived the original "dynamic revolutionary conception" of spontaneous, violent class struggle.[12] It was the action of being in that struggle which brought about a revolutionary consciousness, and this line of thought Mariátegui originally took from Sorel. Thus when we speak of Mariátegui's Marxism, we are surely speaking of a Sorelian Marxism.

But Sorel is only one key source, and himself the mediator of others. We find Mariátegui's thinking on action and vitalism, for example, essentially derived from Henri Bergson. There were others, of course, among them the several important Italian sources. But for the moment we are following the text of the *Defensa* so that we may uncover the basis of Mariátegui's Marxian beliefs. Another important figure introduced in this opening essay was none other than the Belgian reformist Henri de Man, whose *Zur Psychologie des Sozialismus* (1926)—and its French translation, *Au-delà du Marxisme* (1927)—turned him into a celebrity of sorts. De Man's work in fact awakened considerable interest because of its fashionable efforts to apply the ideas of Sigmund Freud and psychoanalysis to the socialist consciousness.

De Man's purpose actually went even further. His basic goal, it seemed, was to destroy the economic foundations of Marxism in order then to make the psychologistic argument that the workers who joined in the class struggle did so not because of material interests but because of an ingrained inferiority complex. Indeed, Mariátegui's own propensity for dealing with psychologistic themes no doubt explains much about why he decided to take de Man's *Au-delà* as a foil against which the *Defensa* would respond in its own fashion and for its own ends.

Mariátegui's design, if we can speak of one, was certainly to use the polemic against de Man as a forum for presenting his own beliefs in a certain style of revolutionary consciousness. That is really the subject of the otherwise outwardly aggressive and polemical style employed throughout the *Defensa*.

A Critique of de Man

The polemic's tone was aggressive from the outset; the *Defensa* lashed at the *Au-delà*, calling it a "defeatist and negative" work. It was more revealing of the reasons behind the shortcomings of German Social Democracy, than it was about Marxism, it said. The "liquidation of Marxism," which it purported to announce, wrote Mariátegui in intense commitment, in reality but revealed the dying out of Marxism in the Belgian's own consciousness.

De Man was challenged on a variety of grounds; for instance, on his narrow conception of the problem of class consciousness. His treatment of the subject wholly ignored the work of Sorel and of the voluntarist revolutionaries who held to the idea of waging a heroically moral and violent class struggle, charged Mariátegui. In other words, the Belgian de Man ignored and remained seemingly indifferent to the "emotional and revolutionary" vitalism sweeping his own times.

De Man's own "case" against a revolutionary Marxism—and here Mariátegui was assuming his favorite role of prosecutor—could best be understood if placed against the experience of the class struggle in his native Belgium.[13] The twin sources of the characterization which followed were Sorel and the Italian radical journalist and liberal philosopher, Piero Gobetti, another premier mediator of ideas.

By now Mariátegui's polemical style should be abundantly clear: he liked to contrast sharp opposites and did so with great decisiveness and intense commitment. It is in his style that we find expressed most openly his adherence to faith and will as powerful adjuncts of intelligence.

De Man and the Belgian socialist tradition served of course as a perfect contrast to the heroic view of revolutionary class struggle. According to both Sorel and Gobetti, the Belgian working class tradition could be traced back to the spirit of the Second International and their commitment to electoral reformism which also meant steering the masses in the direction of cooperativism, and away from the notion of violent struggle.

Unaware of an alternative form of struggle, de Man could not understand how revolutionary consciousness could not be cultivated among workers unless they understood the necessity for waging the class struggle with "passionate and heroic volition."[14] Instead, de Man argued that historical materialism did not leave room, did not allow, for the idea that the workers could exercise their own will. Although de Man did not go so far as to say that Marx had purged the notion of free will from history, he did argue that according to Marx social volition remained subject to the general laws guiding the class struggle. Moreover, in the Marxian tradition, according to de Man, such laws had their basis in a "predetermined reality"—that is, they issued ineluctably from class conflicts originating in the mode of production.[15]

De Man's view of Marxism was reduced to this: the doctrine sprang from nineteenth-century rationalism and German idealism; Marx had borrowed from the exact sciences the principle of causation implicit to the causal materialism found in Darwin; and from Hegel he had taken a teleological notion of history, which saw historical development as inevitably unfolding, out of constant conflict, in a succession of stages toward an ultimate goal.[16]

To all this the *Defensa* countered that Marx had never proposed a philosophy of history; neither had he ever advanced a metaphysical or philosophical materialism.[17] What Marx did was propose a historical method for studying the society of his time, and he based his interpretations on the concrete and empirical study of the capitalism of his day.

Marx had relied (and the style employed here is that of an experienced teacher who is guiding the student through a world of clear-cut opposites), on some scientific and philosophical ideas long since superceded by the biology of de Vries, the psychology of Freud, and the physics of Einstein. But the bankruptcy of the positivism and scientism of Marx's day did not compromise "in the least" the general validity of the doctrine. Indeed, the latter-day influences of "vitalism, activism, pragmatism, relativism" had all made their contribution to the ongoing renewal of Marxism.[18]

Nowhere was it laid down that Marxism was limited to the data and premises held by Marx himself. One chief function of international congresses and meetings was precisely that of providing debate on current problems and for reformulation of theoretical and practical propositions in light of present-day and changing circumstances.

To the positivist and determinist Marxism outlined by de Man, Mariátegui opposed another, one centered around the theme of voluntarist revolutionary experience. In doing so, he particularly dwelled on the subject of "moral ascendancy" and of a "producers' morality"—which came to him via Sorel (who originally took its seed from Proudhon) and also from the general cultural climate surrounding the Italian sources of the early 1920s so favored by him. Indeed, Sorel's impact on *L'Ordine Nuovo* circle and on Piero Gobetti, for example, was transformed, in Mariátegui's case, to virtual articles of faith.

Thus the *Defensa* reduced revolutionary experience to the taking of command over one's own consciousness in the name of a material "producers' morality," an experience designed to create a "moral regeneration." Economic conditions and material interests could not of themselves automatically inspire in the proletariat the will for creating a new socialist society. In effect, the crucial dimension of the class struggle took place at the level of consciousness, and it was there that the new order was born.

But how was this to be realized? For Mariátegui the basic model of developing working-class revolutionary consciousness remained his remembrances of the early contact he had had with the Turinese *L'Ordine Nuovo* circle and his later encounter with the writings of Piero Gobetti. In particular, Antonio Gramsci's proposal for reorganizing workers along the lines of Italian soviets or *consigli di fabbrica* (factory councils), away from the traditional trade union structure, served as the nub for the prescriptive model mentioned here (though Gramsci himself was not directly referred to in the text). Moreover, it was not so much the organizational imperatives which drew Mariátegui's attention in this instance, but rather the emphasis placed on moral regeneration and the notion of taking command over one's own consciousness.

The model invoked, in other words, basically stemmed from the recent reading of Piero Gobetti (who in fact appeared in the text as the mediator of the Turinese experience). What captivated Mariátegui in particular was the virtual puritanical zeal associated with *L'Ordine Nuovo* group in its efforts to promote discipline and a toughening of the ranks. Mariátegui was then very much in the same train of thought himself as evidenced by the well-known statement found in a letter to Samuel Glusberg of April 30, 1927: [If] "violence, authority, [and] discipline" were necessary, "then I am for violence, for authority, for discipline."

"Pride and humility," tolerance, interdependence, solidarity, discipline, were the revolutionary virtues to be transmitted in the factory councils, to which others were added. In Gobetti, Mariátegui found the notion, which he quickly endorsed, that certain Anglo-Saxon qualities—such as maturity, asceticism, persistence, a capacity to believe in precise ideologies and to practice a disciplined political struggle—must be assimilated by the workers as well. In that sense, the socialist struggle was but an extension of the liberal struggle, and the capitalist-liberal values useful to the socialist cause in Europe should be emulated in America.[19]

So much then for de Man's view of revolutionary struggle and his need to confront the opposite view of a voluntarist revolutionary struggle. But according to the *Defensa*, the weaknesses of the *Au-delà* were even more basic, for de Man insisted on seeing capitalism fundamentally as a cluster of attitudes rather than as an economic system. Liberalism, he believed, would eventually lead to the democratization of capital, despite the fact that such a line of thinking had been discredited by theorists as disparate as Lenin and Hilferding.

De Man's abandonment of the most basic Marxist tenets was nowhere more evident than in his discussion of automation and the thinking associated with the American business expert, Frederick W. Taylor. The Belgian generally supported the American thesis on automation, namely that its effects on production were revolutionary and the dislocation it inflicted on workers would not be longlasting. On the contrary, he expected that in the long run automation would produce new employment opportunities for the masses. Henry Ford's well-known admission that he personally could not abide the tediousness of mass-production techniques (but that the common man was different), seemed not to bother de Man.[20]

By now it should not surprise us that the *Defensa* should appeal once again to Sorel for arguments with which to counter de Man's attitude toward Taylorism. Indeed, Sorel, we are told, had some time before revealed the psychologistic effects of capitalism on workers' consciousness, though de Man remained ignorant of his efforts. In marshalling other arguments against de Man, the *Defensa* returned without hesitation to Sorel. For instance, it referred to him and Renan in dealing with the psychological and social functions of sexuality.

The *Defensa's* critique of de Man was mainly limited to its first section, though its author returned to the Belgian reformist later on in the book. For now, however, we will focus our attention on the succeeding essays dealing with Max Eastman, introduced here as an apostate of the Marxist revolutionary tradition, in contradistinction to the reformist de Man.

Eastman, British Socialism, and Idealist Materialism

Unlike what he found in the *Au-delà*, Mariátegui found much of value in Eastman's *The Science of Revolution*. His discussion of the similarities between Marxism and Freudian psychology especially received attention.

If, according to Eastman, Marxism had demonstrated how political, philosophical, and religious ideas were used by social classes to mask their true economic interests, Freudian psychology relied on the concepts of rationalization, transference, condensation, and sublimation to unmask individual self-interest and impulses.[21] Like Marxism, Freudian psychology had contributed fundamentally to the dismantling of the bourgeois idealist-rationalist edifice constructed in the eighteenth century. And so like Marxism, Freudian psychology too now faced the organized opposition of bourgeois culture.[22]

Similarly, the criticism of paneconomism leveled against Marxists by bourgeois intellectuals resembled the criticism of pansexualism aimed at the Freudians. Eastman correctly pointed out, however, that just as Marxism did not simplistically assume a position of economic determinism but viewed economic forces as operating dialectically, in similar fashion Freud had propounded a rigorously dualist theory of instincts.[23]

Still, the similarities of the two doctrines notwithstanding, Eastman showed how the followers of Freud had proven incapable of overcoming their own class biases. For instance, their resistance to Marxism had reached such a point that some Freudians interpreted any revolutionary attitude as merely disguising a neurosis.

But if Mariátegui followed Eastman on such questions—revealing in the process, of course, common interests as well as a relatively open frame of mind and ready willingness to break with established conventions—time and again he chided him for having abandoned Bolshevism.

Following this initial, and generally friendly, treatment of Eastman he returned to his polemic against de Man. Three articles dealing with the *Au-delà* (one only indirectly) followed in succession. The first disputed de Man's claim that British socialism refuted the basic premises of Marxist doctrine. But the brunt of the attack was really aimed against British trade unionism, especially for its efforts in dampening militancy. The other piece, really a brief review, focused on a recent publication of Emile Vandervelde (prominent leader of Belgian socialism) which referred admiringly if ambiguously to de Man's *Au-delà*.

But the succeeding essay stood out, and in many important respects embodied the main thrust of the entire book. In it Mariátegui confronted the problem of an "idealist materialism," which was reduced to the bourgeois critique that Marxism, due to its materialist principles, lacked humane ideals. The essay originally appeared in May 1929, only two months before Mariátegui published his three-part tribute to Gobetti (whose influence is clearly reflected here) mentioned earlier.

It is in this essay that the famous displacement of Engels from the holy revolutionary trinity takes place; instead of Engels, Sorel is installed alongside Marx and Lenin. But the text revealed no apparent self-conscious effort to slight Engels; rather the purpose seemed to be to exalt, through historical example, the intense moral dedication characteristic of the newly-named trinity, which we are told, compared favorably with that of any religious hero or ascetic of the past.[24] Marxist materialism, Mariátegui insisted at the outset with great vehemence, was not lacking in the means for dealing with all of the moral, spiritual, and philosophical challenges of the age.

Mariátegui's flat assertion to the contrary, it is nevertheless the case that he essentially relied on non-Marxist sources for supporting his, to say the least, polemical argument. The *Defensa* resolved, or attempted to resolve, the question of Marxist ideals with a long discussion of Gobetti's conception of *praxis* or action. As has been pointed out by Robert Paris, Mariátegui may have assimilated the germ in the process—albeit in a refined form as rendered by Gobetti—of Giovanni Gentile's actualism, or philosophy of praxis.

In the hands of Gobetti, Gentile's notion of praxis, to be found scattered in multiple writings including the celebrated text on *La filosofia di Marx* (1899), became a powerful philosophy of assuming moral responsibility for one's actions. Mariátegui may have remained oblivious to the derivative nature of Gobetti's thought on this point—expressed in this instance in his *La Rivoluzione liberale* (1924)—for his usual references to Gentile were most uncomplimentary because of the latter's Fascist beliefs and collaboration.

In any event, the long characterization of Gobetti's thought included here rested on Gobetti's assumption that the displacement of Christian dogma by liberalism in modern times represented a great leap in the collective consciousness of mankind. As a result of the historic liberal triumph, the great masses of people had become more and more reliant on their own inner convictions and volition, thus acquiring a great capacity for taking action and for self-improvement. But to the liberal thesis were added some refinements, such as Gobetti's fundamental moral passion.

The rational-liberal thesis notwithstanding, Gobetti remained attached at bottom to certain moral attitudes. Indeed, in his view, all political questions essentially reduced to moral questions and vice-versa. Moreover, he further believed all individuals basically responded to such questions most realistically through their actions (hence his inclination toward the Gentilian notion of reality as action). Matter and spirit, in effect, interacted dialectically in action or practice, and this became ultimately a "spiritualization of matter."[25]

Gobetti had perceived all political and moral choices as reducing to a question of human responsibility and action, concluding that "it is we who make our own history." But that history developed, or unfolded, out of a continuing process of class struggle. So a revolutionary ethics emerged, prizing above all the idea of struggle, for "we live in struggle and only through struggle are tempered the capacities of each one of us."[26]

It was in light of this analysis of action in the world that Mariátegui asked who the real idealists, in the full sense of the word, were: the idealists of the bourgeoisie or the materialists of revolutionary socialism?

His understanding that ideas could operate in society independently (that is, not strictly tied to the material structure), and that they could thereby be crucial in triggering social change, came through most clearly in this essay. So did the origins of that understanding, which tied him intimately to the Italian experience, and, as shown by several references in the *Defensa* and elsewhere to Nikolai Bukharin as well.

Youth, the Intellectuals, and the Postwar Reaction

The final two sections of the text, really unrelated to the bulk, were not without their own interest. The first, dealing with postwar youth and intellectuals in general, amounted to Mariátegui's own farewell to youth (a theme also present, incidentally, in the closing paragraphs of the literary essay in the *Siete ensayos*).

Up to this point, Mariátegui's references to the youth movement had always been quite favorable. Here the tone and substance of his outlook changed.

Using some recent writings of Pierre Drieu la Rochelle, André Chamson, and Marcel Prévost as the catalysts for his discussion, Mariátegui commented that the youthful spontaneity of 1919, had represented a reflection of, rather than a solid contribution to, the revolutionary movement of the times. One must look, in other words, beyond the radical posture of youth in the postwar period, and examine their actual contributions to the process of revolutionary change. Doing so would yield primarily evidence of a spirited longing and impatience for change, but little else. As Chamson had written, in 1919 the young looked for and expected "a purification of the world, a rebirth."[27] Although imbued with Marxist rhetoric, they had lacked a serious and strong commitment to Marxism.

Still, some members of the generation, like the dadaists, had evolved from the stage of student rhetoric to revolutionary suprarealism. In Italy, figures like Antonio Gramsci and Umberto Terracini represented the best examples of tenacious dedication to the ideals of youth; in Germany, Ernst Töller, J. R. Becher, and George Groz played a similar role. But none of them now believed that the young would make the revolution. More responsible and mature, they were now simply committed to the ranks of socialism.[28] (We should keep in mind that much of Mariátegui's criticism here could be read as applying to the Peruvian experience, and most particularly to Haya de la Torre and the so-called aprista deviation.)

Mariátegui's accusation of lack of passion, commitment, and maturity on the part of youth was also aimed at intellectuals like Emmanuel Berl and Julien Benda. Berl was especially taken to task for hiding behind, as the *Defensa* suggested, the Myth of Pure Intelligence. Berl believed that intellectuals must resist any commitments that would compromise their higher duty to "lucidity." Thus, an intellectual could never become a man of the party because he could not renounce his intellectual autonomy. In Mariátegui's eyes such a position came down to the fact that intellectuals wanted to be *of* the revolution without being *in* it.[29]

To succeed as a responsible individual, responded the *Defensa,* an intellectual must commit himself to principles capable of transforming him into an agent of historical change. Dogma, for instance, had not impeded Dante from becoming one of the greatest poets of all times, nor Lenin from becoming a great revolutionist and statesman. Marxism, in fact, offered intellectuals the possibility of freedom and advance, for Marxist dogma was not an itinerary but a compass.[30]

Sorel appeared as a model one final time. Unlike de Man, the Frenchman had not repudiated Marxism a priori. Though outside the discipline of the party, he had remained loyal to a discipline of class consciousness and class analysis, and like Lenin he had proven that Marxism provided the only means for following in the path of Marx.[31] (Elsewhere Mariátegui noted Sorel's later association with a reactionary nationalism and fascism, but here he remained the paragon of revolutionary virtue.)

Eastman again became a target of attack because of his claim that Marx had not succeeded in purging his philosophy of German metaphysics and idealism. But by making this argument, said Mariátegui, Eastman was really showing his own preference for the anti-Hegelianism of William James. The poverty of Eastman's criticism could not be better demonstrated than on the grounds that he himself had failed to propose any new bases for a better science of revolution.[32]

The final section of the book impressionistically portrayed the prevailing crisis of the liberal imagination, which now found itself thrown into doubt and disillusionment by the postwar right-wing reaction. Up until then the liberals had generally remained staunchly loyal to the ideals of progress and democracy. But the outcome of the negotiated peace had overturned their former hope.

All kinds of reactionary ideologies, including fascism, had proliferated in the era of capitalist stabilization brought about by the Dawes Plan. This rightist resurgence had succeeded in Italy and not France, according to the Peruvian, because France lacked the philosophical and literary culture that Italian fascists were able to draw upon. Ironically, this included Sorel, who was "so diversely interpreted" in Italy as to become, he said, one of the favorite authors of the right as well as the left.[33]

Despite its current wave of success, fascism could never assume the leadership of western capitalism, concluded the *Defensa*. Its roots were too closely linked to Latin culture and Roman Catholicism, as opposed to western capitalism, which was fundamentally Protestant, individualist, liberal, and Anglo-Saxon. Thus while the French neo-Thomists and German racists might debate over who would now lead the West, that question had already been answered: the United States was the center of world capitalism and held the key to the future of the European and world economy.

The United States's economic strength stemmed from its vast industrial capacities and the great resources of its finance capital.[34] In addition, the convergence of various historical elements—including the absence of a feudal class and the triumph of Yankee capitalism during the Civil War—assured American capitalism of an untrammeled future.

Among the more perceptive intellectuals of the right, the Spaniard Ramiro de Maeztu had grasped that the United States and the Soviet Union had emerged as the two poles on which contemporary world history turned. They represented universalizing historical tendencies with antagonistic ends; but the ultimate victor, predicted Maeztu, would be the United States.

Maeztu's confidence in the United States's ability to prevail over Moscow rested partly on his assessment of the industrial potential brought about by Henry Ford, who had introduced new methods of production based on standardization and Taylorism. Ford's success revealed that North American industrial capitalism remained strong vis-à-vis finance capital, although Ford's anti-Semitic attacks on finance capital presaged a coming struggle between the two forces. At any rate, it remained clear that American capitalism had yet to confront any crisis of the magnitude recently experienced by European capitalism (by the time this was being written, however, such a crisis was just around the corner).

This final passage dealing with American economic might is one of the few written by Mariátegui which gives us an idea of how he interpreted the changing postwar role of the United States. But the basic focus of the final essay was on rightist reaction, originally conceived as the primary part of the work.

Since then, however, his interests had shifted to the problem of revolutionary consciousness, and by the time the final essay of the *Defensa* appeared in June 1929, Mariátegui and the Lima group were already deeply involved in making a revolutionary political movement of their own—one that was geared toward the peculiar Indo-American milieu of Peru.

8

Peruanicemos al Perú:
Toward a Nationalist Indigenista Revolution

> La nueva generación siente y sabe que el progreso del
> Perú será ficticio, o por lo menos no será peruano,
> mientras no constituya la obra y no signifique el
> bienestar de la masa peruana, que en sus cuatro quintas
> partes es indígena y campesina.[1]

The last photographs of Mariátegui show him physically exhausted, his life visibly shrinking away, though the sharp look in
the eye and the thin smile remain.

He virtually lost himself in work during the four years following the appearance of *Amauta* (1926–30), as if aware that he did
not have much time. Aside from his intellectual and literary
pursuits—publishing *Amauta*, and writing *Siete ensayos, Defensa
del Marxismo*, and numerous other articles, essays, and tracts—
he was deeply involved politically. As we have mentioned,
during this period he founded, with his Limeño circle of intellectuals and working-class radicals, a Peruvian socialist party, the
Partido Socialista del Perú (PSP); a Peruvian labor confederation,
the Confederación General de Trabajadores del Perú (CGTP);
and a working-class newspaper, *Labor*.

All of his work now reflected a great sensitivity to the historic
rights of the native Peruvian people and of all those whose toil
produced the wealth of the country. This emphasis on race
combined with a class outlook gave his socialist perspective an
original slant. It also inescapably led to the conclusion that a
Peruvian revolution lacking in the participation of the indigenous
masses simply could not be.

As Mariátegui's thinking on an indigenista revolutionary nationalism took shape in the late 1920s, it had the effect of cutting
him off from many of his contemporaries. But indigenismo was
not solely responsible for that happening; his way of approaching

147

politics—"at the same time intellectual, emotional, and practi-cal"[2]—further set him apart from the beaten path of his peers and of others as well.

When the *Siete ensayos* appeared in 1928—and incorporated a radical indigenista and class perspective—in Lima it mostly received a brief and lukewarm review from Luis Alberto Sánchez and some brief reviews in the *Mercurio Peruano*. A decidedly cooler reception awaited his major work than that given earlier to *La escena contemporánea*.

In time, the standard of a Peruvian nationalist revolution rooted in a socialist movement and his voluntarist conception of a revolutionary consciousness, also led to his ostracism, as we shall see, from the ranks of the international left.

Race and Class

Our reading of the basic data all points to the fact that the design for a nationalist revolution came together as Mariátegui worked out his race and class analysis of the national question (a process not completed in the *Siete ensayos*).

Not until the very late 1920s did he succeed in bringing together a comprehensive statement on race and class, and in the usual fashion, non-Marxists contributed to the process. In this instance the aristocratic Marchese Vilfredo Pareto's *Les systèmes socialistes*, in particular, supplied Mariátegui with a general historical account of racism.

But the key to his integration of a class analysis with a race interpretation is to be found in Nikolai Bukharin's *Historical Materialism: A System of Sociology* (first published in Moscow in 1921). Bukharin's text showed him, as he himself pointedly revealed, how the circumstances and status of a given race depended on their relation to the "movement of the productive forces."[3]

Applying such basic principles to Peru, Mariátigui returned to his earlier treatment of gamonalismo, finding now how the mode of production explained the interrelating functions between race and socioeconomic status. Most basic to his views were the origins of gamonalismo which could be traced back to the Conquest, when a system of large estates owned by whites and run by subservient native labor had been implanted by the Spaniards. Across the centuries that system had produced the well-known gamonalismo, wherein "the race factor . . . [had become] dynamically related to the class factor."[4]

This social process, produced by such fundamental divisions existing among Peruvians as those of class and race, had its ideological counterparts. Race, in fact, served as a crucial underpinning of the ruling-class ideology. Notions of racial superiority still served to justify their exploitative relations to the native people,[5] and bourgeois intellectuals still often complained about the "inferiority and primitiveness" of the native race.

Upper-class ideology, which he referred to as an "incurable and sickly *pasadismo,*" (ideological attachment to the colonial past) held that the national history of Peru originated with the Conquest. While occasionally expressing a "lingering sentiment" for the natives, *pasadismo* traced Peru's roots to the Iberian peninsula, to the virtual exclusion of the indigenous legacy.

The Indian was not the only casualty of the prevailing situation; the mestizo also suffered from the basic race and class divisions of the country. The view of the mestizo world that emerges is grim indeed. In fact, it contrasted sharply with what Mariátegui described as the creole tendency to portray the mestizo as a "new social type"; a type for whom skin color no longer mattered. This white-washing of the mestizo, which he attributed to the most progressive sectors of the creole bourgeoisie (ideologues like Manuel Vicente Villarán, Francisco García Calderón, and Víctor Andrés Belaúnde), had been so successful that even mestizos themselves had bought their arguments.

In reality, the mestizos were a tragic group, who found their consciousness caught in the middle of a world bisected by skin color. Therein precisely originated their deepest conflicts; in the fact they were in the middle but sided with the whites in every respect. Assimilated into the white, urbanized, westernized world of modern Peru, the mestizo could take pride in his successful mastering of the intellectual and technical requirements imposed by western culture. But he could never really absorb the European's "complex of beliefs, myths, and emotions," the essential constituent elements of their white identity running, in the Nietzschean sense, "in the blood." Lacking, in other words, in their most fundamental nature, the mestizo could therefore only aspire to a life of imitation.

In countries marked by "Spanish pauperism"—the special form of social backwardness bequeathed to Peru by Spain—that imitation translated into a peculiar form of social dependency. Generally, the typical mestizo petit bourgeois depended on the government bureaucracy for his livelihood. In return for some form of security, the mestizo aped the ideology and culture of the white ruling class in order to advance in the creole world. In the process he had to repudiate all indigenous ties; indeed, to such a degree did his rejection go that it even produced a form of "self loathing."[6] More than once Mariátegui noted how even so-called revolutionary elements in Lima occasionally revealed a strong racial prejudice against the native people.

Because the mestizo and other racially mixed peoples in Peru tried to identify with the white world rather than with the indigenous, Peruvian society was split into those who rejected "the popular . . . the national," and the vast masses of native people. This basic contradiction stemmed from Peru's Hispanic colonial heritage, which emphasized the supremacy of white Europeans over the Indian.

Capitalist imperialism further reinforced Peru's internal class and race contradictions; it "fatally" conditioned the existing structures of relations, resulting in a hegemonic bloc of *internal colonialism* made up of creole and mestizo bourgeois and middle-class elements. And just as the mestizo middle-classes aped the creole bourgeoisie, the latter did the same vis-à-vis the white imperialist forces. International class solidarity (the identification of the Peruvian ruling classes with the foreign capitalist class), transformed the "national bourgeoisie into a docile instrument of Yankee and British imperialism."[7]

In contrast to the whites and mestizos who readily compromised national interests to foreign imperialism, Mariátegui found the native people wholly alienated from the present form of national integration and development. From this he drew the conclusion that only the Indian had not "broken with his past." Living in a milieu which "conserved his customs, his emotional life, and his attitude toward the universe," the Indian remained in contact with his traditions and his cultural identity. From such sources he drew his strength. While some might say indigenous life was primitive and backward, or insist that the original structure of Indian society had been deformed and uprooted, they could never deny its continuing social and cultural vitality.[8]

It is on such principles that the Lima radical circle based its politics, which in addition to producing a form of indigenista revolutionary nationalism also looked to some kind of cooperation with the international movement.

To date, no one faulting the Peruvians for their nationalist posture has suggested that the *Amauta* group excluded international activity from their plans. On the contrary, the journal's format itself suggested at the level of theory an "open Marxism"; that is, a Marxism foreign to sectarianism. Similarly, their Peruvian nationalist posture remained open to broader international contacts. Mariátegui enunciated a kind of party dogma when he proposed that the liberation of the native people of Peru could never be achieved without the assimilation of western "science and technology." But this opening to the West and to the international workers' movement had to obey their own ways of doing things, "their own style." And that style, as we know, was indigenous.

Nationalism and Internationalism

Mariátegui's radical indigenista nationalism led him off the beaten path not only in relation to his own generation and society, but also in respect to the international socialist movement. The path he charted, which evolved from his reading of the Peruvian past and his own personal history, hinged on the differences existing between the colonial and the industrialized world. Which to him essentially meant the socialist struggle must take a different form in colonial areas. That much he established as early as 1923, during several references made at the UPGP lectures. At that time, in applying his schema to the situation of Peru, he concluded that Peru belonged to a *semicolonial* group of countries enjoying some political but not much economic independence. To that extent at least he subscribed to the Third International's policy on the colonial world.

In the following years, Mariátegui's interests in nationalism deepened. For example, in 1925 he wrote several essays on the common theme of nationalism and vanguardism, in which he analyzed the variety of nationalisms existing, going from right to left.

The early writings already contained the germ of his idea that in Peru a revolutionary form of nationalism, rooted in socialist principles, was the strategy local conditions most required. A very basic condition made this so:

[In] societies [like Peru] that are politically and economically colonial . . . through force of circumstance and without rejecting any of its principles, [socialism] acquired, out of historical necessity, a revolutionary nationalist character.[9]

Just as earlier the western bourgeois idea of the nation had inspired the Latin American wars of independence, now the same idea, in socialist dress, was affecting "all of those societies that exploited by a foreign imperialism, struggle for their national liberty."[10]

The unproductive nationalism of previous generations stemmed from the central fact that independence had not been the product of a true democratic-bourgeois revolution. As a result, it now seemed that the historical tasks generally associated with the democratic–bourgeois revolution—such as the breaking-up of the large feudal estate—must now be accomplished by the socialist revolution.

In his own words:

Socialism does not appear in our history by chance, imitation, or fashion as many superficial minds have supposed, but as a historical fatality. . . . On the one hand, we who profess socialism propose logically and coherently the reorganization of the country on a socialist basis . . . [and] proclaim that at this moment in our history it is not possible to be effective nationalists and revolutionaries without being socialists . . . [because] the economic-political regime which we combat has gradually been converted into a force of internal colonialism by foreign capitalist imperalists . . . On the other hand, there does not exist and never has existed, a progressive bourgeoisie with a national vision that, professing itself liberal and democratic, inspired its politics in the postulates of its doctrine.[11]

To this fusion of nationalism and socialism he further added the unique stamp of Peruvian indigenismo. Race enters in at this point, and it served a pivotal function. It was pivotal indeed, for the native majority must necessarily represent the critical mass of any future revolutionary process. This is why Mariátegui could say as early as 1927, in his debate with Sánchez:

> No one who sees the content and essence of things can be surprised by the confluence or amalgamation of indigenismo and socialism. Socialism orders and defines the revindication of the masses, of the working class. And in Peru the masses—the working class—are four-fifths indigenous. Thus our socialism . . . [must declare its] solidarity with the native people. . . . [In] this vanguard . . . there exists absolutely nothing of an "exotic nationalism"; it is nothing but a "Peruvian nationalism."[12]

Yet this merging of an indigenista nationalism with the goal of socialist revolution did not mean that one of the main tenets of the socialist movement—the "dialectical negation" of nationalism—had been dropped by Mariátegui. In due course he acknowledged that internationalism as a "higher stage of development" eventually must supercede nationalism as a "historical necessity."[13] At the same time he also understood socialist internationalism as not implying "the standardization of all societies and all men according to one unique model." All of these thoughts correspond to the actual steps followed by him and by the *Amauta* cadre, as they proceeded to put together first a national political party—the PSP—and then a national labor confederation—the CGTP.

Organizing the PSP and the CGTP

Mariátegui and his group made contact with the international socialist movement while they were still laying the groundwork for the Peruvian socialist party and the labor confederation. Their first contact with the Third International came in the wake of two measures passed by the Second Workers' Congress held in Lima in 1927—one proposing the organization of the CGTP, and the other that Julio Portocarrero (a young textile worker from Vitarte) be sent to Moscow as the Peruvian delegate to the Fifth Congress of the Red International of Labor Unions.

Once in Moscow, Portocarrero received from the Comintern an itemized set of directives for the Lima group. Of its seven basic points—which touched on the nature of the Peruvian proletariat and peasant masses and included some criticism of APRA—the most important one stressed that a communist party affiliated with the Third International ought to be organized in Peru.[14]

Mariátegui received this directive, and other contacts with the International followed—he began to receive *La Correspondencia Sudamericana*, the official organ of the Latin American Bureau of the International set up in Buenos Aires. But these contacts failed in and of themselves to persuade him to found a political party. What did precipitate action on that front was not international pressure, but rather APRA's Mexico City declaration that it was not simply an alliance but a party. In that sense, the consideration of local conditions always remained the primary reality to take into account. International considerations remained secondary, at least up to then.

Thus on a quiet Sunday on September 16, 1928, six persons met on a desolate beach near the road leading to the Playa de la Herradura on the outskirts of Lima. Mariátegui did not attend this initial meeting, but it was chaired by his chief collaborator on such matters, Ricardo Martínez de la Torre. The six members of the group included four factory workers, one traveling vendor, and one white collar professional.[15]

The group laid down a table of organization for a Peruvian socialist party. They decided: (1) to create a socialist, not a communist party (the PSP), which would be organized by conscientious "Marxist" elements and affiliated with the Third International; (2) to set up a labor cell, the counterpart of the party, to carry out the directives of the Red International of Labor Unions (also called the Profintern); (3) to form a "secret cell of seven" (the original six plus Mariátegui), which would constitute the executive committee of the party; and finally, (4) to hold another meeting on this subject. Thus the initial proposal already contained the makings of the idea of a communist core group being organized within a socialist party, a notion that immediately made the Lima group suspect in the eyes of the International.

Several weeks later, on Sunday, October 7, the second meeting took place—this time in Lima at the home of Avelino Navarro, perhaps the group's most effective labor organizer. Mariátegui attended, and he was elected secretary general of the new party.[16]

Mariátegui himself drew up the meeting's minutes, which included a most careful listing of the group's purpose, which was (1) to develop class consciousness among urban workers and campesinos; (2) to organize factory and hacienda syndicates, and those syndicates into federations, and ultimately those federations into a national confederation; (3) to build a socialist party made up of workers and peasants; (4) to register all the syndicates with the government's labor office so as to avoid police action; (5) to follow the tactic of the united front and accept petit bourgeois membership in both the party and labor organizations, so long as everyone identified with the idea of class solidarity; and finally, (6) to form organizational committees and cells in all working-class areas for the purpose of national coordination.

As these points reveal, Mariátegui and his group sought to establish what has been called a "broad based" party—one open to petit bourgeois, middle-class elements committed to a legal Marxism.

Martínez de la Torre maintained to the end that this second meeting of October 7, 1928, and the summary of its proceedings were the founding date and document of the Peruvian revolutionary movement. The issue of which meeting held primacy, the first or the second, had some bearing on a question that was to arise later: whether Mariátegui had meant to establish a Peruvian socialist or communist party. Martínez insisted that the former had always been their unswerving purpose.

At any rate, after the October meeting the party's two syndical secretaries, Avelino Navarro and Jorge Portocarrero, launched efforts to organize the CGTP as decided. That was no easy task, for since the alleged June 1927 "communist plot" and police raids and arrests of that year, the labor movement had been in disarray.

By January 1929, however, considerable progress had been made in putting it back together. On several occasions in the late 1920s the chief organ of the communist trade union movement, the *Trabajador Latino Americano* (published in Montevideo by the Confederación Sindical Latino Americana) described the revitalized activities of the Peruvian Federación Ferrocarrilera del Perú, the Federación Textil del Perú, the Federación Gráfica del Perú, and five other federations. One article associated their success with the efforts of the "Editorial Amauta" and the working-class newspaper Labor.

Founded in November 1928, Labor served to disseminate information on organizing throughout the country. Published biweekly, it sought to reach some 19,000 members of the Federación Obrera de Lima,[17] embracing all of the organized workers' groups in the Lima area (who made up roughly one-quarter of the nonagricultural labor force of 58,000 industrial workers and 28,000 mine workers reported for Peru in the late 1920s).[18] Within a fairly short time, Labor was reaching between six and eight thousand workers, many of whom passed the paper around from hand to hand.[19]

By mid 1929, El Trabajador Latino Americano was reporting support for the proposed CGTP from at least five major labor organizations in Lima. And the May Day issue of Labor carried a manifesto, written by Mariátegui, which announced the formation of a Comité Pro 1° de Mayo to serve as the organizing committee for a CGTP. It especially stressed the strategy of organizing workers by individual industry and factory, rather than by trade or profession.

The Lima movement quickly attracted support from labor groups in other parts of the country. Casiano Rado, for example, one of the principal leaders of the Cuzco workers' cell—which had established independent contact with the South American Communist Bureau in February 1927[20]—came to the capital for discussions, as a result of which he consented to joining the efforts of both the PSP and CGTP. Other cooperating groups appeared in Lambayeque and Chiclayo in the north; Morococha, Juaja, Huánuco, and Cerro de Pasco in the central sierra; and Arequipa and Cuzco in the south.

The movement emphasized not only political involvement on the part of the workers, but also the enhancement of "proletarian culture" as well. Toward this end the working-class newspaper Labor was made an aesthetically attractive publication like Amauta, with its columns broken up by sharp and impressive indigenous graphics.

Direct education of the working class also received high priority. Wherever an affiliate of the CGTP was set up, an Oficina de Auto-Educación Obrera (Office for Workers' Self-Education) also appeared (the headquarters of the educational association was established in Lima). Each educational cell offered either a basic or an advanced course of study. The basic program included courses in Peruvian history and geography, world history and geography, Spanish, and syndicalism. The upper level courses included sociology, the history of social ideas, economics, biology, and syndicalism.[21]

Building popular culture and class consciousness went hand in hand with the task of elaborating a political program. Mariátegui worked out a nine-point program for the PSP in 1928, point four of which identified the party's politics as Marxist-Leninist and proposed the adoption of a Leninist "method of combat."[22] But at the same time, one point reaffirmed the independent stance of the party, saying:

> [The] socialist party adapts its praxis to the concrete circumstances of the country, although the same national circumstances are subordinated to the rhythm of world history.[23]

This seemed to suggest that although the PSP would cooperate with the International, the party reserved an area of decision for its own—which only added to the tension already existing between the Peruvian socialists and the Comintern.

In the meantime, the International had proceeded slowly in developing its South American activities. A regional Secretariat had not been established until late 1925-early 1926 and *La Correspondencia Sudamericana*, the chief party organ, did not appear until April 1926.[24] At the time the Latin American working the closest with the International Bureau had been Victorio Codovilla, chief of the Argentine party. Buenos Aires thus became the center of contact between the Comintern and the various Latin American communist organizations. Usually, the Bureau sent representatives to each country to announce international meetings, distribute travel funds, or make other party arrangements.[25]

Such a representative came to Peru in 1929 to arrange for delegations to attend two upcoming international meetings, to which Mariátegui's cadre was invited, despite the emerging differences between them and the South American Bureau. In fact, the trade union conference in Montevideo and the First Congress of Latin American Communist Parties in May-June 1929 in Buenos Aires can be seen as the acid test of Mariátegui's reconciliation of nationalism and socialism. To some extent these meetings represented a showdown between the path being followed by the Peruvian cell and the official line of the Comintern.

The degree of importance attached to these meetings by Mariátegui is reflected in the careful preparations that were made. The executive committee of the party reviewed the situation and decided to send Julio Portocarrero as head of a delegation of four to Montevideo, and Dr. Hugo Pesce as chief representative to the Buenos Aires conference (Portocarrero would be joining him there). Pesce was brought into the secret communist cell just prior to the Buenos Aires meeting for consultation.[26]

Two of the principal items on the Buenos Aires agenda were the role of the middle classes in a socialist revolutionary movement and the race question. One can say therefore that the Congress became a most appropriate and dramatic forum for airing the unique ideas being pursued by the Peruvian comrades. Mariátegui himself drafted three important position papers relating to these issues: "Antecedents and Development of Class Action in Peru," "The Problem of Race in Latin America," and "An Anti-Imperialist Point of View." Martínez de la Torre and Portocarrero also prepared a PSP report analyzing the social and political situation in Peru.

At the Montevideo meeting things went well for the Peruvian delegates, and Portocarrero was elected to the executive committee of the Confederación Sindical Latino Americana. But in Buenos Aires they fared differently.

Pesce and Portocarrero joined thirty-eight other Spanish American delegates and numerous observers at the historic congress, which presented the first opportunity for the International Secretariat to coordinate its policies in Latin America.

From the beginning the presiding officers of the meeting, and especially Victorio Codovilla, referred to the Peruvian party in highly critical terms. Codovilla opened the first session of the General Assembly with the Bureau's general analysis of the situation in Latin America, and his remarks included criticism of the Peruvian comrades for not giving sufficient attention to the Tacna-Arica dispute existing between Peru and Chile. Later, when it was Pesce's turn to reply, he tactfully refuted Codovilla's charges.

From then on the dispute broke out in the open, revolving primarily around the fact that Mariátegui had established a Peruvian socialist party (PSP) rather than a communist party (PCP) as directed by the Comintern.

Things began to heat up when Portocarrero presented Mariátegui's thesis on antiimperialism. He started out by saying that the Peruvians had come to Buenos Aires "to resolve an issue." A good portion of the discussion focused on the differences between the PSP and APRA, the nature of the class struggle in Peru, and the role of the middle class in the revolution. The crux of the argument, however, was the clear indication that national parties were in a better position to judge local conditions than the Comintern, and therefore "the directives issued by the South American Secretariat of the Communist International must differ in accordance with the different conditions of each region."[27]

Along these lines, he noted that their decision to organize a PCP rather than a PSP involved a tactical decision based on their own judgment of the Peruvian situation. (What he did not say was that they wanted to draw support for the party from the middle class, which they felt would never join a PCP.) Their intentions, said Portocarrero, were for a core communist cell to exercise control over the party's open activities. No longer reading from Mariátegui's text, he summarized their position by saying:

> The socialist party is based on our group and is entirely committed to the ideology of the Communist International. We are, and we declare ourselves to be, communists above everything else; we desire that the workers' movement in Peru carry the imprint of the Communist International.[28]

Portocarrero's speech quickly drew the fire of those presiding. Codovilla led the attack, but the strongest criticism came from the others, especially Comrade Luis (code name for Jules Humbert-Droz), who then held the number-two spot in the Profintern. He characterized the tactic of the secret communist cell within a PSP as "dangerous," arguing that a multiclass party with working-class, peasant, and petit bourgeois membership could easily escape the control of the communist leadership unless the party were openly under communist discipline. Moreover, he said, if a legal communist party could not be organized in Peru, then an illegal or clandestine one should be created (which was indeed what the Peruvians were precisely doing, creating an underground PCP).[29]

Pesce's turn to be roasted came next as the result of his reading of Mariátegui's thesis on the race question. One argument made was that while capitalism had introduced wage labor and modern technology to Peru, it had failed to erase the feudal character of the large estate and thereby had "generated instability" in the relations between labor and property.

Further, as native workers from the sierra increasingly entered the wage-labor market in the sierra mining centers and on the coastal export-agriculture haciendas, the changing social relations, were leading to the creation of a new proletariat. Although it was extremely difficult to organize these workers (because the mining companies and hacendados immediately discharged anyone distributing party propaganda), nevertheless it was precisely in those places where the indigenous population was slowly being proletarianized that organizing must be given priority.

Because the native miners retained their ties with the rural peasantry it was up to them to disseminate "class propaganda" when they returned to their communities seasonally.[30] Mariátegui felt that only such indigenous organizers proved effective with the Indian rural peasants, who distrusted whites and mestizos and had to be approached in their own language.

Against the orthodox view of a passive native population offering no resistance to white exploitation, Mariátegui's address contrasted a portrayal of the long history of indigenous insurrections in Peru. Not for a minute did he question the potential of the native population for fueling a future revolutionary insurrection.

> It will no doubt take time for an indigenous revolutionary consciousness to form; but once the Indian makes the socialist idea his own, it will provide him with a discipline, a tenacity and strength that few proletariats from other areas could match.[31]

The thesis further proposed that the country's reconstruction should rest solidly—though not exclusively—upon an indigenous foundation. He took this position not out of a sentimental or romantic infatuation with the Inca civilization of the past, but because of the revolutionary potential of "the Indian of today."[32]

When Dr. Pesce finished presenting Mariátegui's paper, it was attacked for explaining the race question solely in terms of the feudal exploitation of the Indians by the mode of production of the large estate. It was also criticized for not following the Leninist line that the Indian problem, like all race problems, was actually a "national question" that could only be resolved through a separatist movement of self-determination rather than a multiclass revolutionary movement such as that proposed by the PSP.

Mariátegui did not understand, they said, that the Indian movement must evolve toward a dictatorship of the indigenous proletariat, rather than the establishment of an indigenous democratic-bourgeois state with all of the contradictions inherent in such politics.[33] The Peruvian delegates were even told they were using the term peasant incorrectly; the word properly referred to a small property-holder or renter, while the term agricultural worker was used when talking about agricultural wage labor.[34]

Codovilla delivered the lengthiest criticism, at the end of which he exclaimed: "And if the Communist International directs that in all countries communist parties must be organized, why should Peru be an exception?"[35]

Under the circumstances, Pesce and Portocarrero were models of firmness and tact. In a reply not entirely free of some sarcasm, Dr. Pesce pointed out that the indigenous question must be construed above all as a class question. To propose nativist self-determination and separatism amounted to viewing the entire issue solely in terms of race alone. Such a strategy would also exclude the non-Indian and mestizo proletariat from the revolutionary struggle.[36] But while the indigenous masses figured as the salient bloc in the national movement, he noted, the party wished to incorporate nonindigenous social sectors including members of the petit bourgeoisie—as long as they all subscribed to the idea of a workers' class struggle.

As a result of these differences between the PSP and the

ideological stand of the International, the Bureau decided to reject the party as an affiliate and set aside the question for further consultation.[37] Codovilla relented in the end, however, acknowledging that the Peruvian delegation had contributed "most intensely" to the congress. Droz, who reputedly held Mariátegui in high regard, added that the Peruvians had taken important steps toward "the assimilation of communist ideology." There is no reason to doubt the genuineness of their remarks, for earlier no less a light than Zinoviev had made this comment:

> Mariátegui has a brilliant mind; he is a true creator. He does not seem like a Latin American; he does not plagiarize, he does not copy, he does not parrot what the Europeans say. What he creates is his own.[38]

Mariátegui was not overly surprised to learn what had happened in Buenos Aires. They had all pretty much expected the opposition, and were prepared to stick to their guns. As Martínez de la Torre and Pesce, two of Mariátegui's closest confidants, reported, the party was committed to a policy of tactical flexibility; a long-term organizing strategy; and the goal of a broad-based party dedicated to the class struggle.[39] Portocarrero as well as Antonio Navarro Madrid, who served as *Amauta's* secretary,[40] agreed with this assessment of their position. They intended to retain control of the movement and not yield to external pressures.[41]

In the meantime, the party's organizing effort continued at its hectic pace, and the government harrassment followed close behind. When *Labor* carried the story of a walkout by 15,000 miners at Cerro de Pasco in Morococha in late 1929, the paper was closed down and Mariátegui was arrested briefly. From then on his home was under constant surveillance and the authorities opened all of his mail.[42]

One effect of the stepped-up police repression was to isolate Mariátegui, for from then on fewer and fewer visitors dared to come by except on the most urgent matters, but the PSP and CGTP maintained their organizing momentum nevertheless.

The CGTP had been officially founded on May 17, 1929, by a Provisional Committee made up of accredited delegations from numerous syndicates.[43] In fact, when Portocarrero spoke at the Montevideo trade union meeting of the Confederación Sindical

Latino Americana he did so as head of a CGTP delegation, and his report already indicated the broad range of organizing efforts the CGTP had begun.[44]

There Portocarreo had catalogued the numerous causes the CGTP was pursuing, from the general problems affecting agricultural workers[45] to the issue of child and female labor. On the latter point, one of the earliest manifestos of the CGTP Provisional Committee described how women workers and juvenile laborers were "cruelly exploited."

Partly as a result of such interest in issues directly affecting young workers and students, members of these groups enthusiastically devoted their energy to helping the movement. In 1929, for example, the party was joined by Pompeyo Herrera, José D. Montesinos, Moisés Arroyo Posada, Julio del Prado, and Jorge del Prado[46]—who saw Mariátegui put the finishing touches to the first manifesto of the CGTP Provisional Committee.[47] The youths received organizing assignments immediately; Jorge del Prado, for example, started in the Callao area working with maritime laborers, and later went on to Morococha when the miners' Federation was set up.[48]

By 1931, the CGTP claimed a total membership of 60,000 industrial, agricultural, and mining workers.[49] And the PSP reported active cells in Callao, Cuzco, and Arequipa, as well as in many lesser towns and cities. The party's ten regional committees and two thousand members, not counting the Federation of Communist Youth, included industrial workers (45%), artisans (17%), and native peasants.

The Last Days

The growing success of the Peruvian Socialist Party and the labor confederation contrasted sharply with the declining course of Mariátegui's health throughout 1929. Since the amputation of his leg in 1924 he had suffered from recurrent illnesses, on the average of every six months, and a lingering malaise[50] for which his doctors were forever after him to rest. One major source for reconstructing the effect that the deterioration of his health had on his outlook on life during the final years is the series of remarkably revealing letters he wrote to his Argentine friend,

Samuel Glusberg, between 1927 and 1930.[51] They suggest an increasing frustration and anxiety apparently unknown to his Lima associates.[52]

In one of his first letters, written in April 1927, Mariátegui referred to his "unstable health" and noted that the amputation had left him "sick and mutilated." After the police raid of September 1927 he wrote to his friend again, mentioning a recent "rheumatic arthritic attack" for which he had taken a brief holiday to Chosica, some fifty miles from damp and gray Lima. He also expressed concern over *Amauta's* future and said that if the journal could not be published in Lima he would consider leaving for Buenos Aires.[53] From then on, he talked more and more about the idea of leaving Peru in his communications with Glusberg.

Mariátegui apparently did not write again until July 4, 1928, when he exuded optimism and glossed over the fact that he had been bedridden for several months. A leading Lima surgeon, he told Glusberg, had assured him of good health within eight to ten months.[54] On November 7, 1928, he commented on the publication of the *Siete ensayos* and discussed his new manuscript. He remarked that he was thinking of changing its name from "Defense of the West" to "Defense of Marxism," and furthermore proposed that Glusberg arrange for its publication in Buenos Aires instead of Spain "to save time."[55] In closing, he again spoke of a possible visit to Buenos Aires within six months.

Almost every succeeding letter included a reference to his declining health. On March 10, 1929, for example, he complained of a bothersome and prolonged "neuralgia." It was on this occasion that he described the *Defensa* as reaching "conclusions unfavorable to Marxism," and as probably not being acceptable for publication by the Buenos Aires group, La Vanguardia.[56]

The following letter (June 10) again dealt mainly with publishing matters, but in the final paragraph revealed an uncharacteristic impatience and bitterness. In Lima, Mariátegui wrote, a tacit but continual campaign of repression faced him daily, which he despised for its "stupidity, its mediocrity, its *arrivismo*";[57] he longed to breathe "the air of a free country." He specifically pointed to the stoney silence that had greeted the *Siete ensayos:* with the exception of a brief note by Luis Alberto Sánchez and some "affectionate commentaries" in the provincial newspapers, the book had generally been ignored.[58] Mariátegui saw this as part of a movement "to block me in my work, to besiege me economically, to asphyxiate me with violence."[59]

The campaign of repression intensified daily as people coming to see him were harrassed by the police, most of his mail was not only opened but frequently confiscated, and even *Variedades* and *Mundial,* the two weeklies that were the chief source of his personal income, were pressured—unsuccessfully—to discharge him.[60]

After letters to Glusberg on June 20, and August 21, Mariátegui did not write again until November 7, 1929, when he informed his Argentine correspondent of an impending visit by Waldo Frank. Two weeks later, on November 21, he told of the mass arrests that had included a round-up of some 180 people, many of them labor leaders from Cerro de Pasco. Soon afterwards, when he sent another letter, he seemed to have reached the breaking point, saying, "I cannot remain here. I will only stay the time necessary to prepare for the trip. I will leave Peru any way I can."[61]

Waldo Frank's visit had an extraordinary effect on Mariátegui. He wrote Glusberg an emotional letter in December 1929, saying that Frank's presence had confirmed his intention to leave for Buenos Aires—although he saw the trip as only a temporary interruption of his political work in Peru.

Another person reinforcing Mariátegui's plans to leave Lima was Eudocio Ravines, who had arrived in the capital in February 1930 directly from Moscow. Ravines had broken with Haya de la Torre after the Brussels Anti-Imperialist Congress of February 1928 and subsequently had fallen in with the French radical Barbusse, who in turn had put Ravines in touch with the communist movement. Eventually, he had wound up in Moscow, where, at the Fifth Congress of the Red International of Labor Unions of 1927, he had met Portocarrero.[62] Apparently, Ravines came to Peru in 1930 as an agent of the International with instructions to steer the PSP toward becoming a PCP.[63]

A few days after Ravines's arrival in Lima he had a brief meeting on the outskirts of the city with Mariátegui, whom he had previously known only casually. Accompanied by Pesce, Mariátegui reached an agreement with Ravines on certain basic principles and issues. They did not see eye to eye, however, on the need, as Ravines urged, to accelerate the pace of the Peruvian movement's organizing activities, to institute greater party discipline, or to radicalize the PSP. While on such issues they disagreed then, and continued to remain at odds throughout their relationship, at no time did Ravines ever openly challenge Mariátegui's leadership. And Mariátegui admired Ravine's quick intelligence and political skills.[64]

Ravines's arrival came at an opportune time, in that his enthusiasm and ability enabled him to assume quickly many of Mariátegui's political responsibilities, thereby allowing Mariátegui to decide to leave definitely for Buenos Aires. On March 1, 1930, he recommended to the Executive Committee that Ravines be appointed secretary general of the PSP,[65] arranged for Martínez de la Torre to remain as his personal representative in the capital and to assume charge of *Amauta*, and even devised a clandestine communication network.

Glusberg, in the meantime, had agreed to coordinate arrangements in Buenos Aires for Mariátegui's arrival. They wrote each other frequently and set a tentative date for his departure in April. A letter from Lima of March 6 described the political intrigue in the capital surrounding the penultimate days of the Leguía dictatorship and the frequent police raids which Mariátegui said he hoped would not interfere with their plans.

Several other letters followed. But shortly after the last one of March 25, Mariátegui suddenly fell ill. The doctors made an initial diagnosis at home and decided to move him to the Clínica Villarán, where he was attended by six physicians, led by Dr. Fortunato Quesada.[66] He underwent emergency surgery twice, but a rampant staphylococcus infection continued to spread. *Amauta*, as well as newspapers in the capital and the provinces, published daily medical reports on his worsening condition. In the second week of April his physicians realized that they could not control the infection, which finally entered his bloodstream. Only intermittently conscious in the final days of his three-week fight for life, early on April 16 he awoke alert and spoke briefly to his wife and close friends. At about 8:50 in the morning he died.

On April 17, at four in the afternoon, all of the trolley and motor transport of Lima stopped for five minutes in his honor. His funeral, which had been arranged by the CGTP, drew one of the most massive demonstrations of public sentiment ever seen in the city, and his passing was mourned nationwide.

After Mariátegui's death, the socialist labor movement remained prostrate for weeks. Then the arrival of an important memorandum from the Political Secretariat set the wheels of politics in motion again.

The International's message reopened the issue of whether the Peruvian party should be a socialist or communist organization. It basically repeated what had been said earlier in Buenos Aires: that the PSP incorporated too broad a social base; that it embraced "intellectuals and petit bourgeois" elements not acceptable to a communist party; and that the political profile of the group came dangerously close to that of APRA. The International concluded by directing that a communist party be established immediately.[67]

Ravines called the central committee of the party into session at a farm above Chosica in May 1930, to formulate a response. As secretary general he presided over the debate, with he himself taking a position in favor of the name change. Martínez de la Torre argued vehemently against it. In the end, however, Ravines succeeded in persuading them to reach a unanimous decision to establish a communist party. Even Martínez de la Torre went along, under protest;[68] but not long afterward, on July 29, 1931, he resigned from the organization he had helped to found. From then on he tenaciously insisted that Mariátegui had not intended to organize a PCP, at least not for a long time.

Meanwhile Ravines, now secretary general of a flaming new PCP, assumed command over the political party and the labor movement that had been carefully nurtured by Mariátegui over many tireless years of cautious effort.[69] Acting upon entirely different premises than those inspiring the group's earlier efforts, Ravines set about organizing the Morococha miners for armed action. In the months that followed, the movement was quickly destroyed by police and military repression.

At the same time, other impatient leaders were battering at the doors of the government itself, although with quite different objectives in mind. On August 22, 1930, the Arequipa military garrison led by Comandante Luis M. Sánchez Cerro revolted. Two days later—August 24—Leguía, ill and weary and no doubt despondent, resigned and turned over his government to a military cabinet.

Thus the eleven-year reign of dictatorial power was brought to

a close. From the distance that time brings, we are just beginning to see how Leguía's fall was largely the result of global
economic pressures relentlessly wearing upon the weak social
structures of not only Peru, but other Indo-American semicolonial states as well. The Great Depression had already seized the
world in its debilitating grip.

Léguía's resignation also marked the end of an era, a period in
many ways comparable to the European epoch roughly spanning
the years 1789–1848, during which, in the words of Eric J.
Hobsbawm, the "double revolution" took place—the French
Revolution and the British Industrial Revolution.[70]

And just as this double revolution introduced an entirely new
vocabulary in the West—such as *self-determination, nationalism,
industry, factory, working class, proletariat, statistics,* and
sociology—so, too, in Peru these same terms appeared and attained an ever more concrete and vital meaning between 1870
and 1930. Much in the same way that the double revolution had
unleashed the forces of nationalism earlier in Europe, this era
launched the age of modern Peruvian nationalism. And José Carlos Mariátegui was certainly one of the prime movers—intellectually and politically—of that volatile new age.

Epilog

Much of the literature on Mariátegui has suffered from a basic misconception, one rooted in the insistence on approaching him essentially from the perspective of European Marxism.[1] Focusing on the degree to which he conforms or not to orthodox doctrine, these studies often boil down to a consideration of whether or not he was a Marxist.[2]

But such a narrow approach deals with only one side of the man and his work. In this book we have taken a broader view—we have sought out the historical Mariátegui, asking such questions as how the Peruvian absorbed a Marxist perspective and how his unique understanding of Marxism affected his political activities. These questions, in turn, led us to inquire into such matters as the concrete social, political, and economic factors that affected his outlook, and how those conditions came about.

Thus we came to discover what was most original and creative in Mariátegui's life history—how his personal search for an identity, his Peruvian culture, and the global influences of his age led him down the path of revolution. We have explored how his inner experiences and his external world combined to affect his application of certain Marxist methods and concepts, and helped produce a Peruvianized Marxism.

Mariátegui's special brand of Marxism was not a breach of the faith, he himself felt, but rather a necessary adaptation. He always remained very much aware of the fact that Marxism was a doctrine derived from a European experience, and that its application in the colonial world meant confronting a different set of problems. Such thoughts must have been heavy in his mind when he wrote that

Marxism is a method that anchors itself fully in reality, in actual events. It is not, as some erroneously suppose, a body of rigid predictions, applicable in the same fashion to all historical climates and social latitudes. Marx took his method from the very entrails of history.[3]

Along these lines, we have attempted to describe the world in which Mariátegui lived. As we have said, all of his work is really autobiographical in that each experience, each achievement, represents basically a facet of his personal response to his national surroundings.

His early awareness of certain dimensions of Peruvian culture gradually was enriched by an understanding of the broader national problems that demanded attention. His nationalistic outlook did not develop only after his European apprenticeship, as he pointed out in a message accompanying his famous theses presented at the First South American Communist Party Congress, but rather had started while he was still working for *La Prensa, El Tiempo*, and *La Razón*.[4]

Mariátegui grew up, in fact, in a milieu permeated with nationalistic fervor. When José de la Riva Agüero wrote in *La historia en el Perú* that his purpose was not "to create a national consciousness . . . [but to] rouse it from the almost unconscious state in which it dreamily sleeps,"[5] he was indulging a youthful impatience and dissatisfaction. For the fact was otherwise: since the 1870s the tempo of the nationalist movement had been picking up.

Indeed, seldom have two successive generations of outstanding intellectuals (those of 1900 and 1919) *both* found themselves so completely dominated by one passion—that of wanting to define and guide their country's nationhood. And so Mariátegui, as a member of the second generation, adapted Marxism to what he perceived as being a very powerful historical current and, indeed, necessity in his culture, that of nationalism.

Such is the context for the shaping of his view that

Indigenismo does not dream of utopian restorations. . . . In no country is socialism an anti-nationalist movement. . . . [Moreover] the function of the socialist idea changes in countries politically or economically colonized [where it becomes] a revolutionary nationalism.[6]

Although the form of revolutionary nationalism developed by Mariátegui represented a departure in some respects from Marxist-Leninist orthodoxy, it still incorporated the essence of the doctrine that material and class forces are primary determinants of society. In this respect, then, his historical materialist emphasis separated him from previous generations of Peruvian nationalists.

Jorge Basadre was perhaps one of the first to perceive, and acknowledge, that his emphasis on material and class forces produced an entirely new way of looking at Peru. Even Víctor Andrés Belaúnde, who otherwise broadcasted great reservations about the *Siete ensayos*, nevertheless admitted that Mariátegui had transformed thinking about the native people by linking their situation to the "problem of the land"[7]—the property system and mode of production of the large estate (gamonalismo) holding the Indians in semifeudal bondage.

Mariátegui's thinking on the agrarian question was without doubt one of his most useful contributions, but it was not an isolated one. In the wake of the Mexican Revolution, progressive Latin American intellectuals had turned, especially throughout the 1920s, to this issue and the related one of the revolutionary potential of the rural peasantry. Evidence of this trend may be found in *El Repertorio Americano*, published in Costa Rica, which drew the participation of the likes of Haya de la Torre, José Vasconcelos, José Ingenieros, and many others.

Actually, the agrarian question transcended a purely Latin American area of concern, for the official attitude of the Third International was defined as early as the Sixth Congress when they agreed that the Indians represented "the most important revolutionary reserve of energy existing in Latin America," and that in the Mexican case the proletariat had been "revolutionized thanks to the peasant revolutionary movement."[8]

Mariátegui's own interest in the Mexican Revolution may be traced to one of his first statements on the subject, made in January 1924, when he observed that in that country the expansion of latifundismo (read gamonalismo in Peru) at the expense of the indigenous peasant communities had resulted in their proletarianization.[9] Later in the *Siete ensayos* he carried this analysis to its logical conclusions in relation to Peru.

All this meant he defined the national question in terms of the agrarian issue, saying that the resolution of both the agrarian and native questions entailed the "liquidation" of the vestiges of Peruvian feudalism embodied in the system of gamonalismo.

Such a task essentially called for a democratic-bourgeois revolution; but—and here we enter into an area of controversy—because of the country's peculiar conditions such a revolution was no longer to be accomplished by the bourgeoisie, but rather by an indigenista socialist movement of national liberation.[10]

To some degree, such ideas paralleled some incomplete views on the subject of nationalism found in Marx and Lenin. Marx's understanding of the function of nationalism in backward colonial areas has been divided into his "earlier views" (up to the late 1860s), not at all favorable to colonial societies, and his "later" support for nationalist anticolonial movements. Moreover, by 1877, Marx was actively considering the possibility that in Russia the capitalist stage of national development might be skipped, and the reorganized rural village commune could serve as the core of a socialist society.[11] Such views were not that far apart from the Peruvian's thesis, that in his country the indigenous community might play the same role in the anticolonialist revolution.

Once Marx had embraced the idea of worldwide proletarian revolution, however, he seldom referred to nationalism, except in negative terms. Though Lenin later returned to such questions from a more progressive standpoint, he, too, could not see fully nationalism from the perspective of the colonial and semicolonial world. It was not possible perhaps for even Lenin to understand the driving nationalist necessity embedded in the consciousness of anticolonial revolutionaries for self-expression and self-affirmation. Thus, Mariátegui could write with a great deal of passion that the national revolution in Peru must insure that

> Our economy, our political organization, our social architecture, our literature and our art, the forms of our lives must be ours, created by us and for us. The greatness of our countries will inevitably correspond to the degree that they are able to recreate themselves. . . . As for us, we believe and feel the creative potential of our race.[12]

Nevertheless Mariátegui's analysis brought him into conflict not only with the international communist movement, but also with the APRA and Haya de la Torre. While Haya de la Torre accepted the premise that in Latin America "the content of the antiimperialist struggle is antifeudal," he did not grasp the revolutionary potential of the indigenous rural masses. Indeed, he saw even the Peruvian urban proletariat "as young . . . an infant unable to lead himself."

The break between Haya de la Torre and Mariátegui, as between the PSP and APRA, hinged on this vital discrepancy—which, in turn, pointed to many others. The relationship between Mariátegui and the apristas is another area in which other commentators have come to quite a different interpretation than we have presented here. Some, in fact, have even considered Mariátegui to have been a "founder of APRA."[13] But that is certainly an excessive and inaccurate statement. It is true that Mariátegui had at first backed APRA, as he himself indicated several months before the final break with the apristas. Writing to Haya de la Torre on April 14, 1927, he said:

I see that X [sic] has not interpreted correctly my views on APRA. I do not understand truly how he could believe me to be opposed to it. When I first learned of its program I wrote you and said I found it all right. . . . The best proof that I am not absolutely against APRA is that I have given it my adherence *in principle*, accepting your proposal to *Amauta* [the proposal for a united front of intellectual and manual workers made in December 1926 and April 1927], and above all participating, and not passively or simply as a commentator, in the organization of APRA in Lima.[14]

But there never existed an APRA organization in Lima in the twenties to speak of, and Mariátegui certainly did not promote one. Moreover, at the height of his disagreement with Haya de la Torre in 1928 he had no difficulty in saying:

APRA must be categorically and officially defined and organized as an alliance or united front but not as a party.[15]

Like Haya de la Torre, however, Mariátegui knew that the middle class must be brought into any revolutionary movement. And so he incorporated into the PSP the most progressive elements of the middle class—university students and intellectuals, for example. But it is difficult to sustain the charges of populism made on the basis of the multiclass constituency of the PSP, or for that matter on the grounds that he saw the communistic foundations of a new Peru as resting on the traditional collectivist ayllus of the ancient Indian culture.[16] For all of Mariátegui's work was always very clearly and openly oriented toward the working class, despite his reluctance to abandon middle-class participation and the importance he assigned the rural peasantry.

Furthermore, he relentlessly insisted on the adherence of all sectors involved in the revolutionary movement to the principles of class struggle. In Peru, he wrote,

> the Leguiísta process is the political expression of our manner of assimilating capitalist development, and if something opposes it diametrically, if something is its antithesis and its negation, it is justifiably our socialism, our Marxism, that struggles to affirm a politics based on the interests and principles of the worker and peasant masses, of the proletariat, not of the unstable petit bourgeoisie.[17]

Does this mean, as Miroshevsky has maintained, that Mariátegui saw the conflict between the peasantry and the landholding bourgeoisie as the basic contradiction of Peru?[18] In a sense, yes, because it was the feudalism embodied by the system of the large estate that held the key to the most basic problems of national development.

The resolution of this contradiction fell upon the shoulders primarily of the working classes, Mariategui held, recognizing the political limitations of the middle classes. He realized that the upper classes had sucked the middle class into its network of economic interests. Thus he remained convinced that neither the bourgeoisie nor the petit bourgeoisie would stand for an antiimperialist political program, and therefore the path of socialism led by a working-class vanguard offered Peru the best chance of success.

Hence he had no difficulty with the stand of the International that the Peruvian socialist party should be organized around a "worker and peasant bloc." Indeed, his perception of the revolutionary potential of such a united force could not have been unaffected by the sheer numbers involved. In the late 1920s, statistics showed only some 100,000 workers in Peru; but there

were about 1.5 million comuneros living in some 1,562 indigenous communities.[19]

Mariátegui was also a realist. Given the circumstances in Peru,
he was not about to accept the International's policy of the so-called
third period during which all ties with the middle class and intellectuals were to be cut.[20] In that sense, then, the PSP was a kind of
intermediary between APRA's stress on the middle class as instru-
mental in bringing about a revolution, and the Comintern's insistence on shunning an alliance with the middle class.

On other important questions, Mariátegui's thinking paralleled
that of the International. For example, he agreed that only once
the bourgeois-democratic revolution had been completed would
the proletarian revolution begin.[21] In Peruvian terms, this meant
the capitalist haciendas of the coast would survive the first stage
of socialism, but gamonalismo would not. The new socialist state
would distribute the lands nationalized from the gamonales and
the convents to the native communities of the sierra and to the
yanacones (sharecroppers) on the coast.[22]

In terms of the strategy to be followed for bringing about such
a revolution, Mariátegui distinguished among the rural proletariat—agricultural workers employed on the coastal haciendas; the
peasants—who included the sharecroppers and owners of small
plots; and the Indians—the native population of the rural communities who worked the land six or seven months out of the
year and the rest of the time labored in the mines, on the sierra
latifundios, or on the coastal haciendas.

Each sector called for its own type of organization: the first for
a federation of agricultural workers' syndicates, the second for a
national federation of peasant leagues, and the third for a federation of indigenous communities.[23] Similarly, miners and textile
workers were targeted for a federation of their own.

But there was one program common to all: (1) freedom to organize; (2) suppression of the *enganche* (the system of debt
peonage); (3) wage increases; (4) an eight-hour work day; and (5)
compliance with prolabor legislation.[24]

The success of these organizations and their program in attracting workers can be gauged by looking at the CGTP membership. By 1930 it included 58,000 industrial workers and
30,000 rural workers, peasants, and natives from the indigenous
communities.[25]

Mariátegui concentrated his attention on the mineworkers, whom he considered the bridge to the great peasant masses. He particularly geared the movement's organizing efforts to the mining centers in Junín and La Libertad, belonging to the Cerro de Pasco Copper Corporation and the Northern Peru Mining and Smelting Co. They employed hundreds of wage workers, villagers who returned to their communities part of the year. They were especially open to socialist propaganda, for they were already angered by the haciendas encroaching on their lands. In fact, according to statistics for 1920, 98% of all native insurrections of that year originated in disputes over land; in the Puno area alone, for example, between 1890 and 1924, eleven major uprisings took place.

There are few indications that Mariátegui expected armed struggle to break out, however. He was of course familiar with the role of historical violence, via Sorel if no one else. For example, he wrote to his friend Glusberg in Argentina that there was no avoiding "the historical fatality of violence." At the Buenos Aires congress in 1929, Portocarrero made a reference to arming workers and peasants, but this probably never panned out.[26] Rather, the Lima vanguard stressed organization—the formation of a tight PSP and CGTP network working openly and legally.

Thus far we have emphasized Mariátegui's ideology, strategy, and tactics. But equally unique was his personal style—on the one hand, precise and objective; on the other, exhibiting a strong subjectivist quality. During his adolescence the latter tendency led him to adopt a flamboyant, dandylike life-style and later to enter into a religious phase and a fascination with the theme of death.[27] In his maturity, that special tendency emerged as a Nietzschean quality, an inner identification with the idea of the historical hero, the launcher of new epochs and historical stages. He himself as a leader of the socialist movement in Peru embodied such a larger-than-life charisma.

That charismatic and mystical strain also surfaced at times in a Leninist form—for he issued directives to the party cadres as if they were entering a religious order rather than a political organization:

It is urgent, fundamental, indispensable that we purge opportunism and petit bourgeois demagoguery from our ranks, that we organize our cells with an iron discipline proper to a historic party absolutely subject to the methods, tactics, and objectives defined fully by official Marxism. Without the prior acceptance of the principle of class struggle we cannot admit anyone. Whoever needs to discuss such a basic truth, cannot be one of us. . . . After extended polemics with such elements, we must be inflexible in our principles: Unity of Action, Unity of Theory, Unity of Tactics. Legislative and executive centralism of the party: that will determine whether our class political organization becomes an organic, concrete reality, identified with the class interests of the proletariat.[28]

Mariátegui's grand sense of historical mission gave him a strength and perseverance that allowed him to overcome, to a remarkable degree, the adversities he faced. For example, when his friend Waldo Frank visited him in Lima, he discovered that

Mariátegui lived in a state of perpetual siege. Often his letters never reached him; his papers were wantonly destroyed; in a hundred petty ways his life was miserable for him, and work almost impossible. Yet the heart of the man was so hale that these misfortunes did not touch the bloom of his happy spirit.[29]

His undauntable temperament and charismatic style generated a wide and fervent following. As Waldo Frank reported regarding his experiences traveling from Argentina to Peru, people were anxious to convey their deep feelings to Mariátegui:

"You are going to Lima," they said, "you will see him. Tell him for us that we read him and love him, and that we follow him."

And if the outpouring of public grief at Mariátegui's funeral is indicative of his personal power, then the occasion can indeed be considered high ritual.

But who would have thought at the time of his birth in Moquegua, that isolated corner of Peru, that life held in store for José Carlos Mariátegui such extraordinary experiences? Who, above all, would have thought that his personal history was "to counterpoint certain opposite potentialities," and thereby lift him from the realm of the commonplace "to a unique style" of personal existence?[30]

It must have evolved, in part at least, out of his lifelong affinity for "the open"—for as he wrote in the *Siete ensayos,* only "the universal, ecumenical paths . . . take us ever closer to ourselves."

Appendix A
Principles of a National Agrarian Policy

As an appendix or complement to my study of the land problem in Peru, which I concluded in the last issue of *Mundial*, I now wish to add, in summary fashion, the main features—in accordance with the propositions of my study—which, in keeping with present conditions, an agrarian policy intent on an organic solution to the problem might incorporate. Necessarily this outline has been reduced to a body of general conclusions, from which are excluded any and all detailed or descriptive considerations; it focuses solely on the most important aspects of the question.

1. The point of departure, doctrinal or otherwise, of a socialist agrarian policy can be nothing less than a law of nationalization of the land. In practice, however, nationalization must be adapted to the concrete needs and conditions of the country's economy. Principles in and of themselves are never sufficient. Experience has already shown us how the principles of the Constitution and the Civil Code did not suffice to implement in Peru a liberal, i.e., a capitalist economy, and, therefore, such principles notwithstanding, there continue to exist institutions characteristic of a feudal economy. A policy of nationalization can be initiated even without incorporating in the constitutional charter the principle in a formal sense, should the constitution not be integrally revised. In this respect, the example of Mexico is the most useful that can be consulted. Article 27 of the Mexican constitution defines the policy of the state concerning the ownership of land in this manner: "1. Ownership of all lands and waters found within the boundaries of the national territory belong fundamentally to the Nation, which has had and retains the right to transfer their dominion to individuals, thus establishing private

179

property. 2. Expropriations shall be made solely for the purpose of the public good and by means of indemnification. 3. The Nation shall reserve the right to impose on private property any changes dictated by the public interest, as well as that of regulating the production of those natural resources available for exploitation, in order to distribute equally the public wealth and provide for its conservation. With this objective in view the necessary measures will be dictated for the subdividing of the large estates, for the development of small property holdings, for the creation of new areas essential to the fostering of agriculture, and for preventing the destruction of natural resources and damages which property might suffer at the expense of society. The towns, settlements, and communities lacking land and water, or not having amounts sufficient for the needs of their people, shall have the right to have them granted to them, taking them from the contiguous properties, although this will always be done with respect toward small property holdings. Therefore, the grants of land so far executed in accordance with the Decree of March 6, 1915, is confirmed. The acquisition of these individual properties in order to obtain the forementioned goals will be considered for the public good."

2. In contrast to the policy of our first century, liberal in theory but gamonalista in practice, a new agrarian policy must aim above all at fostering and protecting the indigenous "community". The ayllu, cell of the Incaic State, surviving to this day despite the onslaughts of feudalism and gamonalismo, still reveals enough vitality to be gradually transformed into the cell of a modern socialist State. State policy, as rightly asserted by Castro Pozo, should be directed toward the transformation of farming communities into production and consumer cooperatives. The granting of lands to the communities, naturally, must take effect at the expense of the large estates, always exempting small and even medium-sized landholdings from expropriation, just as in Mexico, so long as their proprietors personally work the land. The availability of disposable lands allows the setting aside of enough lands that will permit the continued and progressive granting of them relative to the growth of the communities. This measure alone would insure the demographic growth of Peru on a much larger scale than any to be achieved through any current "immigration" policy.

3. Agricultural credit, which, only when controlled by the State can promote agriculture in the way most suitable to our national agricultural needs, would constitute according to this agrarian policy the best means of stimulating communitarian production. The National Agrarian Bank would grant preference to the activities of cooperatives, which in other ways would also be aided concurrently by technical and educational bodies of the State for the purpose of maximizing productivity and the industrial instruction of their members.

4. The capitalist exploitation of rural estates where agriculture has been industrialized must be maintained so long as it remains the most efficient system of production, and does not lose its progressive attitude. However, it must remain subject to the strict control of the State in all matters concerning the observance of labor and public health laws, as well as in the fiscal accounting of profits.

5. Small landholdings deserve protection and support in the coastal valleys and in the sierra, where there exist factors economically and socially favorable to their development. The "yanacón" of the coast, when he has lost the socialist habits and traditions of the native is transformed into a type of small farmer in transition, in formation. So long as the problem of insufficient water for irrigation persists, there is no reason to subdivide the coastal farmlands devoted to industrial farming with modern technology. A policy concerning the division of rural estates in favor of small property should never disregard, in any instance, requirements not concerned with increasing production.

6. The confiscation of noncultivated lands and the irrigation and/or fertilizing of barren lands would put large areas of land at the State's disposition, which should be preferentially earmarked for settlement by technically capacitated cooperatives.

7. Those large estates which are not actually being used in a prductive way by their owners, should pass into the hands of the rentees, in accordance with the limitations of usufruct and according to territorial controls imposed by the State in those instances where the exploitation of the soil is to be subject to industrial techniques with sufficient capital and installations.

8. The State would organize the teaching of agricultural education and provide for its maximum diffusion among the rural masses by means of country grade schools, agricultural trade

schools, experimental farms, etc. The education of rural children would take on a definite agricultural orientation.

I am not seeking to establish these conclusions in any kind of fundamental way, but rather to propose a brief outline of some concrete proposals for an agrarian policy consistent with the present conditions of the country, with its actual development thrust, and that of the continent. I do not want it said that from my critical examination of the Peruvian agrarian question there only derive negative conclusions or propositions of a premature or intransigeant dogmatism.

Published in *Mundial*, July 1927.

Appendix B

Programmatic Principles of the Socialist Party

[The Meeting at the Playa de la Herradura, September 16, 1928]

1. To establish the initial cell of the Party, affiliated with the Third International, and whose name shall be the Socialist Party of Peru under the direction of conscientious Marxist elements.

2. To support its counterpart syndical cell which Julio Portocarrero had organized in order to carry out the tasks and directives established at the Fifth Congress of the I.S.R. (International Red Union).

3. The Executive Committee of the Socialist Party shall be formed by the "secret cell of seven."

4. To convene a new meeting at which other elements shall be incorporated.

[The Meeting at Barranco, October 7, 1928]

1. To establish the organizing group of the Socialist Party of Peru.

2. Mariátegui was nominated Secretary General; Portocarrero, Syndical Secretary; Martínez de la Torre, Secretary of Propaganda; Bernardo Regman, Treasurer. Navarro and Hinojosa were nominated to the Syndical Secretariat.

3. The following motion was passed as the order of the day, drawn up by Mariátegui:

"The undersigned declare as constituted a Committee which proposes to work with the masses of workers and peasants, according to the following concepts:

(a) The organization of workers and peasants, along class lines, is the main object of our efforts and propaganda and the basis of our struggle against foreign imperialism and the national bourgeoisie.

(b) For the defense of the economic interests of workers in the city and in the country, the Committee will actively push the formation of syndicates in factories, on haciendas and elsewhere, as well as their federation into industrial syndicates and their confederation into a national central organization.

(c) The political struggle requires the creation of a class party, in whose formation and organization must prevail revolutionary class viewpoints. In accordance with the actual concrete conditions of Peru, the Committee will organize a Socialist Party, based on the organized worker and peasant masses.

(d) To protect themselves against demoralizing repressions and persecutions, the worker and peasant syndicates will register with the Labor Section [governmental agency]. In its statute, the declaration of principles shall be limited to the affirmation of its class character and its goal of contributing to the foundation and maintenance of a General Confederation of Labor.

(e) The syndical organization and the Socialist Party for whose establishment we will be working shall adopt contingently the tactic of a united front, or alliance, with organizations or groups of the petite bourgeoisie, but only in those instances when such groups effectively represent mass movements with concretely defined goals and revindications.

(f) The Committee will proceed with the organizing of committees throughout the republic, and of cells in all centers of work, and contact with them will be maintained according to strict discipline.

The Program of the Party

The Program must be a doctrinal declaration that affirms:

1. The international character of the present economy, which does not allow any country to evade the currents of change brought on by the prevailing conditions of production.

2. The international character of the revolutionary movement of the proletariat. The Socialist Party adapts its praxis to the concrete circumstances of the country; but it obeys an ample view of class and the same national circumstances are subordinate to the rhythm of world history. The revolution of independence of over a century ago was a general movement of all the colonies under Spanish rule; similarly the socialist revolution is a unified movement of all peoples oppressed by capitalism. If the

liberal revolution, nationalist in its principles, could not be effected without the solidarity of the South American countries, it is easy to understand that the same historical law in an epoch of even greater unity and interdependence among nations, determining how the socialist revolution, internationalist in principle, must take place with a more intense and disciplined coordination between the proletarian parties. The manifesto of Marx and Engles summarized the first principle of the proletarian revolution in the historic phrase: "Workers of the World, Unite!"

3. The intensification of capitalist economic contradictions. Capitalism develops in a semifeudal country such as ours, at a time during which, having reached the stage of monopoly capitalism and imperialism, the whole of liberal ideology corresponding to the period of free trade has ceased to be valid. Imperialism does not allow any of these semicolonized countries, which it exploits as markets for its capital and commodities and as sources of raw materials, an economic program of nationalization and industrialization. Instead it forces them toward specialization and monoculture. (Petroleum, copper, sugar, and cotton in Peru.) Crises derive from this rigid determination of national production imposed by the capitalist world market.

4. Capitalism is now in the imperialist stage. It is a capitalism of monopolies, of finance capital, of imperialist wars for the control of markets and sources of raw materials. The praxis of Marxist socialism in this stage is that of Marxism-Leninism, this being the revolutionary strategy in the period of imperialism and monopoly capital. The Peruvian Socialist Party adopts this as its method of combat.

5. The precapitalist economy of republican Peru, which, due to the absence of a vigorous bourgeoisie and because of the national and international conditions that have determined the gradual advance of the country toward capitalism, could not liberate itself under the bourgeois regime, tied as it was to imperialist interests and colonial feudalism. The colonial destiny of the country is therefore reinforced. The emancipation of the country's economy is possible only through the struggle of the proletarian masses, united in the worldwide antiimperialist struggle. Only the proletarian struggle can stimulate first and realize later the tasks of the bourgeois-democratic revolution which the bourgeois regime is incapable of achieving and carrying through.

6. Socialism finds in the existing (indigenous) communities, as

in the great agricultural enterprises, the elements of a socialist solution to the agrarian question; the solution of which will allow in
part the exploitation of the lands by small landholders wherever
sharecropping or small landholdings indicate individual effort
should be allowed while the collectivization is being pursued in
those areas where that type of production prevails. But this alternative, as well as the stimulus that is given to the resurgence of the
indigenous people, to the creative manifestation of its energies and
native spirit, does not signify in the least a romantic or antihistori-
cal tendency of reconstruction or resurrection of Incaic socialism,
which corresponded to historical conditions wholly superceded,
and of which there only remains as a still viable factor within a
technical and scientific mode of production, the habits of cooperation and socialism of the native people. Socialism presupposes
technique, science, the capitalist stage; and its acquisition cannot
signify a step backward in the absorption of modern civilization,
but on the contrary the greatest and most methodical acceleration
of that very absorption.

7. Only socialism can resolve the problem of providing a
democratic and egalitarian education, whereby each member of
society can receive all the instruction to which his capacity enti-
tles him. The socialist education system is the only one that can
fully and systematically apply the principles of the single school,
of the school of work, of the educational communities, and generally of all the ideals of contemporary revolutionary education
incompatible with the privilege of the capitalist school, where
the poor classes are condemned to cultural inferiority and higher
education becomes the monopoly of the rich.

8. Having completed its democratic-bourgeois phase, the revolution devolves in its objectives and in its doctrine into the proletarian revolution. The workers' party, prepared by the struggle
for the exercise of power and the development of its own program, realizes at this stage the organizational and defensive stage
of a socialist order.

9. The Peruvian Socialist Party is the vanguard of the proletariat, the political force that assumes the task of orienting and
directing the proletariat in their struggle for the fulfillment of
their class ideals.

In conjunction with the program, theses will be published on
the Indian question, on the economic situation, on the antiimperialist struggle, which, after they have been debated by the

sections and amended by the Central Committee, will be definitively formulated at the First Congress of the Party.

With its public manifesto, the Party will direct a call to all of its adherents, to the working masses, to work for the following immediate revindications:

Full recognition of free association, gathering, and press for the workers.

Recognition of the right of all workers to strike.

Abolition of the road conscription.

Substitution of the vagrancy law by the articles that specifically considered the vagrancy question in the first draft of the Penal Code put in force by the State, with the sole exception of those articles which are incompatible with the spirit and criteria of the special law.

Establishment of Social Security and Social Welfare by the State.

Compliance with job accident laws, laws protecting women and minors, and of the eight-hour day for farm labor.

Classification of malaria as an occupational illness in the coastal valleys, and the assumption of responsibility for assistance by the landowner.

The establishment of a seven-hour work day in the mines and of other work in insalubrious environment hazardous to the health of the workers.

Obligation by the mining and petroleum companies to recognize, permanently and effectively, all of the rights of their workers guaranteed by the laws of the country.

Salary increases in industry, agriculture, mining, marine and overland transport, and on the guano islands in proportion to the cost of living and to the workers' right to a higher standard of living.

Effective abolition and punishment of the semislave regime in the sierra.

Granting lands from the large estates to the communities for distribution among their members in proportion sufficient to their needs.

Expropriation without indemnification, of all estates belonging to convents or religious congregations for the benefit of the communities.

The right of sharecroppers, renters, etc., who work a piece of land for over three consecutive years, to gain adjudication of the definitive use of their plots by means of annuities not greater than 60% of the prevailing rent agreement. For all those who remain sharecroppers or renters, the amount shall be lowered to at least 50% of this agreement.

Adjudication of all land made usable by irrigation projects to the poor peasants.

Upholding everywhere the rights of employees as recognized by the respective laws. Regulation by a representative commission of the rights of retirement in a form which would not imply any loss of rights now established in the law.

Implementation of minimum wages and salaries.

Ratification of the freedom of religious practice and teaching, at least in keeping with the relevant constitutional article and consistent with the last decree issued against non-Catholic schools.

Tuition-free education at all levels.

These are the principal revindications for which the Socialist Party will struggle at this time. They all represent urgent needs to be met in order to achieve the freeing of the masses, both materially and intellectually. They all must be actively supported by the proletariat and by conscientious sectors of the middle class. The freedom of the Party to act publicly and legally, with the protection of the constitution and of the guarantees that it accords to its citizens, enabling them to produce and distribute their press without restrictions, to hold congresses and debates, is a right revindicated by the very act of publicly establishing this organization. The tightly knitted groups which are directing themselves to the people today by means of this manifesto resolvedly assume, mindful of their historic duty and responsibility, the mission of defending and propagating their principles, and maintaining and advancing their organization, at any cost. And the people whose interests and aspirations we represent, the urban and rural laborers, and the Indian peasants, shall learn to make use of these revindications and of this doctrine, to fight forcefully and persistently for them, and to discover in each struggle the path that leads to the final victory of socialism.

> Long live the working and peasant classes of Peru!
> Long live the world's proletariat!
> Long live the social revolution!

Appendix C

Statutes of the General Confederation of Peruvian Workers

Concerning Goals

Art. 1. The "General Confederation of Peruvian Workers," is the Unitary Central of the syndical organizations of the Peruvian proletariat.

Art. 2. The C.G.T.P. proposes:

(a) to group on the economic front all wage-earners, for the defense of their rights, interests, and revindications.

(b) to orient and stimulate the development of the syndical movement by means of oral and written propaganda, directed toward those not yet organized into their respective syndicates, and creating these if they do not yet exist.

(c) to reinforce solidarity with the Latin American labor movement, by means of the Latin American Syndical Confederation.

(d) to raise class consciousness among the working class.

(e) to organize lectures and other activities of proletarian education, to colaborate in the struggle against illiteracy, to sponsor schools and courses of technical education, to publish newspapers, journals, and books.

Constitution

Art. 3. The C.G.T.P. is hereby established:

(a) by the syndicates, regularly constituted workers of the country, and in agreement with the working-class principle.

(b) by the Local and Regional Federations of Labor.

(c) by the National and Industrial Federations of Labor.

(d) by the Peasant Federations or Leagues.

(e) by the Federations of Indigenous Communities.

Art. 4. Every organization belonging to the C.G.T.P. will be represented in it by means of delegations established according to the following formula:

(a) up to one hundred members by one delegate.

(b) from 100 to 500 members by two delegates.

(c) from 500 to 1,000 members by three delegates.

(d) from 1,000 to 2,000 members by four delegates.

(e) beyond 2,000 members, one more delegate for each 1,000 or fraction thereof.

Art. 5. The C.G.T.P. is represented and administered:

(a) by a Confederal Committee (assembly of delegates, Comité Confederal Nacional, C.C.N.).

(b) by an Executive Committee, made up of a Secretary General, an International Secretary, a Secretary of Propaganda, a Secretary of Rural Workers' Affairs, a Secretary of Indigenous Affairs, a Secretary of Records, a Treasurer, and an Accountant.

Art. 6. Decisions concerning the business of the Confederation will be taken by the delegates' assembly, which will meet once a month.

Art. 7. Special meetings will be allowed when they are requested in writing by a member organization, indicating the object of the meeting, and likewise when the Executive Committee considers it necessary, or when it is asked for by the delegates' assembly.

Art. 8. The Executive Committee will meet ordinarily once a week, and in the case of an ongoing conflict as often as necessary.

Art. 9. To aid the work of the Executive Committee, the Confederal Committee may designate all the commissions it deems necessary; the permanent ones will be for: Propaganda, Organization, Statistics, Culture, Solidarity, the Press, Economic, Youth, Women, Peasant, and Indian. Each commission will work under the responsibility and direction of a member of the Executive Committee.

Art. 10. The regional and local organizations of the country will be able to delegate their representation to militant workers in the capital.

Funding

Art. 11. The funds of the C.G.T.P. will be constituted:

(a) through the ordinary membership dues of the member institutions at the rate of two cents a month per organized worker.

(b) through extraordinary membership dues.

(c) through the contributions of militants, mutual savings, cooperatives, etc.

(d) through the product of the sale of confederal publications, and through all the funds established by the Economic Commission.

Art. 12. The quota will be paid directly by the organized workers in their respective organizations. To facilitate this, the C.G.T.P. will distribute each month the quantity of stamps which it deems necessary for each organization, and these will be attached to the receipt of payment given to each contributing entity.

Art. 13. The membership fees should come together with the statistics ticket, showing in detail the number of members in the organization, dues taken during the respective month, unemployed persons, members who have dropped out, and new members.

Art. 14. Exempted from payment are those organizations which have spent all their resources because of strikes. In such cases the C.G.T.P.'s records will show with an "S" the state of the strike.

Concerning the Congresses

Art. 15. The C.G.T.P. will hold a regular Congress every two years and an extraordinary one when the C.C.N. thinks it necessary or when a third of the member organizations whose dues are paid up request it. In extraordinary cases the C.C.N. may advance or postpone the date of the Congress.

Art. 16. The agenda of each Congress will be formulated definitively by the C.C.N. and communicated to the syndicates three months in advance.

Art. 17. The Executive Committee will publish a general and

economic report of its undertakings at least eight days before the Congress takes place.

Art. 18. All organizations belonging to the C.G.T.P. and those groups invited and approved for representation by the Executive Committee will participate in the Congress.

Art. 19. The relevant regulations of the Congress will determine its rules of participation and operations.

Local Federations

Art. 20. In every locality where three organizations belonging to the C.G.T.P. have been formed, these should form of their own accord with the aid of the C.C.N. a corresponding Local Federation.

Art. 21. These are the functions of the Local Federations:

(a) to develop active syndical propaganda for the purpose of recruiting all the local workers into syndicates.

(b) to unify the actions of the workers in the area for the most effective defense of the dignity and interests of the working class.

(c) to support in all areas the organizing and solidarity aims of the C.G.T.P., throughout the country.

Art. 22. The Local Federation, independent of the dues it contributes to the C.G.T.P. may, according to its own needs and in agreement with the Comité Confederal Nacional, fix the dues deemed necessary to attend to its own fiscal needs.

Regional Federations

Art. 23. In all departments having seven federal organizations or three local federations, there should be established a Regional Federation, having the same structure and aims as guide the local federations in their region.

National and Industrial Federations

Art. 24. The syndicates of a particular industry which exists in various localities of the country, should be tightly linked together creating in each case a corresponding National Federation of Industry.

Concerning Strikes and Solidarity

Art. 25. Before decreeing an important strike movement, or one which threatens to have serious repercussions or compromise the interests of other syndicates, any organization must advise the Executive Committee of the C.G.T.P., informing it of the incidents leading to the strike and the process of the conflict; once the movement is decreed, one or more delegates may intervene in the Strike Committee as advisors.

Art. 26. Whenever a strike supported by a particular organization provokes conflicts with other groups, these should intervene in the Strike Committee of the former group and in the orientation of the struggle in general.

Art. 27. All demands of solidarity made to the syndicates of the C.G.T.P. must be presented through the mediation of this headquarters (with the exception of those cases where it becomes impossible, and the circumstances are unusual.)

Discipline

Art. 28. All syndicates must be governed by internal rules which are not at odds with the present rules.

Art. 29. If a syndicate with no justifiable cause fails to make payments to the central cashier for three consecutive months, it will be denied the right to vote previous to communication from the Executive Committee and pronouncement from the C.C.N.

Art. 30. If a delegate is absent from two consecutive meetings without justifiable cause he will be reminded to appear more regularly, and with the third absence he will end his membership, and his respective organization will so take notice.

Art. 31. Any member who betrays a labor movement will be thrown out of the C.G.T.P.

Art. 32. Any disciplinary measure taken by the syndicates must be communicated to the Executive Committee, before which he or she, may appeal, or those representing him; as a last resort they may appeal to the Comité Confederal Nacional.

Referendum

Art. 33. The Executive Committee may submit to the deliberation of the member syndicates all matters which are serious or unusual and affect the general interests of the organization.

Art. 34. In all cases the Executive Committee shall communicate the causes that motivated a resolution concerning the questions which are submitted to the referendum, and shall immediately communicate the results.

Newspaper

Art. 35. The C.G.T.P. will have its official central organ, and the press commission will take charge of its editing.

Confederal Seal

Art. 36. Each and every member organization of the C.G.T.P. should use the Confederal Seal of the Central on all its documents, with the initials C.G.T.P. Besides this, the motto will be placed below the respective title in each case (Member of the Confederación General de Trabajadores Peruanos).

Art. 37. All initiatives to reform the organizational charter of the C.G.T.P. should be presented before the Executive Committee three months before the Congress. The C.C.N. will refer any project for the modification of the organizational charter to the syndicates two months before the Congress for their consideration.

Art. 38. The Confederación General de Trabajadores Peruanos is indissoluble as long as there are organizations which support it.

Published in *Labor*, September 10, 1929, p. 8.

Notes

Introduction

1. All of the epigraphs heading chapters are from Mariátegui's published works: "in certain historical periods, the idea of the nation . . . becomes the incarnation of the spirit of liberty." "Nacionalismo y vanguardismo," *Peruanicemos al Perú* in *Colección Obras Completas,* 20 vols. (Lima, 1970), 11:75.

2. Armando Bazán, *Mariátegui y su tiempo* in *Colección Obras Completas,* 20:64.

3. P. Macera, *Conversaciones: Jorge Basadre y Pablo Macera* (Lima, 1974), p. 12.

Chapter 1

1. "The times of living with sweetness will return, who knows when." *El alma matinal* (Lima, 1950), p. 22.

2. José Gálvez, *Una Lima que se va* (Lima, 1921), pp. i–iii.

3. Ibid., p. 254.

4. W. M. Mathew, "The Imperialism of Free Trade: Peru, 1820–1870," *The Economic History Review* 21(1968):563.

5. Heraclio Bonilla, "Aspects de l'histoire economique et sociale du Pérou au XIXe siècle," 2 vols. (Ph.D. diss., Université de Paris, 1970), 2:380. See also his *Guano y burguesía en el Perú* (Lima, 1974). Jonathan V. Levin's *The Export Economies* (Cambridge, 1960), cogently interprets Peru's nineteenth-century economy. It is substantially in agreement with the youthful Jorge Basadre's "La riqueza territorial y las actividades comerciales y industriales en los primeros años de la república," *Mercurio Peruano,* January 1928. Other important Peruvian sources in economic history are: P. E. Dancuart and J. M. Rodríguez, eds., *Anales de la hacienda pública del Perú,* 22 vols., (Lima, 1902–8), a nineteenth-century fiscal history based on the laws, decrees, regulations, and resolutions dealing with tariffs, budgets, accounts, and contracts of the government; J. M. Rodríguez, *Estudios económicos y financieros y ojeada sobre la Hacienda Pública del Perú y la necesidad de su reforma* (Lima, 1895); Carlos Jiménez, *Reseña histórica de la minería en el Perú* (Lima, n.d.); Shane J. Hunt, *Some Tasks in Peruvian Economic History, 1830-1930,* Research Program in Economic Development, Woodrow Wilson School, Discussion Paper #25 (Princeton, 1972); Carlos Camprubí Alcázar, *Historia de los bancos en el Perú* (Lima, 1957); Carlos Capunay Mimbela, "Historia del presupuesto nacional desde 1821 a 1899," *Revista de la Facultad de Ciencias Económicas,* 23 (1942); César Antonio Ugarte, *Bosquejo de la historia económica del Perú* (Lima, 1926) and Emilio Romero, *Historia económica del Perú* (Buenos Aires, 1949).

6. W. M. Mathew, "Anglo-Peruvian Commercial and Financial Relations, 1820–1865; With Special Reference to Antony Cibbs and Sons and the Guano Trade" (Ph.D. diss., The University of London (1964), pp. 6, 9.

7. John Lynch, "British Policy and Spanish America, 1783–1808," *Journal of Latin American Studies,* (1969): 13ff.

8. Mathew, "Anglo-Peruvian Commercial and Financial Relations," pp. 16–17.

9. Basil Hall, *Extracts From a Journal Written on the Coasts of Chile, Peru, and Mexico in the Years 1820, 1821, 1822,* 2 vols. (Edinburgh, 1924), 2:86.

10. For a periodization of nineteenth-century economic developments, I have relied

mainly on Mathew, "Anglo-Peruvian Commercial and Finacial Relations," p. 2. Bonilla, with some slight variations, essentially agrees: see his "Aspects de l'histoire economique et sociale," 1:21.

11. Mathew, "Imperialism of Free Trade," p. 563.

12. Ibid., p. 564.

13. Mathew, "Anglo-Peruvian Commercial and Financial Relations," p. 336.

14. Watt Stewart, *Henry Meiggs, Yankee Pizarro* (Durham, N.C., 1946), see especially chapters 3 and 16. For a melodramatic version of Meiggs's methods and the Limanean ambience of his times see: Fernando Casos, *Los hombres de bien* (Paris, 1874).

15. Meiggs' fabulous railroad reached in the short distance of 106 miles the altitude of 15,665 feet at Galera Tunnel. A string of 65 tunnels and 67 bridges were built on the entire line. Stewart, *Henry Meiggs*, pp. 288–327. For Peruvian railway-building see: F. M. Halsey, *Railway Expansion in Latin America* (New York, 1910), pp. 48–60; Federico Costa-Laurent, *Reseña histórica de los ferrocarriles del Perú* (Lima, 1908); Ernesto Malinowski, *Ferrocarril central trans-andino* (Lima, 1869) and *Los Ferrocarriles del Perú* (Lima, 1876), the last two volumes commissioned by Meiggs.

16. José M. Rodríquez Montoya, "Historia de los contratos de guano," *Economista Peruano*, 6 (1921): 108–15 and Levin, *Export Economies*, pp. 91–103.

17. Levin, *Export Economies*, pp. 117–19. See also: Shane J. Hunt, *Growth and Guano in Nineteenth Century Peru*, Research Program in Economic Development, Woodrow Wilson School, Discussion Paper No. 34 (Princeton, 1973).

18. Mathew, "Anglo-Peruvian Commercial and Financial Relations," p. 345.

19. Bonilla, "Aspects de l'histoire economique et sociale," 2:380.

20. Levin, *Export Economies*, pp. 104ff; and Howard L. Karno, "Augusto B. Leguía, The Oligarchy and the Modernization of Peru, 1870-1930" (Ph.D. diss., University of California, Los Angeles, 1970), especially chapter 1.

21. R. H. Tawney, *Religion and the Rise of Capitalism* (London, 1961), p. 63.

22. Romero, *Historia económica del Perú*, p. 374.

23. Marion Gordon Daniels, "Guano, Railroads and the Peruvian Corporation" (M.A. thesis, University of Texas, 1949), pp. 55–70; and Karno, "Augusto B. Leguía," pp. 28–32.

24. Karno, "Augusto B. Leguía," pp. 28–32. For Pardo's reforms consult; Mario E. del Río, *La immigración y su desarrollo en el Perú* (Lima, 1929); Felipe Barreda y Laos, "Las reformas de instrucción pública," *Revista Universitaria*, 14 (1919); and, Evaristo San Cristobal's lyrical biography, *Manuel Pardo y Lavalle: su vida y su obra* (Lima, 1945), pp. 125ff. On the civilistas see the following works: Pedro Dávalos y Lissón's *Leguía* (Lima, 1928) and *Diez años de historia contemporánea del Perú* (Lima, 1930). The last are two indispensable "personal histories" by a man who knew most of the protagonists. Alberto Ulloa Cisneros's *Reflexiones de un cualquiera* (Buenos Aires, 1945) and *Escritos históricos* (Buenos Aires, 1946) are two excellent political journals by a man who bitterly opposed civilismo.

25. Jorge Basadre, "La aristocracia y las clases medias civiles en el Perú republicano," *Mercurio Peruano* 43 (1963):462. Antioligarchic sentiment was so strong that on November 16, 1878, two years after Pardo left the presidency, a Senate guard assassinated him (Pardo was then only forty-five). See F. A. Deglane, *El drama del senado* (Lima, 1878) and the government's findings on the assassination, *El asesinato de Manuel Pardo* (Lima, 1878).

26. For background to the war see: Robert N. Burr, *By Reason or Force* (Berkeley, 1965), pp. 138–66.

27. Daniels, "Guano, Railroads. . . ," pp. 109–48. For particulars of the contract see: "The Peruvian Corporation, Ltd.: Its Origins and History," *West Coast Leader*, October 7, 1931.

28. Bonilla, "Aspects de l'histoire economique," 2:380.

29. Alberto Ulloa Sotomayor's *Don Nicolás de Piérola* (Lima, 1950) is the standard biography.

30. Jorge Basadre, *Historia de la república del Perú*, 10 vols. (Lima, 1961–64), 6:3031.

31. Carlos Camprubí Alcázar, "Un Cubano al servicio del Perú, José Payán," *Revista Histórica* 29 (1966):28.

32. Ulloa Cisneros, *Reflexiones*, pp. 99ff.

33. See L. A. Eguiguren, *Recordando a Manuel Candamo* (Lima, 1909).

34. Basadre, *Historia de la república*, 7:3333.

35. On the displacement of the demócratas see Basadre's detailed, "*Para la historia de los partidos: el desplazamiento de los demócratas por el civilismo*," *Documenta* (1965): 299ff. Karno has posed an interesting question—why did Piérola agree to the Almenara cabinet? See his "Augusto B. Leguía," pp. 62f.

36. After Candamo's death, Augusto B. Leguía became the leading and most dynamic spokesman for such views. Karno, "Augusto B. Leguía," pp. 70–97.

37. W. S. Bolinger, "The Rise of the United States Influence in the Peruvian Economy, 1869–1921" (M.A. thesis, University of California, Los Angeles, 1971), pp. 188–203.

38. J. A. Broggi, "El cobre en el Perú," *Copper Resources of the World, Papers of the Sixteenth International Geographical Congress* (Washington, D.C., 1933), p. 511.

39. Luis Laurie Solis, *La diplomacia del petroleo y el caso de la Brea i Pariñas* (Lima, 1934), p. 102.

40. F. M. Halsey, *Investments in Latin America and the British West Indies* (Washington, D.C., 1918), p. 322; J. Fred Rippy, "British Investments in Paraguay, Bolivia, and Peru," *Inter-American Economics Affairs* 6 (1953):43ff; Max Winkler, *Investments of United States Capital in Latin America* (Boston, 1929), pp. 140–53. Two other important sources on foreign investments for this period are: W. E. Dunn, *Peru, a Commercial and Industrial Handbook*, Trade Promotion Series (Washington, D.C., 1925), and W. E. Dunn, *American Foreign Investments* (New York, 1926).

41. Charles A. McQueen, *Peruvian Public Finance* (Washington, D.C., 1926), p. 21.

42. See ibid., p. 94, for a breakdown of Peruvian currency. The Peruvian silver peso served as the basic currency unit until replaced in 1863 by the silver sol. Gold pesos, always scarce, circulated until 1872. Peso and sol were about equal, the sol being equivalent to about 0.48 percent of the dollar. The Lp., or libra peruana, (ten soles) was equivalent to the British pound sterling (or US $4.86 in 1901). See also Alejandro Garland's *Estudio económico sobre los medios circulantes usados en el Perú* (Lima, 1908), and Rómulo A. Ferrero's *La historia monetaria del Perú en el presente siglo* (Lima, 1963), pp. 3ff. For mining data, see Alberto Salomon, *Peru: Potentialities of Economic Development* (London, 1920), p. 37.

43. Peter F. Klarén, "Origins of the Peruvian Aprista Party: A Study of Social and Economic Change in the Department of La Libertad, 1870-1932" (Ph.D. diss., University of California, Los Angeles, 1968), especially chapters 1–3.

44. Francois Chevalier, "L'expansion de la grande propiété dans le Haut-Pérou au XXe siécle," *Annales* 21 (1966): 821–25.

45. Camprubí Alcázar, *Historia de los bancos*, pp. 38–41. Some of the other leading banks and the year of their founding were: the Banco Italiano (1889), the Banco Internacional del Perú (1897), Banco Popular del Perú (1899), and the Banco Alemán Trans-Atlántico (1905).

46. H. Buse, *Huinco* (Lima, 1965), is a brief but highly readable account of the electrical industry; see also his, *60 años de Empresas Eléctricas Asociades* (Lima, 1966), especially pp. 15f.

47. Garland, *Peru in 1906* (Lima, 1908), pp. 269ff. An Anglo-Peruvian, Garland began

collecting data on Peru's manufacturing industries in 1905. The Ministerio de Fomento took Peru's first tentative industrial census in 1918, published as the *Estadística industrial del Perú* (Lima, 1922). In 1920, the Dirección de Estadística took an industrial census of the Lima-Callao area later published as, *Resumén del censo de las provincias de Lima-Callao,* (Lima, 1927).

48. J. L. Basombrío, "Estudio comparativo de la situación comercial, financiera y económica del país de 1888 a 1938," *Boletín de la Cámara de Comercio de Lima* 9 (1938):195.

49. *Informaciones comerciales, económicas y financieras del Perú,* Ministerio de Relaciones Exteriores, Departamento Comercial, no. 9, (Lima, 1938), 2:224–28. Between 1900 and 1913 exports jumped from 49 million to about 80 million soles.

50. Juan Bromley and José Barbagelata, *Evolución urbana de la ciudad de Lima* (Lima, 1945), p. 93.

51. Garland, *Peru in 1906,* p. 153.

52. Dávalos y Lissón observed how the austere José Pardo cheered his contemporaries simply by returning their greetings with a faint nod of his head. "José Pardo, his brothers and uncles," he wrote, "represented in those years the most firmly established aristocracy in Peru." Dávalos y Lissón, *Diez años,* pp. 132ff.

53. C. W. Sutton, "Land Economies and Reclamation in Peru," *West Coast Leader,* January 14, 1930. By 1920, a foreign analyst observed that "under the most favorable of conditions, Peru is a country financially dependent on Europe. Her merchants have been accustomed to long-term credits, her banks are in the main financed by European capital." L. S. Rowe, *Early Effects of the War upon the Finance, Commerce and Industry of Peru* (New York, 1920), p. 15.

54. For an excellent summary of an important revolt, see Jean Piel, "A Propos d'un soulevement rural Péruvien au début du vingtième siècle: Tocroyoc (1921)" *Revue d'histoire Moderne et Contemporaine* 14 (1967):375–405.

55. George Kubler, *The Indian Caste of Peru, 1795–1940* (Washington, D.C., 1952), pp. 5, 35, 59, 64. Kubler noted that "*White* is a caste designation in Peru, relating to economic class and occupation rather than to biological character." One can generalize from this observation to include the categories of Indian and mestizo, p. 5.

56. J. L. Basombrío, "Estudio comparativo de la situación comercial. . . ," p. 200. In 1918, the Pan American Union estimated the population of Peru at 4.5 million, and that of Lima at 200,000. *Peru: General Descriptive Data* (Washington, D.C., 1918), p. 2.

57. Basadre, *Historia de la república,* 9:4349–87 and Raúl Porras Barrenechea, "El periodismo en el Perú," *Mundial,* July 28, 1921.

58. Rowe, *Early Effects,* pp. 3ff.

59. Ibid., p. 18.

60. Hernando de Lavalle, *La Gran Guerra y el organismo económico nacional* (Lima, 1919), p. 81.

61. Klarén, "Origins of the Peruvian Aprista Party," pp. 56ff.

62. Jorge Basadre, "Un caso en la crisis universitaria Hispano-americana: La Universidad de San Marcos" *La Educación* 5 (1960):62.

63. Outside of Basadre's treatment in *Historia de la república,* there is virtually no objective treatment of the 1914 golpe. All of the literature except Billinghurst's own defense, *El presidente Billinghurst a la nación* (Santiago de Chile, 1915) is slanted against him. For the demócrata version and the view of a participant, see Ulloa Cisneros, *Escritos,* pp. 314–78, in many respects the best factual account. An important collection of speeches and articles representing the views of the conspirators are in *La opinión pública del Perú y el movimiento del 4 de febrero de 1914* (Lima, 1916). Colonel José Urdaniva Ginés, *Una revolución modelo* (Lima, 1954), is an important account of the military's complicity.

64. Basadre, *Historia de la república*, 8:3851–52.

65. A police force garrisoned at Santa Ana initiated the coup and received crucial support from the Callao naval squadron, while the army stood aside neutral and Pardo's Honor Guard failed to defend him. Moisés Pinto Bazurco, *El 4 de julio de 1919* (Lima, 1920), pp. 59, 75ff. Mariano H. Cornejo, a leguiísta in 1919, wrote in 1924 that the coup was not against Pardo, but "against the Congress which represented 20 years of national political sins." "Habla el Dr. Mariano H. Cornejo," *La Prensa*, October 15, 1924. Pardo agreed. In his own defense, published in both Spanish and English, Pardo wrote that the revolution had not been waged against him, but against the Congress. Pardo, *Peru, Four Years of Constitutional Government* (New York, 1920), pp. 216ff.

66. *Discurso de recepción del excmo. Sr. D. Augusto B. Leguía, Presidente de la República, Lima, 12 octubre de 1926*, Academia Peruana Correspondiente de la Real Española de la Lengua (Lima, 1926), pp. 8ff.

67. Karno, "Augusto B. Leguía," pp. 216ff.

68. Quoted in Karno, "Augusto B. Leguía," p. 202. Between 1920 and 1931 North American investors poured 89.6 million dollars into Peruvian bonds. R. J. Owens, *Peru* (London, 1963), p. 170.

Chapter 2

1. "In these societies the idea of the nation has not yet completed its trajectory, or fulfilled its historic mission," "Réplica a Luis Alberto Sánchez," *Ideología y política* in *Colección Obras Completas* (Lima, 1969), 11:221.

2. Other dates have been suggested for these two generations, such as 1905, 1903, 1920, and 1923. See Luis Alberto Sánchez, *Balance y liquidación del novecientos* (Santiago de Chile, 1941); Raúl Porras Barrenechea, *Mito, tradición e historia del Perú* (Lima, 1951); and, César Pacheco Vélez, "Los historiadores del Perú en la generación del 1900" *Fanal* 19 (1964): 2-11.

3. Estuardo Núñez, "Las generaciones post-románticas en el Perú," *Letràs* (1936): 413.

4. Núñez, "Las generaciones post-románticas," p. 413. Among the characteristics Sánchez has ascribed to the radical intellectuals of the 1870s and later, three seem particularly apt: their political radicalism and rabid anticlericalism, their indigenista outlook, and their nationalism and anti-Hispanism. Luis Alberto Sánchez, *La literatura peruana*, 4 vols. (Lima, 1956), 3:1046.

5. Luis Alberto Sánchez, *Don Manuel* (Lima, 1964), p. 65.

6. The standard biography on González Prada is Luis Alberto Sanchez's *Don Manuel*, which must be used cautiously. *Mi Manuel*, by the poet's widow also contains some important personal accounts. Eugenio Chang-Rodríguez's *La literatura política de González Prada, Mariátegui y Haya de la Torre* (Mexico, 1957), is an aprista account of the three men. Basadre's *Historia de la república*, 9:4391–4403, should also be consulted.

7. Marie Louise Telich, "Manuel González Prada, The Social Content of his Writing" (M.A. thesis, Stanford University, 1955), pp. 57–64. See also Francisco Carrillo, "La temática indigenista de las *Baladas peruanas*, " in M. González Prada, *Baladas peruanas* (Lima, 1966), pp. 5–10.

8. González Prada, "Impresiones de un reservista," in *El tonel de Diógenes* (Mexico, 1945), p. 39. In this work, not published until 1945, González Prada briefly traced his remembrance of Lima at the onset of the war. Toward the end of 1880, he recalled, Lima had become a military camp teeming with the movement of horses, of artillery equipment, and of men in sundry uniforms, p. 32.

9. Quoted in Sánchez, *Literatura peruana*, 3:1055. Among the leading members of the Círculo were: poets Carlos G. Amézaga, Germán Leguía y Martínez, Luis Ulloa, Hernán Velarde, and Luis Márquez; critics Carlos Rey de Castro, Alberto Quimper, Alberto

Secada; in theatre, Manuel Moncloa Covarrubias and Carlos G. Amézaga; short story writer Abelardo Gamarra; journalists Luis Márquez, Gamarra, Quimper; folklore writer A. Vienrich; and historians Pablo Patrón and Carlos Alberto Romero. For a charming remembrance of the society, see Manuel Moncloa y Covarrubias's *Los bohemios de 1886* in the series Biblioteca de Cultura Peruana, ed. by Ventura García Calderón (Paris, 1938), first published in 1901.

10. González Prada, *Pájinas libres* (Lima, 1966), p. 29. The best treatment of González Prada's ideas, especially on science and positivism, is in Augusto Salazar Bondy, *Historia de las ideas en el Perú contemporáneo*, 2 vols. (Lima, 1965), 1:10–37. For González Prada's ideas on religion and science consult his two essays, "Jesucristo y su doctrina" and "Catolicismo y ciencia," first appearing in *Nuevas pájinas libres* (Santiago de Chile, 1937). González Prada published two anthologies of his essays and speeches during his lifetime: *Pájinas libres* (Paris, 1894), and *Horas de lucha* (Lima, 1908). Other works appeared posthumously, including *Bajo el oprobio* (Paris, 1933); *Anarquía* (Santiago de Chile, 1936); *Nuevas pájinas libres* (Lima, 1948); *Figuras y figurones* (Paris, 1938); *Propaganda y ataque* (Buenos Aires, 1939); *Prosa menuda* (Buenos Aires, 1941); and *El tonel de Diógenes* (Mexico City, 1945).

11. Augusto Tamayo Vargas, "Clorinda Matto y las veladas literarias del siglo XIX," *La mujer peruana* 1 (1953); and, Mario Castro Arenas, *La novela peruana y la evolución social* (Lima, 1963), pp. 87ff.

12. On the importance of *Aves*, consult Francisco Carrillo, *Clorinda Matto de Turner y su indigenismo literario* (Lima, 1967); Aída Cometta Manzoni, *El indio en la novela de América* (Buenos Aires, 1960); and Clifton Brooke McIntosh, "*Aves sin nido* and the Beginning of Indianismo" (Ph.D. diss., University of Virginia, 1932).

13. González Prada lived in Paris precisely at the time when "the influence of anarchism on artists and writers . . . [was reaching] its peak . . . toward the end of the 19th century." Donald D. Egbert, "The Idea of 'Avante garde' in Art and Politics," *American Historical Review* 73 (1967):359.

14. He began by writing for *La Protesta*, published briefly in Lima in 1902 and later between 1910 and 1923; and also for *Los Parias* which appeared between 1904 and 1909 (articles later published in *Anarquía*, 4th ed., Lima, 1948). In 1914, González Prada and his son Alfredo (the latter edited many of his father's posthumously published books), brought out one number of a radical newspaper, *La Lucha*.

15. González Prada, *Anarquía*, pp. 12, 14.

16. Ibid., p. 72.

17. Salazar Bondy, *Historia de las ideas*, 1:32.

18. González Prada, *Horas de Lucha*, p. 212.

19. González Prada, *Prosa menuda* (Buenos Aires, 1941), p. 156.

20. Manuel Gonzáles Prada first used the term *intellectual* in Peru in 1905. Significantly he was in France in the 1890s, precisely at the time when the term came into general use there as a result of *l'affaire Dreyfus*. See Victor Brombert, *The Intellectual Hero* (Chicago, 1964), pp. 21ff. The term also appeared in the title, although not in the text, of a 1905 pamphlet by Carlos D. Gibson, *Un intelectual* (Arequipa, 1905).

21. González Prada, *Horas de lucha*, p. 50.

22. Manuel Mejía Valera, *Fuentes para le historia de la filosofia en el Perú* (Lima, 1963), pp. 131ff. Mejía Valera indicates the first references to positivism in Lima appeared as early as 1854 in the writings of Sebastián Lorente, and in 1859 in *La Revista de Lima*.

23. Ibid., p. 132.

24. Ibid., p. 133.

25. Salazar Bondy, *Historia de las ideas*, 1:48ff.

26. See Villarán's preface to *Estado social del Peru durante la dominación española*,

(Lima, 1941), p. 9. *El estado* explained Peru's backwardness on the basis of race, and advocated greater racial mixture to improve Peru's population. His doctoral dissertation, entitled "La evolución de la idea filosófica en la historia," was submitted in 1891; he also published two minor works on education: *La educación nacional* (Lima, 1899) and *El problema de la enseñanza* (Lima, 1915).

27. Villarán, *Estado social del Perú*, p. 10.

28. At various times Prado served as a senator, supreme court judge, minister of foreign relations, minister of government, president of El Partido Civil, rector and dean at San Marcos University, historian, philosopher, one of Lima's leading lawyers, and a member of numerous banking and corporate directories.

29. On Prado's pro-American views, see his *La nueva época y los destinos de los Estados Unidos* (Lima, 1918), p. 71.

30. Generally the traditional professions of the law, the clergy, and the military predominated. Villarán, *Las profesiones liberales en el Perú* (Lima, 1900), p. 15.

31. Villarán, "La educación nacional y la influencia extranjera," in *Estudios sobre educación nacional* (Lima, 1922), pp. 58f. Villarán's *Pájinas escogidas* (Lima, 1922), is a comprehensive collection of his social and political writings. For an overview of the pervasive racism characterizing Spanish-American social thought at the turn of the century consult: Martin S. Stabb, *In Quest of Identity* (Chapel Hill, 1967), especially chapter 2.

32. Villarán, *El factor económico en la educación nacional* (Lima 1954), p. 8.

33. Ventura García Calderón Rey, *Nosotros*, (Paris, 1946), pp. 106ff.

34. Other important names associated with the generation are Ventura García Calderón Rey, José Gálvez, Oscar Miró Quesada, Luis Miró Quesada, Felipe Barreda y Laos, Julio C. Tello, and many others. See Sánchez, *Balance y liquidación;* Porras Barrenechea, *Mito, tradición e historia;* and Pacheco Vélez, "Los historiadores del Perú." For a good history of the generation consult Ventura García Calderón Rey, *Nosotros*.

35. García Calderón's father wrote his memoirs of the war debacle of the 1870s, entitled *Memorias del cautiverio* (Lima, 1949).

36. García Calderón Rey, *Nosotros*, pp. 106ff. Belaúnde also wrote "Nos unía el amor a la historia, el sentido de la tradición patria, el afán de buscar el punto de vista filosófico y el gusto por la expresión elegante." *Memorias*, 3 vols. (Lima, 1960), 2:38.

37. García Calderón Rey, *Nosotros*, p. 36.

38. Ibid., p. 32f.

39. César Pacheco Vélez, *Menendez Pelayo y Riva Agüero* (Lima, 1958), pp. 13ff. Pacheco Vélez noted how Riva Agüero was an incessant reader from early childhood, always cultivated a passion for books, and lived a relatively solitary life as a bachelor. Ventura García Calderón reported that at the age of fourteen most members of the generation read a book a day. *Nosotros*, pp. 32.

40. Belaúnde, *Memorias*, 2:58.

41. Ibid., 2:45. Porras Barrenechea, in a perceptive biographic portrait, noted that Belaúnde always suffered an ambivalence and tension caused by "his idealist orientation and positivist methods, by his reverence for tradition and his commitment to progress, by his espousal of democratic principles and his respect for hierarchical authority." "Discurso del Dr. Raúl Porras Barrenechea," *Mercurio Peruano*, January 1944.

42. In 1905, Riva Agüero wrote that "it is imperative that we dedicate ourselves seriously to the study of modern civilization." *Carácter de la literatura del Perú independiente* (Lima, 1962), p. 282. For his more extensive thoughts on reform during those years, see *Carácter*, pp. 296–305, and *La historia en el Peru* (Madrid, 1952), pp. 517–28. The latter he presented as his doctoral dissertation in 1910.

43. García Calderón, *En torno al Perú y América* (Lima, 1954), p. 12 (this is an anthology that includes an extensive fragment from *Le Pérou*).

44. Ibid., p. 42.

45. Ibid., p. 79.

46. Among the San Marcos bachelor and doctoral theses submitted during these years were the following: Pedro Irigoyen, "Inducciones acerca de la civilización incaica"; Julio Tello's celebrated "La antigüedad de la sífilis en el Perú "; Felipe Barreda y Laos, "Vida intelectual de la colonia"; Riva Agüero's two classics "Carácter de la literatura del Perú independiente" and "La historia en el Perú "; Víctor Andrés Belaúnde, "Los modernos sociólogos y el antiguo Perú "; and José Gálvez, "Posibilidad de una geuina literatura nacional."

47. Belaúnde, *Memorias*, 2:55.

48. Quoted in Gabriel del Mazo, ed. *La reforma universitaria*, 6 vols. (Buenos, Aires, 1927), 6:87ff.

49. Belaúnde, "La crisis presente," *Revista Universitaria* 9 (1914):447.

50. Riva Agüero, *Paisajes peruanos* (Lima, 1955), p. 186.

51. Ibid., pp. 116ff.

52. Ibid., pp. x, clvi. Raúl Porras Barrenechea contributed a lengthy introduction to this edition.

53. See Belaúnde's prolog to Mariano Iberico y Rodríguez's *La filosofía de Enrique Bergson* (Lima, 1916), p. ii.

54. Of mid nineteenth-century writers, Luis Alberto Sánchez has written: "They had economic security, either because of their own assets, or because of bureaucratic appointment; they were appointed as consuls abroad, or were presidential secretaries, or served caudillos and legislative groups; or received military pensions; or served diplomatic legations." *La literatura peruana*, 3:963.

55. Both the generation of 1900 and the generation of 1919 were well aware of the differences between them. Of the former group, a youthful Jorge Basadre wrote: "They left books, articles, verses, but no action." After pointing out their differences in socioeconomic status, Basadre further claimed that his generation had a "social consciousness." "Motivos de la época: la emoción social," *Claridad* 2 (1924):12. On November 8, 1933, APRA's *La Tribuna* leveled charges against the García Calderón brothers and the 1919 generation. Replying through *El Comercio*, the García Calderón brothers defended their generation, and eventually Ventura García Calderón published *Nosotros* as a generational defense.

Chapter 3

1. "Was I, in my literary adolescence, the person others thought I was, the person I myself thought I was?" "Una encuesta a José Carlos Mariátegui," in *La novela y la vida*, in *Colección Obras Completas* (Lima 1959), 4:151.

2. Mariátegui himself thought he was born in 1895 and in Lima. Letter to Samuel Glusberg, January 10, 1927. Guillermo Rouillón, in his *Bío-Bibliografía de José Carlos Mariátegui* (Lima, 1963), p. 9, proposed, based on a baptismal certificate, a new date and birthplace. According to the certificate, José Carlos had been baptized on July 16, thirty-two days after his birth, which means that he was born on June 14, 1894. Rouillón also asserted that José Carlos had been born in Moquegua on the southern coast of Peru, not in Lima.

3. Guillermo Rouillón, *La creación heroica de José Carlos Mariátegui* (Lima, 1975), chapter 1.

4. Ibid., chapter 2.

5. The relationship between José Carlos's parents was a complex one. To date the fullest explanation has been that proposed by Guillermo Rouillón, ibid. His mother apparently did not herself know her husband's true identity until 1895, ibid., p. 41. She

kept it from her children thereafter because her husband's father had been an excommunicated anticlericalist, and she was a devout Catholic.

6. Ibid., p. 75.

7. Ibid., p. 45.

8. Letter from Dr. Javier Mariátegui, dated January 19, 1969, Lima, Peru.

9. Ibid.

10. Rouillón, *Creación heroica*, p. 66.

11. After José Carlos's mother found out her husband's true identity she kept it from her children. Ibid., pp. 62–63. The incident with González Prada is related on p. 81.

12. Gastón Roger (pseudonym for Ezequiel Balarezo Pinillos), "José Carlos Mariátegui," *Mercurio Peruano* March-April 1930.

13. Armando Bazán, *Biografía de José Carlos Mariátegui* (Santiago de Chile, 1939), p. 41.

14. Rouillón, *Creación heroica*, p. 118 and Rouillón's prolog to a Chilean edition of Mariátegui's *Siete ensayos de interpretación de la realidad peruana* (Santiago de Chile, 1955), p. xi.

15. Luis Monguió, *La poesía postmodernista peruana* (Berkeley, 1954), pp. 10ff.

16. Ibid.

17. Sánchez, *La literatura peruana*, 4:1215.

18. Quoted in Monguió, *Poesía postmodernista*, p. 28.

19. Sánchez, *La literatura peruana*, 4:1215.

20. Monguió, *Poesía postmodernista*, pp. 48ff. Monguió also points to similar activities in Arequipa.

21. Interview with Humberto del Aguila, Lima, September 20, 1966.

22. *El Turf* (Lima, 1914–18). Beginning with no. 13 of July 3, 1915, Juan Croniqueur and "Debel" appears as editors. A partial bibliography of José Carlos's writings in 1915–16 would include his frequent contributions to *Lulú*, an illustrated weekly for young ladies, for which he wrote "Gesto de spleen" July 28, 1915): 26; "Plegarias románticas III morfina" March 2, 1916): 15; "Interpretación III" (March 16, 1916): 8; "Cuentos de hoy: Rudyard Ring, ganador" (March 23, 1916): 8ff; "El hombre que se enamora de Lily Gant" (May 18, 1916):18–20; "Minuto de encuentro" and "Minuto de confianza" (July 7, 1916): 18; (and December 23, 1915) the same journal reproduced a complimentary article on José Carlos written by Eduardo Zapata López, "Promesas: José Carlos Mariátegui" *Grito del Pueblo* (Guayaquil, 1914).

23. For a discussion of the importance of *Colónida*, see Monguió, *Poesía postmodernista*, pp. 30–31; and Alberto Tauro, "*Colónida* en el modernismo peruano" and "Bibliografía de *Colónida*," *Revista Iberoamericana* 1 (1939): 77–82, 461–67..

24. Genaro Carnero Checa, *La acción escrita* (Lima, 1964), p. 108.

25. For the literary production of the youthful José Carlos see, ibid., pp. 63–94.

26. *El Tiempo*, March 2, 1917.

27. Angela Ramos, "Una encuesta a José Carlos Mariátegui," *Mundial*, July 23, 1926. A variation of this confession of his "search for God," appeared two years later in the *Siete ensayos*, p. 261.

28. Rouillón indicates he eventually found out his father's identity: *Creación heroica*, p. 93.

29. Rouillón related the incident during an interview in Lima, July 25, 1968. Rouillón interviewed don Foción Mariátegui many times, and the elder Mariátegui told him that the young José Carlos always approached him with an unmistakable arrogance.

30. Carnero Checa, *La acción escrita*, p. 84.

31. Interview with Humberto del Aguila, February 19, 1966, Lima.

32. *El Tiempo*, March 2, 1917.

33. Mariátegui, "Voces: un año," *El Tiempo*, July 14, 1917.

34. "El asunto de Norka Rouskaya; Palabras de justificación y defensa," *El Tiempo*, November 10, 1917.

35. Alberto R. Alexander, *Estudio sobre la crisis de la habitación en Lima* (Lima, 1922), pp. 26–46.

36. Sebastián Lorente and Raúl Flores Córdova, *Estudios sobre geografía médica y patología del Perú* (Lima, 1925), p. 106.

37. Interview with Héctor Merel, January 31, 1966, Lima.

38. Interview with Humberto del Aguila, February 19, 1966, Lima.

39. Mariátegui, "Antecedentes y desarrollo de la acción clasista," in Ricardo Martínez de la Torre, *Apuntes para una interpretación marxista de historia social del Perú*, 4 vols. (Lima, 1948) 2:405.

40. Quoted in Alcides Spelucín, "Contribución al conocimiento de César Vallejo y de las primeras etapas de su evolución poética," *Aula Vallejo* (Córdoba, 1962), p. 85.

41. Only two editions of *Nuestra Epoca* appeared: June 22, 1918, and July 6, 1918.

42. *Nuestra Epoca*, June 22, 1918.

43. *Siete ensayos de interpretación de la realidad peruana* (Lima, 1928), p. 260.

44. *Nuestra Epoca*, June 22, 1918.

45. The incident is covered best in Carnero Checa, *La acción escrita*, pp. 117ff.

46. Interview with Humberto del Aguila, February 19, 1966, Lima.

47. "Antecedentes y desarrollo," *Apuntes* 2:405.

48. "Perú en tres tiempos," *Amauta* 4 (1929): 26.

49. In dealing with the December-January 1919 general strike, known as "la jornada de 8 horas," I have followed the interpretation of Héctor Merel, one of the leaders of the vitartinos, as well as of Ricardo Martínez de la Torre. My sources were Merel's "La verdad sobre la jornada de 8 horas," *Indice* 5 (1951) as well as information gathered on three separate interviews with him: January 31, 1966, May 27, 1966, and July 9, 1968. For the most complete history of the eight-hour general strike see Martínez de la Torre, "Asi se conquisto la jornada de ocho horas," *Apuntes* 1:395–461. Martínez corroborates Merel's claim that even though the eight hours were conquered collectively by the working class, it was the Unificación Obrera Textil Vitarte that provided the vanguard and mass of the movement. César Levano's *La verdadera historia de la jornada de las ocho horas en el Perú* (Lima, 1967) disputes that claim, although without adding new evidence. See also Demetrio Flores González, *Medio siglo de vida sindical en Vitarte* (Lima, 1959), pp. 42–49 and Haya de la Torre's special claim as to his role in the event, "La jornada de 8 horas," *APRA* (1946): 26–30.

50. Del Aguila maintained that they only bluffed about buying *El Tiempo*. Interview, October 29, 1966, Lima. But Falcón, who was closer to José Carlos in such dealings, indicated that Aspíllaga did approach them and offer to buy the newspaper for them, but they refused his offer. Later they decided to use the idea of "buying *El Tiempo* as a bargaining factor with Ruiz Bravo." Interview, November 29, 1966, Mexico City.

51. Luis Ulloa, "Carta a los señores J. C. Mariátegui y César Falcón," *El Tiempo*, January 25, 1919.

52. Interviews, del Aguila, February 19, 1966, Lima; and César Falcón, November 29, 1966, Mexico City.

53. *El Tiempo*, April 22, 1919. Probably the work of Luis Ulloa, the new party's program avoided taking a position on the question of private property.

54. According to César Falcón, Isaías de Piérola helped them secure the financial backing of a Cuban businessman. His support was minimal, and the venture soon became self-supporting. Interview, November 29, 1966, Mexico City. Del Aguila, in contrast, maintained that Alfredo de la Piedra, Leguía's cousin, initially helped out financially because of his interest in an anti-Pardo paper. Interview, September 20, 1966, Lima.

55. *La Razón*, 1 (1919): 1.

56. *La Prensa*, August 17, 1918; and Haya de la Torre, "La Jornada."

57. Haya de la Torre not only participated in the December-January general strike but also in Leguía's presidential campaign. According to Héctor Merel, Haya de la Torre campaigned for Leguía in Vitarte in February 1919, at the Salón de Billares, owned by a Vitarte master dyer, don Genaro Agüero. Interview, May 27, 1966, Lima. Haya de la Torre also signed a statement in defense of Leguía which appeared in *El Tiempo*, January 26, 1919. The statement read in part: "In the name of the FEP, which we represent, we protest the ignoble defamation campaign initiated against Señor don Augusto B. Leguía, Maestro de la Juventud. . . ." Eight students signed, including Haya de la Torre and Raúl Porras Barrenechea. Merel also pointed out that don Agustín Ganoza, Haya de la Torre's relative and chief of Leguía's political organization in Lima, appointed Haya de la Torre secretary of the Cuzco Prefecture for support given during the campaign though he apparently did not like the appointment and did not stay in Cuzco long. Interview, May 27, 1966, Lima. Later, in 1920, when Haya de la Torre organized the Cuzco National Student Congress, Leguía's government financed it. Humberto del Aguila reported hearing Haya de la Torre defend Leguía at an incident in the offices of *Mundial*, as late as March 1922 after Víctor Andrés Belaúnde had attacked Leguía at a San Marcos rally. Interview, October 29, 1966, Lima. Later Haya de la Torre denied any dealings with Leguía's regime in his "Autobiográfica," *Repertorio Americano* 17 (1928): 50–52.

58. Martínez de la Torre, "El movimiento obrero en 1909," *Apuntes*1:23–48.

59. For a key source on the beginning of University Reform, see Raúl Porras Barrenechea, "Brillante discurso de agradecimiento pronunció Porras," *La Prensa*, April 25, 1957. Basadre's "Algo sobre la reforma universitaria de 1919," *Letras Peruanas*, 1 (1951) is the indespensable testimony of yet another especially perceptive participant. Other important sources include Luis Alberto Sánchez, *La universidad no es una isla* (Lima, 1961); Enrique Cornejo Koster, "Crónica del movimiento estudiantil peruano, 1919-1926," in del Mazo, *Reforma universitaria*, 6:87–181; and Enrique Ramirez Novoa, *La reforma universitaria* (Buenos Aires, 1956).

60. Porras Barrenechea, "Brillante discurso," *La Prensa*, April 25, 1957. On the causes of Peruvian university reform Carlos Enrique Paz Soldán, a participant, accurately observed that "The First Student Congress of Montevideo was the spark that stimulated the fervor of students in . . . Peru." *De la inquietud a la revolución*, p. 9. In fact the Third Spanish American University Student Congress met in Lima prior to both Palacio's visit and the issuance of the Córdoba Manifesto. The Third Congress contributed much to fomenting interest in university reform at San Marcos. See Alberto Ulloa Sotomayor, "El tercer congreso de estudiantes americanos," *Nuevo Zig-Zag* 49, (1953): 34ff. Del Aguila, one of the initiators of the University Reform, insisted that Palacio's visit though significant was not decisive. Interviews, February 19, and September 20, 1966, Lima.

61. *La Razón*, June 27, 1919.

62. Ibid., p. 47. Del Aguila pointed out that with Gutarra, Barba, and Fonkén in prison, they could have assumed leadership of the movement and turned the strike into a major revolt. But they decided against it because they "got cold feet." During the height of the rioting José Carlos was shot at and very nearly killed. Interview, February 19, 1966, Lima.

63. Alfredo de la Piedra, their friend, apparently delivered the alternatives in polite but firm terms. Interviews with del Aguila, September 10, 1966, Lima; and Falcón, November 29, 1966, Mexico City.

64. Haya de la Torre chided Mariátegui for accepting the grant in his "Autobiográfica," p. 52.

65. Due to personal reasons, Humberto del Aguila decided not to go to Europe, and subsequently took a position with the government. Interview, October 29, 1966, Lima.

Chapter 4

1. "Via the paths of Europe I discovered the country of America from which I had come, and in which I had lived estranged and alienated." *Alma matinal*, p. 212.

2. Bazán, *Mariátegui y su tiempo*, 20: 47.

3. Two recent studies draw special attention to the importance of the initial impact Paris had on Mariátegui: Harry E. Vanden, *Mariátegui, influencias en su formación ideológica* (Lima, 1975), pp. 25–36, and John M. Baines, *Revolution in Peru: Mariátegui and the Myth* (University of Alabama Press, 1972), p. 36. Mariátegui and Barbusse corresponded, and Vanden found six of Barbusse's books in his inventory of Mariátegui's library.

4. Bazán, *Mariátegui y su tiempo*, 20: 54.

5. Half of the Italian dispatches, totaling 47, appeared as "Cartas de Italia," and the other half under different titles such as "Aspectos de Europa," "Del carnet de un peregrino," or "Crónica de Verano." *Cartas de Italia* in Obras Completas (Lima, 1969), vol. 15. This volume does not include the first dispatch, "El problema del Adriático," *El Tiempo*, May 2, 1920.

6. *El Tiempo*, May 2, 1920, and *Cartas de Italia*, 15:37–42.

7. Bazán, *Mariátegui y su tiempo*, 20:65; Núñez, "Jose Carlos Mariátegui," p. 189; and César Lévano, " '. . . la vida que me diste,' Anna, viuda de Mariátegui," *Caretas*, April 14-24, 1969. Bazán mentions the phrase "Peruvian communist cell." Núñez writes of discussions dealing "with the organization of a left-wing political party." Mariátegui himself said, "In Europe I became involved in some socialist activities with some Peruvians." Letter to Samuel Glusberg, January 10, 1927.

8. Mariátegui, *Cartas de Italia*, 15:99.

9. Ibid., 15:49ff.

10. Ibid., p. 158.

11. "The Italian Press," ibid., 15: 123.

12. Lévano, " '. . .la vida que me diste, 'Anna, viuda de Mariátegui," and letter to the author dated Lima, March 24, 1970, from Dr. Javier Mariátegui, youngest son of José Carlos.

13. Questions on the Gramscian influence largely derive from startling similarities between Mariátegui and Gramsci, personal and intellectual, which have been noted by Robert Paris, "José Carlos Mariátegui: une bibliographie; quelques problemes," *Annales*, 21 (1966): 194; Gianni Toti, "Mariátegui armó di una teoria el proletariado peruviano," *El Calendario del Populo*, 20 (1964):6583; and by Antonio Melis, "Mariátegui, primer marxista de América," *Casa de las Américas*, 8 (1968):20. Among other things, Melis pointed to the need for "an organic and documented study of possible direct relations and influences" between the two, without unfortunately providing any new materials himself. Dr. Hugo Pesce, one of Mariátegui's closest intellectual companions, stated that Mariátegui never mentioned Gramsci or referred to his ideas. Interview, September 7, 1966, Lima.

14. Bazán, *Mariátegui y su tiempo*, 20:42.

15. Mariátegui's conversion to Marxism probably occurred sometime in 1921 or early 1922. To Bazán, he confided that: "El marxismo había sido para mi hasta esos días una teoría un poco confusa, pesada, y fría; en esos días vi su luz clara y tuve su revelación. . . ." Bazán, *Mariátegui y su tiempo*, 20:80. Mariátegui did not clarify the nature or occasion of his "revelation."

16. The articles were not written until 1929. Of the three articles—*Mundial*, July 12 and 26, August 15, 1929—the second on "La economía y Piero Gobetti," is the one most often cited.

17. Letter from Umberto Terracini to Robert Paris, dated, November 11, 1964, cited in Paris, "La formation ideologigue de José Carlos Mariátegui" (Ph.D. diss., Université

de Paris, 1969), p. 125. Terracini wrote, "I think that Mariátegui was, in 1919–1922, a young man who frequented the University of Turin, without yet having a very marked personality, and therefore did not distinguish himself very much among those who at the time followed the . . . action of the Turinese workers."

18. Paris speaks of Gobetti as a "constant point of reference." *Mariátegui e Gobetti,* p. 7.

19. Mariátegui, *Siete ensayos,* p. 169.

20. Núñez stresses these points. "José Carlos Mariátegui," p. 193.

21. Rouillón believes Mariátegui actually knew Gobetti personally. Paris did not find any traces of a personal relationship in the latter's papers. *La formation ideologigue,"* p. 125. Interview with Guillermo Rouillón, August 15, 1966, Lima.

22. Robert Paris, *Mariátegui e Gobetti,* Quaderno 12, Centro Studi Piero Gobetti (Torino, 1967), p. 3. See also Núñez, "José Carlos Mariátegui," p. 193. Núñez dwells on personal similarities and influences, while Paris stresses the intellectual influences.

23. *Alma matinal,* p. 151.

24. According to Bazán, Mariátegui met Sorel in Venice. *Mariátegui y su tiempo,* 20:80. George Lichtheim on the other hand writes Sorel never left France, never visited Italy: *From Marx to Hegel* (New York, 1971), p. 103. Although Sorel is not mentioned in the *Cartas,* we know that Mariátegui first encountered his writings in Italy. Paris, "José Carlos Mariátegui," p. 195. Sorel does appear—introduced as the "greatest and most illustrious theorist of syndicalism"—in Mariátegui's first lecture to the Popular University of June 15, 1923. It is probable that Mariátegui did not start reading him systematically until after returning to Peru. *Historia de la crisis mundial* in *Colección Obras Completas* (Lima, 1959) 8:21. Mariátegui mentioned Sorel several times during the lecture series, and his influence is manifest throughout Mariátegui's work, especially in the *Defensa del Marxismo* (cited more than 20 times) and in the *Siete ensayos.* That Mariátegui came to Sorel through Croce, and also through Gobetti is a conclusion that Paris reached in, "El Marxismo de Mariátegui," *Aportes,* 17 (1970): 12,5.

25. Interview with Señora Anna Chiappe de Mariátegui, Lima, May 1, 1966. See also Bazán, *Mariátegui y su tiempo,* 20:80.

26. According to his widow, Mariátegui explained that his work compelled him to return to Peru. Interview with Señora Anita Chiappe de Mariátegui, May 1, 1966, Lima. Humberto del Aguila explained that Mariátegui returned to Peru in 1923 because of the government's decision to cut off his support. At the time del Aguila worked for the government. Interview, October 29, 1966, Lima.

27. Karno, "Augusto B. Leguía," especially chapter 6, pp. 227–54.

28. del Mazo, *Reforma universitaria,* 6:94.

29. *Studium,* 2 (1921): 198.

30. *Primer Congreso Nacional de Estudiantes* (Lima, 1920), p. 12.

31. Ibid.

32. A workers' adult education school had existed in Vitarte since 1912 or 1913. The anarchists originally founded these popular universities, and named the first founded in Peru (Vitarte), Escuela Sindical Racionalista Francisco Ferrer la Guardia, after the Spanish anarchist of that name. In 1916, the same group of Vitarte workers created another, called this time 9 de enero in memory of the Vitarte massacre of January 9, 1915. Interview with Héctor Merel, November 11, 1966, Lima.

33. Luis Alberto Sánchez, *Haya de la Torre y el APRA* (Santiago de Chile, 1954), p. 115.

34. Mariátegui, *Siete ensayos,* p. 6 and "Antecedentes y desarrollo," *Apuntes,* 2 (1948):407.

35. Rouillón, *Bío-Bibliografía,* p. 12.

36. Basadre, *Historia de la república,* 9:4033.

37. The incident is related by Haya de la Torre in "Carta a César Mendoza," in *El proceso de Haya de la Torre* (Guayaquil, 1933), p. 6.

38. Interview with Ricardo Martínez de la Torre, October 18, 1966, Lima.

39. Basadre, *Historia de la república*, 9:4033ff. The funeral of the slain student and worker became the occasion for a great public demonstration at which Haya de la Torre was the main orator. For an account in English quite favorable to the latter, see "The Story of Haya de la Torre," *The Nation*, 118 (1924): 406ff, which includes an interesting early statement by Haya de la Torre entitled, "Is the United States Feared in South America?"

40. Mariátegui, *"El pueblo sin Dios*, por César Falcón," *Peruanicemos al Perú* in *Colección Obras Completas* (Lima, 1970), 11:146.

41. Mariátegui, *La escena contemporánea* in *Colección Obras Completas* (Lima, 1959), 1: 190ff.

42. Mariátegui, "Instantáneas," *Variedades*, March 31, 1923.

43. *Historia de la crisis mundial* in *Colección Obras Completas*, 8:15f.

44. Ibid., p. 21.

45. His lecture notes are available as *Historia de la crisis mundial* in *Colección Obras Completas*, vol. 8. He lectured at the offices of the FEP in the Palacio de la Exposición. Mariátegui saw the popular universities as "escuelas de cultura revolucionaria," or "escuelas de clase." He also saw the popular universities as existing to "elaborate and create a proletariat culture." Bourgeois culture represented a major "counterrevolutionary weapon" used against the working class. As a "revolutionary duty," the intellectual had to contribute to the workers' effort to "conquer their own culture." See José Carlos Mariátegui, "Las universidades populares," *Claridad*, 1 (1924): 5.

46. *Historia de la crisis mundial*, in *Colección Obras Completas*, 8:78.

47. Ibid., 8:135.

48. Ibid., 8:129.

49. Ibid., 8:141.

50. Ibid., 8:143.

51. Ibid., 8:144.

52. Ibid., 8:145.

53. *Conversaciones: Basadre y Macera*, pp. 93, 96.

54. Interview with Esteban Pavletich, November 9, 1966, Lima. Bazán first met Mariátegui shortly after his return from Europe at the Popular University. Mariátegui apparently made a decisive impression on everyone there. *Mariátegui y su tiempo*, 20:82.

55. Bazán, *Mariátegui y su tiempo*, 20:93–95.

56. Basadre, *Historia de la república*, 9:4202.

57. *Claridad*, 1 (1924):1.

58. In *Ideología y política*, in *Colección Obras Completas* (Lima, 1969) 13:107.

59. Dr. Hugo Pesce, who became one of Mariátegui's closest intellectual and political confidants, first met him at the clinic, which was owned by his father. Pesce, who met Mariátegui in September or October 1924, had just returned from Italy where he had been studying medicine. Even before Dr. Pesce met Mariátegui he had been curious about him because of the articles he published on Italy. Dr. Pesce's first reaction to the articles had been that their author was either a plagiarist or a brilliant man. When his father told him that Mariátegui was staying in the clinic, he went to see him at once. His first impression was of a thin, small man with brilliant eyes. The eyes, he recalled, immediately caught your attention. After this meeting and their conversation, Pesce became convinced that Mariátegui knew Italy as did few Italians. Interview, June 25, 1966, Lima.

60. From then on Mariátegui suffered physical relapses about every six months. He never fully recovered from this crisis, and his exhaustive work load compounded the

deterioration of his health. Interview with Señora Anita Chiappe de Mariátegui, 1 May 1966, Lima.

61. Alberto Ulloa S., *"La escena contemporánea* por José Carlos Mariategui," *Mercurio Peruano*, January 1926.

Chapter 5

1. "I returned from Europe with the intent of founding a journal . . . this journal will bring together the new men of Peru. . . . ", *Amauta*, 1 (1926): 3.

2. Mariátegui wrote the lead essay, "El alma matinal" or "The Dawning Spirit," in early 1928 but most of the articles were writen in 1924–25. Only one article in the series, "El problema de las élites," (January 9, 1928) is not of this period. *Alma matinal*, pp. 51–57.

3. Vanden found the fifth edition of *Réflexions sur la violence* (Paris, 1921) in Mariátegui's collection. *Mariátegui, influencias*, p. 137.

4. *Alma matinal*, p. 19.

5. Ibid., p. 24.

6. Ibid., p. 28f. Mariátegui often quotes from his favorite authors without giving a precise citation.

7. Ibid., p. 28.

8. Ibid., p. 31.

9. Ibid., p. 34.

10. Ibid., p.31.

11. *Signos y obras, Obras Completas* (Lima, 1959), 7:118.

12. Ibid., p. 119.

13. Interestingly, both Sorel and Croce searched for the meaning of Marxism in Marx's "inmost thoughts." See H. Stuart Hughes, *Consciousness and Society* (New York, 1961), p. 87.

14. So busy was he that he handled his affairs mostly through appointments and—an interesting fact for the times—with the aid of three telephones. C. Lévano, " . . . La vida que me diste," p. 26.

15. Jorge Basadre, who visited Mariátegui's home, observed that "in his library [one] could find books and newspapers on literary, political, and social topics that were not available elsewhere in Lima." *Peru: problema y posibilidad*, p. 196.

16. Señora de Mariátegui reported that on the evenings when her husband had to turn in an article she would keep her ears cocked for the sound of the typewriter. Invariably she reported he typed his articles at the last possible moment, but once he started he typed without stopping. When he finished she would run with the copy to the offices of *Variedades* or *Mundial* (often around 11:00 P.M.). Interview, May 1, 1966, Lima.

17. By then, one article later incorporated into the *Siete ensayos* already had been published: "Economía colonial," *Mundial*, January 8, 1925.

18. Basadre, *Historia de la república*, 9:4203. An example of Mariátegui's wit comes at the expense of Victorio Codovilla, the Argentine communist. Mariátegui once asked rhetorically in conversation: "what is it about Codovilla that makes him a communist?" The reply, "only his title and salary." Interview with Martínez de la Torre, November 18, 1965, Lima.

19. Quoted in Monguió, *La poesía postmodernista perunana*, p. 63.

20. Ibid., p. 79.

21. Originally the essay appeared in *Revista Universitaria* (1907). See also Villarán, *Páginas escogidas*, pp. 3–8.

22. Monguió, *La poesía postmodernista peruana*, p. 92.

210   NOTES

23. Ibid.

24. Maurilio Arriola Granda, *Diccionario literario del Perú* (Barcelona, 1968), p. 443.

25. María Wiesse, *José Carlos Mariátegui* in *Colección Obras Completas*, 10:38. Alberto Tauro has suggested that friends persuaded Mariátegui to abandon *Vanguardia* as a title because of its alarming connotation. Tauro, *Amauta y su influencia* in *Colección Obras Completas* (Lima, 1960) 19:38.

26. *Peruanicemos al Perú*, 11:30.

27. Ibid., p. 32, emphasis mine.

28. Ibid., p. 51.

29. Humberto del Aguila reported Mariátegui was very sensitive about questions concerning his father. Interview, September 20, 1966, Lima.

30. *Alma matinal*, pp. 102ff.

31. Ibid., pp. 93, 104.

32. Telich, "Manuel González Prada," pp. 61–64.

33. *Peruanicemos al Perú*, p. 65.

34. "Presentacion de Amauta," *Amauta*, 1 (1926): 3.

35. For the best bibliographical analysis of *Amauta*, see Tauro, *Amauta y su influencia* 19:11–17. It explains the appearance and development of important sections such as *Libros y Revistas, El Proceso del Gamonalismo*, and *Vida Económica*. Contrary to Mariátegui's own declaration that the journal would only accept material from contributors with like views, *Amauta* welcomed virtually anyone with talent. So much was this the case that the poet Serafín Delmar once kidded Mariátegui saying that *Amauta* was like "an omnibus, anyone can get on." To which Mariátegui instantly replied, "Yes, that may be true, but so far you haven't been able to get on." Interview with Ricardo Martínez de la Torre, November 18, 1965, Lima.

36. For articles published on economics see Tauro, *Amauta y su influencia*, 19:118–25.

37. Quoted in Paris, preface to *7 Essais d'interprétation de la réalité péruvienne* (Paris, 1968), p. 19.

38. Ibid.

39. Escalante's article also appeared in *Mundial*, under the title of "Literatura indigenista," March 4, 1927.

40. All of Sánchez's articles appeared in Mundial: "Batiburrillo indigenista. . . ," (February 18, 1927); "Respuesta a José Carlos Mariátegui," (March 4, 1927); "Ismos contra ismos," (March 18, 1927); and "Más sobre lo mismo," (March 25, 1927). Mariátegui replied twice in *Mundial* with "Intermezzo polémico," (February 25, 1927) and "Réplica a Luis Alberto Sánchez," (March 11, 1927); and once in *Amauta*, "Polémica finita," 2(March 1927). Two other articles involved inconsequentially in the polemic were: Guillermo J. Guevara's "Opportunismo indigenista," *La Sierra* (April 1927), pp. 4ff and Manuel M. González's "Una polémica interesante," *Mundial* (April 4, 1927). Sánchez was the first to criticize Mariátegui for "applying foreign ideas to Peruvian conditions," an argument later used as the standard anti-Mariátegui line by the APRA.

41. Included in Mariátegui's reply to Sánchez, "Réplica a Luis Alberto Sánchez," *Mundial*, March 11, 1927.

42. Interview with Humberto del Aguila, October 29, 1966, Lima.

43. Martínez de la Torre insisted on this point. Mariátegui, he reported, often and openly referred to the leguiísta regime as a "positive" force in that it represented capitalist interests breaking up semi-feudal property structures. Interview, Martínez de la Torre October 12, 1966, Lima.

44. For a brief discussion of Leguía's land and water policies, see Karno, "Augusto B. Leguía," pp. 239–46.

45. For the fullest narrative of this incident, see Carnero Checa's *La acción escrita*, pp. 195–200. Among the individuals writing to Leguía in defense of Mariátegui and for

lifting the government sanctions against *Amauta* figured Romain Rolland, Barbusse, Gorki, Lunatcharsky, and Waldo Frank. Diego Meseguer Illan, *José Carlos Mariátegui y su pensamiento revolucionario* (Lima, 1974), p. 157.

46. The FOL emerged out of the disintegration of the Federación Obrera Regional (FOR) founded by the anarchists in 1919. It was organized after the 1919 general strike "for the lowering of food prices" with the end of establishing a national labor organization with regional federations in the northern, central, and southern regions. Because the Lima labor movement was the strongest, ultimately only the Lima regional federation was organized at the First Workers' Congress of April 1921. See Martínez de la Torre, *Apuntes*, 1(1948):48-50, and Mariátegui's "Mensaje," *Amauta* 1 (1927): 35ff. According to one estimate, at the time of its founding the FOL had about 3,200 members. J. L. Payne, *Labor and Politics in Peru* (New Haven, 1965), pp. 35ff and Basadre, *Historia de la república*, 9:4212 ff.

47. Mariátegui, "Mensaje," *Amauta*, 2 (1927): 36.

48. Martínez de la Torre reported that all their organizational meetings, the mass meetings, were public and open and that the names of the informers who came were known to them. Interview, September 8, 1927, Lima.

49. "Prisión del Señor José Carlos Mariátegui," *La Prensa*, June 10, 1927.

50. "La conjuración comunista," *La Prensa*, June 11, 1927.

51. Not all of the results of the June 1927 raids turned out negatively. Due to the incident Mariátegui recruited the able worker, Julio Portocarrero, a working-class leader from Vitarte who later became one of his principal collaborators. While imprisoned on San Lorenzo, Armando Bazán, then Mariátegui's secretary, met Portocarrero, and after talking with him invited him to meet Mariátegui after he was released. This led to the collaboration that lasted until Mariátegui died. Interview with Portocarrero, July 21, 1968, Lima. Portocarrero also became the distributor of *Amauta* in Vitarte, receiving and selling sixty issues of each edition.

52. For the best available chronology and narrative on the years 1923–28, see Sánchez, *Haya de la Torre y el APRA*, pp. 158–231.

53. According to Esteban Pavletich, Haya de la Torre also relied on a fictitious news agency called Agencia Columbus, which he claimed he carried "in my pocket." Interview with Pavletich, July 18, 1968, Lima. For an example of one of Haya de la Torre's news releases on himself see Chonk Sheik, "Declaraciones de Haya de la Torre," *Reportorio Americano*, (1927): 344. Allegedly "declarations" made by Haya de la Torre in a "speech of October 11, 1926 during a kuomintang dinner in London," the article quotes him as stating that "the APRA is the only antiimperialist party similar to the Kuomintang."

54. For one version of his life-style and manner of travel, see Eudocio Ravines, *The Yenan Way* (New York, 1951), p. 19.

55. See letter dated October 3, 1923, which appears in *Por la emancipación*, p. 22.

56. Many years later Vasconcelos bitterly recanted his earlier views. See "Política peruana," *Novedades*, November 5, 1948, where he remarked, "there is probably no other case in the history of Hispanic America, of an individual of such mediocre qualities having created and maintained for so many years such a powerful political group."

57. Sánchez, *Haya de la Torre*, p. 162.

58. "What is the A.P.R.A.?" *The Labour Monthly* (1926), :756.

59. "La realidad de América Latina," in *Por la emancipación*, p. 199.

60. For Haya de la Torre's trail from Lima to Mexico City, see Sánchez, *Haya de la Torre*, pp. 137–45.

61. *Por la emancipación*, p. 23.

62. Sánchez, *Haya de la Torre*, pp. 158ff.

63. del Mazo, *La reforma universitaria*, 6:166.

64. For the two earliest references to the five points see "Letter to M. J. Chavarría,"

Repertorio Americano, (1926):382; and "What is the A.P.R.A.?," both of which appeared in December 1926.

65. "Sentido de la lucha anti-imperialista," *Amauta* 2 (1927): 39.

66. His Peruvian roots, particularly his remembrance of the ruins of Chan-Chan outside his native Trujillo, moved him very early in life to think that, "something unjust had happened in these arid lands, some tremendous cruelty was responsible for these tombs, these dry wells, these desolate streets, these silent houses." *Espacio-tiempo-histórico, cinco ensayos y tres diálogos* (Lima, 1948), pp. vii–x.

67. "¿Hispanos, latinos, panamericanos o Indoamericanos?," dated "Berlin, October 1929," in *Construyendo el Aprismo* (Buenos Aires, 1933), p. 14.

68. Luis Eduardo Enríquez, *Haya de la Torre: La estafa política más grande de América* (Lima, 1951), pp. 9ff.; and Sánchez, *Haya de la Torre*, p. 170.

69. At the Brussels Congress, Haya challenged the Third International saying that the APRA (a paper organization), would refuse to join the World Anti-imperialist League because "it is an organization completely controlled by the III International, [existing] not for the good of the anti-imperialist struggle, but for the service of communism." *El anti-imperialismo y el Apra*, pp. 48–49. Perhaps the earliest reference to the APRA conceived as a national party was Haya de la Torre's remark that, "The APRA is the only anti-imperialist party similar to the Kuomintag." In Chonk Sheik, "Declaraciones," *Repertorio Americano* (1927): 344.

70. Martínez de la Torre, *Apuntes,* 2:(1948):290. Pavletich, who was in Mexico at the time participating in the events reported that Haya de la Torre wrote the *Plan.* Interview, July 19, 1968, Lima.

71. Martínez de la Torre, *Apuntes,* 2(1948):290.

72. Ibid., p. 296.

73. Ibid., p. 298f. Magda Portal participated in the Mexico City episode and typed Haya de la Torre's reply to Mariátegui. She abandoned the APRA in the late 1940s because she could no longer support his "deception of the people." Interview with Esteban Pavletich, November 9, 1966, Lima. Pavletich, also present when Haya de la Torre dictated the letter to Magda Portal, broke with the APRA in 1929. See Magda Portal, *¿Quiénes traicionaron al pueblo?* (Lima, 1950), p. 11.

74. Martínez de la Torre, *Apuntes,* 2(1948):298ff.

75. *Apuntes,* 2:(1948)336–37.

76. "Antecedentes y desarrollo," in Martínez de la Torre, *Apuntes,* 2(1948):408. For the best testimony from someone close to Mariátegui concerning his attitude toward the APRA and on the role of *Amauta* as the vehicle by which Mariátegui tried to keep the 1919 generation together on basic principles, see Jorge del Prado, *Mariátegui y su obra* (Lima, 1946), p. 28. Del Prado writes: "Nevertheless Mariátegui considered that the moment had not arrived for separating or breaking with those elements [the APRA]; that their anti-imperialism represented, in effect, the positive aspect and point of contact which could serve, if not for recasting their views anew or re-orienting them toward the correct path, at least to maintain, for the time being and perhaps even a prolonged period, joint efforts during the initial phase. From it followed that, on the one hand, he made a supreme effort to keep the APRA as an *Alianza* or *frente único anti-imperialista,* while, on the other, he brought out *Amauta* to give it a clear ideological definition." This statement by del Prado illuminates further Mariátegui's own words, "In September 1926 *Amauta* appeared as an organ of that movement [the APRA], and as a forum for 'ideological definition.'" Martínez de la Torre, "Antecedentes y desarrollo," *Apuntes,* 2(1948)408.

77. *Amauta,* 29 (1930): 95.

78. "Aniversario y balance," *Amauta* 3 (1928): 1. "Antecedentes y desarrollo," in Martínez de la Torre, *Apuntes,* 2(1948):299. After the break with Haya de la Torre,

Mariátegui and the Lima group circulated a collective letter explaining their differences with the "Plan de México" and with Haya de la Torre. Pavletich reported that after writing his letter to Mariátegui, Haya de la Torre also dictated a letter to Manuel Seoane in Buenos Aires who was then thinking of organizing a Socialist Party along the lines of the one founded by Juan Bautista Justo and Alfredo Palacios. In the end, Seoane decided to stick along with Haya de la Torre. Interview, July 19, 1968, Lima. Ravines reported that Haya de la Torre always harbored a special "personal dislike" for Mariátegui and Manuel Seoane. Interview with Ravines, July 16, 1968, Lima.

Chapter 6

1. "The history of Republican Peru has been written, ordinarily and almost invariably, as political history in the narrowest and most self-seeking meaning of the term." "Preface to *El Amauta Atusparia*," *Ideología y política* in *Colección Obras Completas*, 13:184.

2. "Abraham Valdelomar y el movimiento *Colónida*," *Mundial*, December 9, 1924, and "Economía colonial," *Mundial*, January 8, 1925.

3. As early as 1924 he had suggested that the national question represented the leading political question of the country. "El problema primario del Perú," *Mundial*, December 9, 1924.

4. Paris, "El marxismo de Mariátegui," p. 15.

5. *Siete ensayos*, pp. 7ff. Louis Baudin's *El imperio socialista de los Incas* (Santiago de Chile, 1955), p. 10, characterized the realm as both "agrarian collectivism" and "state socialism." For a one-sided critique of the *Siete ensayos*, see Baudin, "*Siete ensayos de interpretación de la realidad peruana*, por José Carlos Mariátegui," *Revue de l'Amerique Latine* 19 (1930): 555–56.

6. *Siete ensayos*, p. 7.

7. Ibid.

8. Ibid., pp. 7–9.

9. Ibid.

10. Ibid., p. 10.

11. Ibid.

12. Ibid., p. 14.

13. Ibid., p. 27. Peculiar to Peru and to other Andean countries such as Bolivia, the terms gamonal and gamonalismo refer to a particularly exploitative form of latifundismo. Martha Hildebrandt writes that, "El gamonalismo como sistema resulta, pues, una forma local—y actual—de feudalismo." "Gamonal," *El Comercio*, April 12, 1964.

14. *Siete ensayos*, p. 35.

15. Ibid., p. 25.

16. Ibid., p. 64.

17. Ibid., pp. 56–58.

18. Ibid., pp. 74–75.

19. Ibid., pp. 56–58.

20. Ibid., p. 60. Richard N. Adams, another student of the Muquiyauyo community interested in its "progressivism" reached a somewhat different conclusion. Adams identified the customs of the Muquiyauyinos as so distinct—and "noticeably of Spanish derivation or influence"—that they could not be considered culturally "in the same category as the Indian of Cuzco or Puno." Adams further notes that a number of writers have referred to the Muquiyauyinos as mestizos. In the sense postulated by Adams, Mariátegui too would have considered them mestizos. *A Community in the Andes* (Seattle, 1959), p. 213.

21. *Siete ensayos,* p. 27. This proposal appears in the *Siete ensayos* only in a prelimi-nary fashion.

22. Ibid., p. 29.

23. Ibid., p. 77.

24. Ibid.

25. Ibid., p. 85.

26. Ibid., p. 91.

27. Ibid., p. 114.

28. Ibid., p. 112.

29. Ibid., p. 132.

30. Ibid., p. 123.

31. Ibid., pp. 129–30.

32. Ibid., p. 130.

33. Ibid., p. 140.

34. Ibid., p. 141.

35. Ibid., p. 146.

36. Ibid., p. 153.

37. Ibid., p. 160.

38. Ibid., p. 166.

39. Ibid., p. 168.

40. Ibid., p. 177.

41. Ibid., p. 173.

42. Ibid., p. 176.

43. Ibid., p. 178.

44. Ibid., p. 177.

45. Ibid., p. 183.

46. Ibid., p. 196.

47. Ibid., p. 203.

48. Ibid., p. 211.

49. Ibid., p. 232.

50. Ibid., p. 251.

51. Ibid., p. 257.

52. Ibid., p. 253.

53. Ibid., pp. 260–61.

54. Ramón Doll, "Política sociológica: *Siete ensayos de interpretación de la realidad peruana,* por José Carlos Mariátegui," *Mercurio Peruano,* (May-June 1929).

Chapter 7

1. "Who are the idealists, in the superior, abstract meaning of the word; the idealists of bourgeois society or the materialists of the socialist revolution?" *Defensa del marxismo* in CQTLECCIón *Obras Completas,* 5:87.

2. *Apuntes,* 2 (1948):403.

3. *Alma matinal,* p. 152.

4. *Defensa del marxismo,* p. 19.

5. Letter to Samuel Glusberg, publisher of *Babel,* an Argentine literary journal, dated January 10, 1927. Copies of these letters were personally obtained from Señor Glusberg in 1968.

6. Mariátegui assembled the manuscript in 1930, just before his death. A pirated and incomplete edition appeared in Chile in 1934. Empresa Editorial Amauta published the first authorized and complete edition in the *Colección Obras Completas,* vol. 5 (Lima, 1959). References cited here are to the second edition (Lima, 1964).

7. This has been argued especially by Vanden, *Mariátegui, influencias,* pp. 41ff. Vanden catalogs the numerous volumes of Marx and Lenin that he was able to account for in his inventory, pp. 126–27 and 129–30.

8. The reference, while not included in the *Defensa,* is of the same period. *Signos y obras,* 7:116.

9. Sorel maintained correspondence with Antonio Labriola, who introduced historical materialism to Italy, and later with Croce. Lichtheim, *From Marx to Hegel,* p. 100.

10. *Defensa del marxismo,* p. 17.

11. Ibid.

12. Ibid., p. 16.

13. Ibid., p. 43.

14. Ibid., p. 51.

15. Ibid., p. 55.

16. Ibid., pp. 37–38.

17. Ibid., p. 36.

18. Ibid., p. 41.

19. Ibid., p. 53.

20. Ibid., pp. 28–29.

21. Ibid., p. 68.

22. Ibid.

23. Ibid., p. 69.

24. Ibid., p. 85.

25. Ibid., pp. 11ff.

26. Ibid., p. 86.

27. Ibid., p. 93.

28. Ibid., p. 95.

29. Ibid., p. 102.

30. Ibid., p. 105.

31. Ibid.

32. Ibid., p. 111.

33. Ibid., p. 126.

34. Ibid., p. 127.

Chapter 8

1. "The New Generation feels and knows that progress in Peru will be false, or at least not Peruvian, so long as it does not involve the participation and signify the well-being of the Peruvian masses who are four-fifths indigenous and peasant." "El progreso nacional y el capital humano," *Mundial,* October 9, 1925.

2. *Ideología y política,* 13:217.

3. "Motivos polémicos: raza, economía, y cultura, en la cuestión indígena," *El Nacional,* January 18, 1930.

4. *Ideología y política,* p. 31.

5. "El problema de las razas en América Latina," in *Apuntes,* 2(1948):435.

6. "El indio mestizo," *Mundial,* August 24, 1928.

7. "El problema de las razas en América Latina," *Apuntes,* 2(1948):437.

8. "El indio mestizo," *Mundial,* August 24, 1928.

9. "Nacionalismo y vanguardismo," *Mundial,* November 27, 1925.

10. Ibid.

11. In his prolog to Luis E. Valcárcel's *Tempestad en los Andes* (Lima, n.d.), pp. 14–15.

12. *Ideología y política*, p. 217.

13. "Israel y Occidente; Israel y el mundo, *Repertorio Hebreo*, 1 (1929):7.

14. *Apuntes*, 2 (1948):392.

15. Ibid. Those in attendance were: Julio Portocarrero, Avelino Navarro, Hinojosa, Borja, Bernardo Regman, and Martínez de la Torre. The first four were workers; Regman, a traveling vendor; and Martínez de la Torre, an accountant.

16. Ibid. Julio Portocarrero and Avelino Navarro were elected to head the Syndical Secretariat; Martínez de la Torre, secretary of propaganda; and Regman, treasurer.

17. Ibid., p. 67.

18. Interview with Antonio Navarro Madrid, August 24, 1966, Lima.

19. S. Semionov and A. Shulgovski, "El papel de José Carlos Mariátegui en la formación del Partido Comunista del Perú," *Hora del hombre*, 1 (1960):71.

20. Ibid., p. 71.

21. *Ideología y política*, p. 217.

22. Ibid., p. 399.

23. Ibid.

24. According to Martínez de la Torre they regularly received about twenty issues of *La Correspondencia Sudamericana*. Letter, March 17, 1967.

25. Ibid., Martínez de la Torre adamantly denied that they ever received "the gold of Moscow," except for travel expenses of delegations to international meetings. The 1927 Moscow trip of Bazán and Portocarrero, however, was partially paid by contributions from Limeño labor groups.

26. According to Pesce, the Buenos Aires delegation was selected in March. When Pesce was told he had been selected to attend, he also was informed that a communist cell existed within the PSP. Subsequently, Pesce became a member of the group. Their adherence to the Comintern, although marked by a strong sense of independence, Pesce maintained, was unquestioned. Interview, October 28, 1966, Lima.

27. *Apuntes*, 2 (1948):420.

28. Ibid., p. 423.

29. Ibid., p. 425. Criticism of the Peruvian theses mainly came from the Mesa Directiva, and Codovilla led the attack. Few of the Spanish American delegates intervened in criticism of the theses. Interview with Hugo Pesce, September 7, 1966, Lima.

30. *Apuntes*, 2 (1948):464–65.

31. Ibid.

32. "La máscara y el rostro," *Mundial*, September 18, 1925.

33. *Apuntes*, 2 (1948):474–47. This statement misrepresents Mariátegui's position. See *Ideología y política*, pp. 80–81.

34. Quoted in "El papel de José Carlos. . . ," *Hora del Hombre*, p. 79. Also consulted was the: *El movimiento revolucionario latinoamericano: versiones de la primera conferencia comunista latinoamericana Junio de 1929* (Buenos Aires, 1929).

35. *Apuntes*, 2 (1948):428.

36. Ibid.

37. Interview with Martínez de la Torre, September 8, 1966, Lima. In a letter of September 12, 1964 to professor Robert Paris, Jules Humbert-Droz reported that Mariátegui and the Lima group were "condemned and rejected" by the International after the Congress. "Formation idéologigue," p. 298.

38. Ravines, *Yenan Way*, p. 70.

39. Interview with Dr. Hugo Pesce, October 28, 1966, Lima. Pesce also indicated Mariátegui was thoroughly familiar with the Twenty-one Points adopted at the Second Congress, July and August 1920. The Twenty-one points were designed to eliminate reformism, and the sixteenth read: "All the decisions of the congresses of the Communist International as well as the decisions of its Executive Committee are binding on all par-

ties belonging to the Communist International." Point seventeen began: "all parties that wish to . . . join must change their names. Every party that wishes to join the Communist International must be called: Communist Party of such and such a country . . . " Any members rejecting in principle the conditions and theses of the International were to be expelled from the party.

40. Interview with Portocarrero, July 21, 1968, Lima, and with Navarro Madrid, August 24, 1966, Lima.

41. Interviews with Pesce, October 28, 1966; Martínez de la Torre, September 8, 1966, Lima.

42. Letter from Mariátegui to Samuel Glusberg, dated September 30, 1927.

43. *Apuntes,* 3 (1948):14.

44. Ibid., pp. 55–70.

45. Ibid., pp. 73–82.

46. Jorge del Prado, "Mariátegui, Marxista-Leninista," *Dialéctica,* 3 (1943): 53.

47. Ibid., p. 43.

48. Ibid.

49. "El papel de José Carlos. . . ," *Hora del Hombre,* p. 71.

50. According to his wife, Mariátegui suffered relapses every year, sometimes every six months. Interview, May 1, 1966, Lima.

51. The name Enrique Espinoza served as Samuel Glusberg's pseudonym. As Espinosa, Glusberg published fragments of the letters in "José Carlos Mariátegui a través de su correspondencia," *Trinchera* (Buenos Aires, 1932):40–69. In August 1968, I obtained a set of these letters from Glusberg in Santiago de Chile. He also informed me their correspondence had been more extensive, but he had only retained copies of the 1927–30 period. The letters are at times of a personal nature, often revealing Mariátegui's state of mind during his last years, plagued by illness, increasing government repression, rising suspicions, and his growing responsibilities and general fatigue.

52. According to Martínez de la Torre, Mariátegui remained vigorous and confident to the end. Interview, September 8, 1966, Lima.

53. Letter from Mariátegui to Glusberg, September 30, 1927.

54. Ibid., July 4, 1928.

55. Ibid., March 10, 1929.

56. Ibid.

57. Ibid., June 10, 1929.

58. Ibid. For Sánchez's review see: "Siete ensayos de Mariátegui," *Mundial,* December 7, 1928, which appeared about two months after the publication of the *Seven Essays.*

59. Letter from Mariátegui to Glusberg, November 21, 1929.

60. Interview with Martínez de la Torre, October 12, 1966, Lima. In the letters to Glusberg of September 30, 1927 and June 10 and 20, 1929, Mariátegui asked that replies be addressed to his wife, or to his son Sandro. Another time he gave his mother's home as return address.

61. Letter from Mariátegui to Glusberg, November 29, 1929.

62. Portocarrero maintained that he did not meet or see Ravines in Moscow. Ravines holds a different view. *The Yenan Way,* pp. 57ff.

63. Ibid.

64. Interview with Dr. Hugo Pesce, September 7, 1966, Lima.

65. *Apuntes,* 2 (1948):486.

66. The other physicians were: Doctors Constantino Carvallo, Guillermo Gastañeta, Eduardo Goicochea, Hugo Pesce and Carlos Roe. Signed memorandum from Dr. Hugo Pesce, dated October 28, 1966. I am indebted to Dr. Hugo Pesce for his diagnosis of the causes of Mariátegui's death as well as of his early illnesses. Since his youth Mariátegui

suffered from a chronic ailment of his right knee. In 1924, an acute infection in that knee required amputation of the leg. From 1925 to 1929, he suffered from a chronic infection with intermittent manifestations ("superative foci"). It is possible, according to Dr. Pesce, that the infection was of a "staphylococcal nature." In April 1930, an overt staphylococci infection appeared which resulted in emergency surgery, but the infection could not be controlled. Eventually it affected his bloodstream, kidneys, and was mortal. On the basis of Dr. Pesce's diagnosis, a physician at the University of California, Los Angeles Medical School suggested that Mariátegui may have suffered from a chronic osteomyelitis since early youth. He also suggested that a diabetes of juvenile form may have anteceded the osteomyelitis. Later in an interview of August 31, 1968, in Lima, Dr. Pesce said that Mariátegui might have had a "kind of inflammatory tuberculosis," and disputed the suggestion of an "infantile diabetic" condition.

67. *Apuntes*, 2 (1948):497–508.

68. *Apuntes*, 2 (1948):508, 513. After the Chosica meeting, another took place with a greater number of delegates attending from different parts of the country. That meeting may have taken place in Lima on May 28, 1930. Sometime after Mariátegui's death, Ravines proposed the line, "we must finish with *Amautismo.*" Interview with Dr. Hugo Pesce, September 7, 1966, Lima. Since the Buenos Aires Congress the South American Bureau had been seeking to undermine the Lima group by dealing directly with provincial contacts, the Cuzco group being a case in point. Interview, Antonio Navarro Madrid, August 24, 1966, Lima.

69. On the subject of his return to Peru, his integration into Mariátegui's circle, and the events following Mariátegui's death, Ravines remained silent. *Yenan Way*, p. 89.

70. E. J. Hobsbawm, *Las revoluciones burguesas* (Madrid, 1971), p. 11.

Epilog

1. See Doll, "Mariátegui y el marxismo;" Melis, "Mariátegui, primer marxista de América," *Casa de las Américas;* Paris, "El marxismo de Mariátegui," *Aportes;* Meseguer Illan's *José Carlos Mariátegui y su pensamiento revolucionario;* and, Francisco Posada Zárate, *Los orígines del pensamiento marxista en Latinoamérica: política y cultura en José Carlos Mariátegui* (Madrid 1968).

2. Such is the tone of Paris's "El marxismo de Mariátegui," shrouded in his usual suspended ambiquity which seems in the end to conclude that Mariátegui was not a Marxist.

3. "Mensaje al congreso obrero," *Amauta* 2 (1927): 35.

4. *Apuntes*, 2 (1948):403.

5. *Historia en el Perú*, p. 524.

6. "Nacionalismo y vanguardismo," *Mundial*, November 27, 1925. This is one of the most important texts for understanding Mariategui's grasp of a revolutionary nationalism.

7. Víctor Andrés Belaúnde, *La realidad nacional* (Lima, 1964), p. 11.

8. Quoted in Paris's *préface* to 7 *Essais d'interprétation de la réalité péruvienne* (Paris, 1968), pp. 16–17. The statement is from October 1928.

9. "México y la revolución," *Variedades*, January 5, 1924.

10. Prolog to Luis E. Valcárcel's *Tempestad en los andes* (Lima, pp. 14–15.

11. Horace B. Davis, *Nationalism and Socialism* (New York, 1967), pp. 66–68.

12. Quoted in Meseguer, *José Carlos Mariátegu . . .* , p. 192.

13. Paris's *préface*, p. 17.

14. Quoted in: Carlos Manuel Cox, "Reflexiones sobre José Carlos Mariátegui," *Claridad*, July 1934.

15. The statement is from the letter circulated to the APRA cells abroad. *Apuntes*, 2 (1948):301.

16. See V. M. Miroshevsky's "El 'populismo' en el Perú, papel de Mariátegui en la historia del pensaminento social latinoamericano," *Dialéctica*, 1 (1942): 45; and Paris's *préface*, pp. 19–21.

17. Letter from Mariátegui to M. Arroyo Posadas, Jauja, Perú, dated July 30, 1929, quoted in Arroyo Posadas, "A propósito del artículo 'El populismo en el Perú,' de V. Miroshevsky," *Dialéctica*, (1946): 13.

18. Miroshevsky, "El 'populismo' en el Perú," p. 48.

19. Abelardo Solis, *Ante el problema agrario peruano* (Lima, 1928), p. 223; and Paris, "José Carlos Mariátegui et le modèle du 'communisme Inca'," p. 1072.

20. Martínez de la Torre, *Apuntes*, 2 (1948):416–17.

21. Ibid., p. 400; and *El movimiento revolucionario latinoamericano . . .* , p. 98.

22. "Principios de política agraria nacional," *Mundial*, July, 1927; and *Apuntes*, 2 (1948):401.

23. *Labor*, September 7, 1929.

24. *Apuntes*, 2 (1948):464.

25. Paris's *préface*, p. 28.

26. *Apuntes*, 2 (1948):421.

27. Rouillón, *La creación heroica*, p. 87; Carnero Checa, *La acción escrita*, p. 80; and Eugenio Chang-Rodríguez, *La literatura política de González Prada*, pp. 151–59. According to an important personal recollection, Mariátegui as an adult man "was not free from a certain fear of illness and a fear of death." Testimonial communicated via M. Michel Barton, from Dr. Jean Otten, Geneve, Switzerland, who lived in Mariátegui's home as a boarder between December 1925 and July 1928. Dated September 10, 1975.

28. Arroyo Posadas, "A propósito del artículo," p. 30.

29. Waldo Frank, "A Communication, José Carlos Mariátegui," *The New Republic*, 58 (1930): 182; Angela Ramos, who met Mariátegui when he returned from Europe and became a close friend, reported how he had an "immediate impact" on people, communication, January 29, 1973; according to Dr. Otten, the dominant traits of his personality were "integrity and sincerity." He further described him as a man with a "golden heart," who if he sometimes appeared calculating it was because of his "carefully thoughtful approach to all problems." Testimonial, September 10, 1975.

30. Erik H. Erikson, *Gandhi's Truth* (New York, 1969), p. 41.

Bibliographical Essay

It is not the purpose of this essay to list all the sources consulted in the preparation of this study of José Carlos Mariátegui and Peru during the years 1870–1930, but to indicate and comment on some of the principal sources used in Part Two. For a comprehensive account of all the sources used the reader is referred to the footnotes. Of the various bibliographies consulted, I will mention only three: Alberto Tauro, *Amauta y su influencia* (Lima, 1960); Guillermo Rouillón, *Bio-Bibliografía de José Carlos Mariátegui* (Lima, 1963); and Jorge Basadre, *Introducción a las bases documentales para la historia de la República del Perú con algunas reflexiones*, 2 vols. (Lima, 1971).

Primary Sources

Mariátegui's Complete Works

Colección Obras Completas was prepared in various editions by the Empresa Editora Amauta, and includes *Amauta, Labor, La Razón, Nuestra Epoca,* the column *Voces,* and some articles from the periods 1914–19 and 1923–30. Here I will not identify the various editions that I used of some works, but the footnotes do. *Obras Completas* includes *La escena contemporánea* and the *Siete ensayos;* the two works Mariátegui prepared for publication but did not see published, *La defensa del marxismo* and *El alma matinal;* and the hundreds of articles (including the lecture notes of the UPGP series and a novel) that Mariátegui published around common themes, like *Peruanicemos al Perú* and *Figuras*

221

y aspectos de la vida mundial (asterisks denote the volumes organized by Mariátegui).

*Vol. 1:   *La escena contemporánea*
*Vol. 2:   *Siete ensayos de interpretación de la realidad peruana*
*Vol. 3:   *El alma matinal y otras estaciones del hombre de hoy*
*Vol. 4:   *La novela y la vida: Siegfried y el profesor Canella*
*Vol. 5:   *Defensa del marxismo*
*Vol. 6:   *El artista y la época*
*Vol. 7:   *Signos y obras*
*Vol. 8:   *Historia de la crisis mundial*
 Vol. 9:   *Poemas a Mariátegui*
 Vol. 10: *José Carlos Mariátegui, etapas de su vida,* Por María Wiesse.
*Vol. 11: *Peruanicemos al Perú*
*Vol. 12: *Temas de nuestra América*
*Vol. 13: *Ideología y política*
*Vol. 14: *Temas de educación*
*Vol. 15: *Cartas de Italia*
*Vol. 16: *Figuras y aspectos de la vida mundial*
*Vol. 17: *Figuras y aspectos de la vida mundial*
*Vol. 18: *Figuras y aspectos de la vida mundial*
 Vol. 19: *Amauta y su influencia,* Por Alberto Tauro.
 Vol. 20: *Mariátegui y su tiempo,* Por Armando Bazán.

Amauta (Journal. Thirty-two numbers between September 1926 and August-September 1930. Ricardo Martínez de la Torre assumed the direction of the last four numbers.)

Labor (Newspaper. Ten numbers, edición en facsímile, Lima 1974.)

La Razón (Newspaper. Twenty-eight numbers consulted, May 14, 1919, to July 22, 1919.)

Nuestra Epoca (Journal. Two numbers, June 22, 1918, and July 6, 1918.)

Voces (Newspaper column. Entire series consulted; beginning July 17, 1916, and written almost daily, until January 23, 1919, in *El Tiempo*.)

Articles (all written by Mariátegui and listed chronologically.)

Juan Croniqueur. "Del momento. La muerte de Juarés." *La Prensa* (August 3, 1914).
———. "Nuestro teatro y su actual período de surgimiento." *La Prensa* (January 3, 1914).
———. "Del momento. Recordando al prócer." *La Prensa* (March 12, 1915).
———. "Del momento. Lima a los ojos del Sr. James Bryce." *La Prensa* (April 15, 1915).
X.Y.Z.. "Un discurso." *La Prensa* (April 30, 1916).
Juan Croniqueur, "Cartas a X," *La Prensa* (June 7, 1916).
———. "El crimen del balneario," *El Tiempo* (July 30, 1916).
José Carlos Mariátegui. "Oración al espíritu inmortal de Leonidas Yerovi," *El Tiempo* (February 17, 1917).
El cronista criollo. "La procesión tradicional," *El Tiempo* (April 12, 1917).
"La cuestión del Ruhr y la gran crisis europea," *La Crónica* (April 15, 1923).
"El ocaso de la civilización europea," *Claridad*, 1 (May 1923). (Mariátegui published several versions on the theme of this article, including the preceding citation, and spoke about it in interviews upon his return from Europe.)
"La crisis universitaria." *Claridad*, 2 (May 1923).
"Las universidades populares." *Claridad*, 4 (January 1924).
"Lenin," *Claridad*. 5 (March 1924).
"Palabras de Mariátegui." *Claridad*, 6 (September 1924).
"La conjuración comunista." *La Prensa* (June 11, 1927).
"Prologue" to Luis E. Valcarcel's *Tempestad en los Andes* (Lima 1927).
"The New Peru," *The Nation* (January 16, 1929).
"Israel y occidente; Israel y el mundo." *Repertorio Hebreo* (April-May 1929).
"Respuesta al cuestionario no. 4 del 'S. de C.P.'." *La Sierra* (June 1929?).
"El problema de palestina." *Repertorio Hebreo* (July-August 1929).
"Raza, economía y cultura en la cuestión indígena," *El Nacional* (Mexico City: January 18, 1930).
"Carta al Sr. Dr. Raúl Porras Barrenechea," *Mercurio Peruano* (March-April 1930).

In addition, Ricardo Martínez de la Torre's *Apuntes para una interpretación marxista de historia social del Perú*, 4 vols. (Lima, 1948) and *El movimiento revolucionario latinoamericano: Versiones de la primera conferencia comunista latinoamericana Junio de 1929* (Buenos Aires, 1929), especially the former, contain important primary source documentation, written by Mariátegui. *Apuntes*, especially volume 2, contains some important letters, several autobiographic memoranda, all the important documents pertaining to the organizing of the PSP and the CGTP, the theses to the Buenos Aires Party Congress, parts of the proceedings contained in *El movimiento revolucionario*, and so forth. Some of these documents have been reproduced in vol. 13 of the *Obras Completas, Ideología y política*, but the *Apuntes* remain a central evidentiary source for students of Mariátegui's 1920s activities.

Manuscripts

In August 1968, I obtained copies of nineteen letters exchanged between José Carlos Mariátegui and Samuel Glusberg from the latter in Santiago de Chile. Sr. Glusberg indicated they had exchanged more letters between 1927 and 1930, but these were all that he kept. Glusberg first published some fragments of this correspondence under the psuedonym, Enrique Espinoza, in: "José Carlos Mariátegui a través de su correspondencia," *Trinchera* (Buenos Aires, 1932). The dates of the letters are: January 10, 1927; April 30, 1927; September 30, 1927; July 4, 1928; November 7, 1928; May 10, 1929; June 10, 1929; June 20, 1929; August 21, 1929; November 7, 1929; November 21, 1929; November 29, 1929; December 18, 1929; February 9, 1930; February 18, 1930; February 26, 1930; March 6, 1930; March 11, 1930; March 25, 1930.

Interviews and Testimonials

The interviews were done mostly in 1966 and during the summer of 1968. They were not recorded because I discovered that taping inhibited the flow of the discussion. All interviews are identified by dates and places. Interviews which stand out because of personal contact with Mariátegui and quality of the information were: for the pre-1919 and European period, Humberto del Aguila and César Falcón; for the period of the UPGP lectures and Haya's Partido Nacionalista incident, Esteban Pavletich and Euodocio Ravines; for Mariátegui's years of maturity 1924–30, the indispensable sources were Dr. Hugo Pesce and Ricardo Martínez de la Torre. They were the individuals closest to Mariátegui. Pesce knew his medical history intimately, and Martínez de la Torre acted as Mariátegui's chief of staff and political representative. Perhaps Martínez de la Torre was closer to Mariátegui's thinking than Pesce, who was more of an internationalist. The former was also more integrated into the operations of Mariátegui's publishing ventures and political activities. Finally, the two Ravines interviews were remarkable due to his incredible perceptiveness and quality and range of the information. These two interviews were especially useful for understanding the relationship between Haya de la Torre and Mariátegui.

Humberto del Aguila, February 19, 1966; September 20, 1966; October 29, 1966; Lima.
Luciano Castillo, July 15, 1968, Lima.
César Falcón, November 29, 1966, Mexico City.
Anita Chiappe de Mariátegui, May 1, 1966; July 26, 1966; and September 26, 1966, Lima.
Ricardo Martínez de la Torre, November 3, 1965; November 18, 1965; September 8, 1966; October 12, 1966; October 18, 1966, Lima.
Héctor Merel, January 31, 1966; May 27, 1966; July 9, 1968, Lima.
Antonio Navarro Madrid, August 24, 1966, Lima.
Esteban Pavletich, November 9, 1966 and July 19, 1968, Lima.
Dr. Hugo Pesce, June 25, 1966; September 7, 1966; October 28, 1966; August 31, 1968, Lima.
Julio Portocarrero, July 21, 1968, Lima.
Eudocio Ravines, October 20, 1966 and July 16, 1968, Lima
Guillermo Rouillón, August 15, 1966 and July 25, 1968, Lima.

Several testimonials facilitated even more information of a personal nature. Dr. Hugo Pesce gave me a signed statement summarizing his medical diagnosis of Mariátegui's always problematic health and illnesses since his adolescence, dated October 28, 1966. On the basis of his diagnosis, medical sources at the UCLA Medical School indicated he may have suffered from a "diabetic condition of juvenile form that later turned into a chronic osteomyelitis." In 1968, Pesce commented on their suggestions. Angela Ramos, a close friend of Mariátegui's since 1923, sent me a testimonial of her remembrances, most of which shed further light on Mariátegui's personality. On September 10, 1975, Dr. Jean Otten transmitted via Michel Barton, Geneva, an invaluable communication. Otten lived in Mariátegui's home from December 1925 to July 1928, struck a very close friendship with Mariátegui and Pesce, and became a kind of nurse to Mariátegui. Because of Otten's discreet manner, Mariátegui established a very close personal relationship with him even to the point of seeking him out whenever he felt particularly frustrated and like letting off steam and crying. At times Mariátegui would break "into terrible bursts of white anger," but they did not last long and then he returned to his quiet even shy way of being. Dr. Otten felt that his physical handicap and his smallness "affected him psychologically." Other testimonials invaluable to this study were one from Dr. Javier Mariátegui, the youngest of four sons, dated January 19, 1969, which supplied me with important information on his father's childhood, the ultimate source apparently being his uncle, Sr. Julio César Mariátegui. Martínez de la Torre, an invaluable and patient source, responded to my queries with a communication of March 17, 1967, in which he once more clarified questions dealing with the International and the Buenos Aires conference.

Secondary Works

Books and Dissertations

The literature on Mariátegui can be easily divided into two camps; the early works of individuals who knew him and who wrote more frequently than not from a political point of view, and more recent and scholarly works. Of the early works, those by members of the generation of 1919 stand out, and especially the writings of Luis Alberto Sánchez and Jorge Basadre.

For Mariátegui's family origins, early childhood, and coming of age up to 1919, there is no better source than Guillermo Rouillón's *La creación heroica de José Carlos Mariátegui* (Lima, 1975), vol. 1. Earlier, in his *Bio-Bibliografía,* Rouillón made known his uncovering of Mariátegui's true birthdate and birthplace, unknown even to Mariátegui. Rouillón's recent volume is based on countless personal testimonials and interviews, among the most valuable being those from Mariátegui's own mother and his uncle, Juan Campos La Chira. This initial volume of a projected larger work is a mine of factual information, some of which I corroborated independently. Frequently, however, the author assumes an omniscient style, purports to know his subject's most inner thoughts, and at times even reconstructs unsubstantiated dialog. Nevertheless this is an indispensable work.

In 1964, Genaro Carnero Checa, a longtime militant of the Peruvian Communist Party, published *La acción escrita* (Lima), the first serious book-length study of Mariátegui by a Peruvian. Carnero Checa's originality was to interpret Mariátegui's life history from the perspective of his professional career as a journalist. The substance of the work is his review of Limanean journalism, and Mariátegui's place in it, during the years 1914–19, but his coverage of the years 1920–30 is also adequate. A source used by Carnero Checa, and invaluable in its own right, is Luis Monguió's *La poesía postmodernista peruana* (Mexico City, 1954). Monguió's study is a crucial source for considering the changing currents and undercurrents of Peruvian literature from 1900 to the 1920s. His treatment of the *Colónida* circle, of the prewar and postwar literary mood, of the upsurge of *indigenismo* and *vanguardismo* in the 1920s is incomparable. More specifically, he situates Mariátegui quite beautifully within the literary milieu of his times. Monguió moreover writes about literature with a concern for the social and political context of individuals and groups. Just as important, but written from a different vantage point, is Luis Alberto Sánchez's lovely *Valdelomar o la belle époque* (Mexico City, 1969). Sánchez, one of the great stylists of twentieth-century Peruvian letters, gives us a gossipy, informative, brilliant reconstruction of Valdelomar's literary coming of age, including some important references to Valdelomar's friendship with Mariátegui. Sánchez knew personally many of the principals, and writes with an uncanny ability for creating a sense of mood and place. Of course, he also writes from a social and political perspective, and his works should always be read critically.

In addition to works principally dealing with the years 1914–19, we have general or particular interpretations and assessments dealing with the years of maturity, 1920–30. Luis Alberto Sánchez has referred to Mariátegui in most of his major works including: *La literatura peruana*, 5 vols. (Lima, 1965–66); *Haya de la Torre o el político* (Santiago, 1936); and his magisterial *Testimonio personal: memorias de un peruano del siglo XX*, 3 vols. (Lima, 1969). Everytime Sánchez writes about Mariátegui he fortunately has something new to say, or takes a different tack making all of his references an important source. Sánchez is not a very adequate source for an interpretation of the Mariátegui-Haya de la Torre split, which he deals with mainly in personal terms. Nor is Sánchez a good source for establishing chronology. But his writings are indispensable; one especially memorable recollection being his physical description and characterization of Mariátegui in his early 1920s in the *Testimonio personal*, vol. 1. Sánchez is especially good for understanding relationships among individuals, for insights into personality and incisive descriptions, and for an almost incomparable firsthand knowledge of most things of importance in Peruvian public life since World War I. Jorge Basadre has also given us his appreciation of

Mariátegui in two of his principal works, *Perú: problema y posibilidad* (Lima, 1931), and in his indispensable *Historia de de la República del Peru*, 11 vols. (Lima, 1968). Basadre, almost alone, has consistently insisted on the unique and indeed original quality of Mariátegui's thought since the first appearance of *Problema*. His concern for solid evidence and for accuracy makes of his various summaries remarkably lucid portraits. Of all the descriptions that I gathered from sundry sources on Mariátegui's personal style in the mid and late 1920s, the one that seemed the truest was Basadre's appearing in the *Historia*, 9:4203. With incredible brevity Basadre evoked his look, his mannerisms, the quality of his speech, his sense of humor, and the way he carried himself, making of his description an extraordinary portrait. Most recently, in his *Conversaciones* with Pablo Macera (Lima, 1974), Basadre has emphasized once again, in the strongest terms he has ever used, his view on the originality of Mariátegui's contribution to Peruvian social thought, something he first proposed in *Problema*.

Armando Bazán, whose *Biografía de José Carlos Mariátegui* (Santiago, 1939) later became a part, in a revised and expanded edition, of the *Obras Completas* with the title, *Mariátegui y su tiempo*, vol. 20, also knew Mariátegui personally. Indeed Bazán served as his secretary for a time, and knew him since his return from Europe (they met after the first UPGP lecture). To Bazán he confided some of his most private thoughts about his European experiences, and how they had affected him personally. Specially important is his confession to Bazán about when he "became" a communist in his own consciousness. Another biography, useful mostly for what it reports about everyday scenes at the Mariátegui household, is María Wiesse's *José Carlos Mariátegui* (Lima, 1959), later also incorporated into the *Obras Completas* as vol. 10. María Wiesse visited the Mariátegui home frequently with her husband, the painter José Sabogal. To the Wiesse biography we owe the story of how Mariátegui almost died during the illness of 1924 because his mother, ultrareligious, would not allow the doctors to amputate his leg. Only when Mariátegui's wife appeared and gave her approval were the doctors able to operate, which saved his life.

In contrast, Ravines, who first met Mariátegui during the excitement of 1919, and later became a close political ally for a while after his break with Haya de la Torre of 1927, gives us a thoroughly engaging political recollection. Moreover the work, *The Yenan Way* (New York, 1951), is an invaluable source for Latin American left-wing politics during the post–World War I period. Ravines offers some remarkably lucid testimony on the 1920s, including exceptionally perceptive estimates of individuals and of the Aprista network and its milieu. At the same time, Ravines contributed considerably to circulating the gloss that Mariátegui was "only an intellectual" and a "mystic" in the 1930s and 1940s, which is also done in the *Yenan Way* though in a subdued fashion. Jorge del Prado's *Mariátegui y su obra* (Lima, 1946), offers one last contribution by someone who knew Mariátegui. It offers some useful information on how Mariátegui viewed the APRA, and on the intensive organizational efforts of 1928 and 1929. Del Prado, then a university student, joined Mariátegui along with other students and were promptly recruited as organizers. Del Prado worked initially in the Callao area, and later in Morococha.

We now pass on to a very partisan literature. It includes books by: Harry Kantor, *The Ideology and Program of the Peruvian Aprista Movement* (Berkeley, 1953); Víctor Alba, *Historia del comunismo en América Latina* (Mexico City, 1954); Eugenio Chang-Rodríquez, *La literatura política de González Prada, Mariátegui y Haya de la Torre* (Mexico City, 1957); Robert J. Alexander, *Communism in Latin America* (New Brunswick, 1957); and Rollie Poppino, *International Communism in Latin America* (London, 1964). There are numerous other titles. Chang-Rodríguez's study is representative of this literature, his main purpose being to show Mariátegui was not a communist but a disciple of Haya de la Torre and an Aprista. Chang dedicated seventy-four pages to Mariátegui, in which he provided a general survey of his life starting with childhood. Unfortunately, his book offered no new data, not even from the Aprista side.

Augusto Salazar Bondy's *Historia de las ideas en el Perú*, 2 vols. (Lima, 1965) is a very different kind of work. Salazar Bondy, at once sympathetic and critical, presents a discussion of Mariátegui's ideas that is outstanding for its fairness and balance. Salazar Bondy did not situate Mariátegui within his corresponding intellectual milieu, either nationally or internationally, in a dynamic fashion. Moreover, his exegesis is perhaps excessively academic. But for those interested in the philosophical roots of Mariátegui's thought this is still one of the best available sources.

John M. Baines recently published the first book-length study of Mariátegui done in this country: *Revolution in Peru: Mariátegui and the Myth* (University, Ala., 1972). Here the author too assumes a sympathetic attitude toward his subject, but in this case he never really establishes contact with him or his reality. Instead what we get is an evaluation of Mariátegui's role as a "transitional figure," viewed so from a comparative politics perspective, one which unfortunately is seriously lacking in historical accuracy. One of the main redeeming features of the work is that Baines figures among the first commentators to call attention to the importance of Henri Barbusse to Mariátegui's intellectual and personal development. In contrast, Harry E. Vanden has given us a very useful book, *Mariátegui, influencias en su formación ideológica* (Lima, 1975). Vanden's original contribution rests on his meticulous inventory of the books in Mariátegui's personal library, and his discussion of the problem of intellectual influences from this vantage point. The book contains some excellent information, but his meticulous methods of collection do not yield significant new directions of inquiry at this time, though he continues apparently to work on a larger project. It does confirm and expands on Baine's suggestion regarding the importance of Barbusse. The project of reconstructing Mariátegui's library presents several problems, among them, as both Pesce and Martínez de la Torre suggested, the fact that Mariátegui lent out many of his books which were never returned.

The final title of this section, which also appears as a disertation, is the excellent book by Diego Meseguer Illan, *José Carlos Mariátegui y su pensamiento revolucionario* (Lima, 1974). Meseguer gives us a sophisticated discussion of Mariátegui's thinking and its European sources. The particular strength of his work lies in its familiarity with the European intellectual and political context of Mariátegui's formation. This is perhaps also its particular weakness, that it emphasizes Europe at the expense of Peru. We are much indebted to Meseguer nonetheless for a truly excellent discussion of the European sources of Mariátegui's creative Peruvian synthesis.

Dissertations

In this category we find the most able exegesis available to date on Mariátegui's intellectual formation: Robert Paris's "La formation ideólogigue de José Carlos Mariátegui," Thèse présentée por le titre de Docteur de Troisième Cycle à l'Ecole Pratique des Hautes Etudes [VI° Section], Paris, 1969. Without question Paris's thesis represents the most critical historical analysis written from a Marxist perspective. His knowledge of Marxism and of the figures principal to Mariátegui's intellectual formation, e.g., Gobetti, Sorel, Croce, Nietzsche, etc., combined with his own exceptional talents for criticizing the text and discourse results in a most sophisticated performance. But his work, varied and extensive, as we shall see is not without some problems. First of all there is the quality of his own writing style, perhaps an excessive version of the *Annales* style with its half-finished questions . . . broken sentences . . . the inconclusive syntax, its parentheses. Second, the perspective of the author is Althusserian, which, as Mariátegui might have said, conflicts "in spirit" to the school of praxis of which Mariátegui was a representative. Consequently Paris, in his scientific approach, adheres religiously to the text analyzing the subtlest of nuance. But Mariátegui, the historical person, never appears, and his existential historical reality remains inconclusive. Hence his uniqueness as a Peruvian nationalist is underplayed and hardly recognized. But even with its flaws, Paris's work is a truly remarkable achievement in textual criticism, and his dissertation broke new ground in evidence provided from interviews or letters from European figures, such as Umberto Terracini. Another important dissertation already appeared above as a published work, Diego Meseguer's "L'Idee de revolutión dans la pensée de José Carlos Mariátegui," Thèse présentée pour le titre de Docteur de Troisième Cycle à l'École Pratique des Hautes Études (June 1969), 2 vols. Since I already commented on this work above I will not repeat myself here. I submitted my own dissertation to UCLA in 1967, entitled: "José Carlos Mariátegui, Revolutionary Nationalist; The Origins and Crisis of Modern Peruvian Nationalism, 1870–1930." As its cumbersome title suggests, the approach was clearly that of Mariátegui as nationalist; as a figure very much the product of a uniquely nationalist age,

232   *BIBLIOGRAPHICAL ESSAY*

the era 1870–1930. Very recently, Elizabeth Garrells received approval (1974) for her doctoral dissertation submitted to Harvard University: "The Young Mariátegui and His World (1894–1919)."

Katherine Bierlmeier submitted in 1946 to Columbia University one of the first graduate theses done in this country on Mariátegui. The title of her work was, "José Carlos Mariátegui, Modern Interpreter of Peru."

Pamphlets

Robert Paris published his first extended treatment of Mariátegui's intellectual formation as a pamphlet entitled, *Mariátegui e Gobetti*, Centro Studi Piero Gobetti (Torino, 1967). His first-hand knowledge of the Italian and generally European period during which Mariátegui lived and traveled in Europe allowed him to situate Mariátegui incomparably. This is the standard discussion of the problem of Gobetti's influence as a personal model and intellectual kindred spirit. Francisco Posada's *Los origenes del pensamiento marxista en latinoamérica* (Havana, 1968), offers a less original but still useful commentary on Mariátegui's Marxism and his aesthetics. Its major flaw lies in that instead of letting his subject be himself, Posada follows in the tradition of focusing on his "errors" as a Marxist theorist and on whether or not he was a Marxist. Posada views Mariátegui wholly from the perspective of European Marxism, and hardly touches on the nationalist strain of his thought. The method of the writer is to focus wholly on the text, and his outlook indicates an Althusserian affinity.

La formazione ideologica di José Carlos Mariátegui, Estratto dagli Annali della Foundazione Luigi Einaudi, vol. 4 (Torino, 1970), by Robert Paris, summarizes the beginning chapters of his doctral dissertation. Here Paris deals with the pre-1919 epoch, using the standard sources. Two other interesting pamphlets are: Julián Huanay's *Mariátegui y los sindicatos* (Lima, 1956), and Gaetano Foresta's "Pirandello e Mariátegui," *Nuova Antologia di Lettere, Arti e Scienze* (1967): 513–26. Huanay's pamphlet is a delight. He knew Mariátegui, and worked with the Lima vanguard as a syndicalist organizer. His pamphlet, a collection of some basic articles and workers' manifestoes, is done with en-

dearing simplicity and affection. More than a source of information, it provides evidence on the feeling workers had for
Mariátegui. Foresta's pamphlet is a brief, not very original, but
interesting discussion of Mariátegui's appreciation of Pirandello.

Articles

Mentioned here are only some of the leading articles consulted, those which contributed to an understanding of various
aspects, noted in the commentary, concerning Mariátegui's
youth and maturity.

Alberto Ulloa S., *"La escena contemporánea* por José Carlos
Mariátegui," *Mercurio Peruano,* January 1926, a brief review,
contains an interesting biographic reference to Mariátegui's early
"promise," as perceived by those working with him at *La
Prensa.* Ulloa's review reflects the praiseful reception given to
Mariátegui's first published book, which established him as a
leading voice of the Limanean intelligentsia in the mid 1920s. J.
Guillermo Guevara's "Oportunismo indigenista," *La Sierra,* 1
(1927), in contrast, reflects a contrary view. Guevara, director of
La Sierra, an indigenista journal, and an Aprista fellow-traveler,
leveled a stinging personal attack against Mariátegui, to which
the latter never replied. In 1929, nevertheless Mariátegui published an important reply to a questionnaire in *La Sierra.*

Federico More's "José Carlos Mariátegui y la generación infor-
tunada," *Mundial,* April 19, 1930, is written in an entirely different spirit. Occasioned by Mariátegui's death, this eulogy called the generation of Yerovi, Valdelomar, and Mariátegui "mis-
fortuned," because they all died young, before producing their
most mature work. More's eulogy is particularly poignant for its
moral passion, inasmuch as his own outward personal style was
one of great cynicism. He wrote: "Entre nosotros—vale decir,
entre los escritores peruanos—Mariátegui ha sido, apesar de su
juventud, el más serio, el más disciplinado, el más limpio." Several months after Mariátegui's death, Alberto Ulloa S., one of
the few true liberals in Peru, published the important "José Carlos Mariátegui," *Nueva Revista Peruana,* ll (1930), which provides us with a beautiful reconstruction of the ambience at *La
Prensa* during the years Mariátegui worked there and with a remarkably prescient interpretation of Mariátegui's life history.

Ulloa gives us a perceptive portrait, presenting Mariátegui as a
nationalist who came to his nationalism via his interpretation of
international contemporary events. Ulloa further suggests, and
correctly I believe, that Mariátegui's own personal style was
greatly influenced by the style of *La Prensa;* especially its prin-
cipled political posture, its worldly understanding of things, its
quiet elegance and sensitivity to form. And it is in fact true that
Mariátegui had a great respect and admiration for the personal
style of those he called the "true liberals," whom he viewed as
"revolutionary figures" in the sense that to the degree that
liberalism fulfilled itself to that degree it paved the way for
socialism. Ulloa also attributes the "improvisational" nature of
Mariátegui's thought and writings to a journalistic style, and also
dwells on his tendency towards a mysticism and a "Christian
humility." This is unquestionably an indispensable source written by someone who knew him well. Estuardo Núñez also knew
Mariátegui personally, and his "José Carlos Mariátegui y su ex-
periencia italiana," *Cuadernos Americanos,* 6 (1964) is just as
important. Núñez covers a different aspect of Mariátegui's development, his romance with Italian culture (he greatly admired
Italian renaissance art for instance for its simplicity and clarity).
Núñez even suggests that Mariátegui perfected his writing style
in Italy: "A clear style, crystaline, sharp, dynamic, incisive,
lacerating." Núñez, who worked on *Amauta,* brings to the essay
a personal slant but also the authority of his scholarly, critical
outlook. This is another vital source, though I will mention one
reservation. The author perhaps overemphasizes the importance
of Italy to Mariátegui's intellectual formation at the expense of
the French influence. Barbusse and *Clarté,* both represented as
we have seen iconic experiences for him, as Armando Bazán
clearly showed.

When the University of Texas decided to publish an English
version of the *Siete ensayos,* they naturally turned for an introduction to the one man who has written in the most consistently
balanced manner about Mariátegui, Jorge Basadre ["Introduction," *Seven Interpretive Essays on Peruvian Reality* (Austin and
London, 1971)]. Basadre's biographic sketches are deservedly
famous; he employs the perspicacity of a novelist for developing
character, and has a brilliant gift for evoking mood and clean
description.

With Carlos Manuel Cox, "Reflexiones sobre José Carlos Mariátegui," *Claridad*, July 1934, we return to polemical aprista literature. For propagandistic reasons, the APRA has actively sought to on the one hand discredit Mariátegui for being a "Europeanized" and mystical intellectual and not a "man of action," and on the other insisting that he was an aprista, which he most definitely was not. Mariátegui, as Cox's own article clearly indicates, endorsed the proposal for an APRA, which he understood conceptually as a united front. Later, when Haya presented the APRA as a middle-class revolutionary national party Mariátegui immediately broke with Haya and the APRA. Cox's article is important because of two quotations from a letter written by Mariátegui to Haya, which should be read as an endorsement of the APRA as a united front. Juan Vargas's three articles—"En defensa de José Carlos Mariátegui, marxista," *Claridad*, August 1934; "José Carlos Mariátegui y la realidad de América Latina," *Claridad*, August 1936 and September 1936— do a better job of pilloring the APRA than of defending Mariátegui against the assertions of the Cox article of 1934.

With Ramón Doll's "Política sociológica: *Siete ensayos de interpretación de la realidad peruana,* por José Carlos Mariátegui," *Mercurio Peruano*, May-June 1929, we turn to the significant articles written by people who did not know Mariátegui. Doll followed his review of the *Seven Essays*, with "Mariátegui y el marxismo," *Crítica* (Buenos Aires, 1930). Of the two, the latter is the most original and perceptive. Doll writes from a liberal-social democratic standpoint, most notably in the review of the *Siete ensayos*, and also from a Europeanist perspective. Not surprising, his style is most reactive when dealing with the indigenismo of the seven essays which he calls "bold" and "utopian." The review is nevertheless somewhat contradictory in that it also conceives the work as a "bolshevik work." More important is the review of the *Defensa*. In *Crítica*, Doll interprets Mariátegui's text with uncommon perspicacity, and gives us a sharp and feeling portrait of Mariátegui on the verge of becoming a Marxist man of praxis. Doll distinguishes, in the mode of Croce, between the Marxist intellectual and the Marxist man of action; the writer of the *Siete ensayos* he sees as being representative of the former and of the *Defensa* of the latter. In looking at the *Defensa*, he focused mostly on its polemical style, saying it smacked of a man who has abandoned theory and who prizes praxis more highly.

Less interesting but nonetheless worthwhile are two French reviews: Louis Baudin's "*Siete ensayos de interpretación de la realidad peruana*, par José Carlos Mariátegui," *Revue de l'Amerique Latine*, 19 (1930), and Francisco Contreras, "Lettres hispano-américaines. L'esprit colonial et le désarroi continental," *Mercure de France*, 241 (1933). Baudin's critique is not particularly enlightening, very reactive, and he reads much meaning into the *Seven essays*. Perhaps the fundamental problem lies in that Baudin would have Mariátegui write in an academic style. Writing from the perspective of a cold rationalism, Baudin reproaches Mariátegui his moral passion which he largely interprets as "mysticism." Contreras's review gently criticizes Mariátegui's indigenismo but mostly limits itself to reconstructing admirably the anti-colonialist attitude of the *Siete ensayos*.

V. M. Miroshevsky's "El 'populismo' en el Perú, papel de Mariátegui en la historia del pensamiento social latinoamericano," *Dialéctica*, 1 (1942), surely represents the most controversial interpretation of Mariátegui done by a Russian Marxist scholar. Miroshevsky's essay, originally published in the 1930s, reflected the criticism voiced by Codovilla and Ravines; namely that Mariátegui had misunderstood the revolutionary potential of the urban proletariat, that he had evolved from a petit bourgeois socialism to become a propagandist for a "peasant socialist revolution." Miroshevsky added a number of other propositions, sufficiently controversial to elicit an editorial clarification from the *Dialéctica* staff and also the heated responses of: Jorge del Prado, "Mariátegui, marxista-leninista," *Dialéctica* 3 (1943) and of M. Arroyo Posadas, "A propósito del artículo, 'El populismo en el Perú,' de V. M. Miroshevsky," *Dialéctica* 17 (1946). Both reacted very strongly to Miroshevsky, an attitude perhaps reflective of their party situation in Peru at the time. Among the barbarities alleged by Miroshevsky, were two saying how Mariátegui saw the fundamental contradiction of Peruvian society in terms of the conflict between the "indigenous peasant community dwellers" and the "bourgeois white large estate owners," and that he never abandoned "his romantic nationalist posture." Instead of focusing their rejoinders on such substantive points, del Prado and Posadas stress Mariátegui's credentials as a Marxist-

Leninist. But their articles, besides shining with an admirable loyalty to Mariátegui's memory, are important because they knew and worked politically with Mariátegui. Del Prado gives us some informative estimates of their organizing efforts and adds some significant data revealing of Mariátegui's political attitudes. Posadas's includes a quotation from a letter he received in Jauja from Mariátegui, dated July 30, 1929, that is a very damaging estimate of the APRA, and another from a party directive drafted by Mariátegui.

In 1955, Guillermo Rouillón contributed a prologue to a Chilean edition of the *Siete ensayos de interpretación de la realidad peruana* (Santiago, 1955). Though not as important as his later *Bio-Bibliografía* where he presented data based on a baptismal record altering the birthdate and birthplace of Mariátegui, this brief sketch included some little known personal information on Mariátegui's childhood, always the strong point of Rouillón's writings on Mariátegui. S. Semionov and A. Shulgovski's "El papel de José Carlos Mariátegui en la formación del Partido Comunista del Perú," *Hora del Hombre*, 1 (1960) [which first appeared in the Moscow publication, *La Historia Moderna y Contemporánea* (1957)] is a study in contrast to the earlier Miroshevsky article. Semionov and Shulgovski approach Mariátegui from the standpoint of national movements of liberation in colonial and neocolonial areas. Theirs is a tightly reasoned argument. Working in the Russian archives, they also offer us some original data from the publications: *La Correspondencia Internacional* and *El Trabajador Latinoamericano*, dealing with organizing activities in Peru and also with the structure that the party and the CGTP were taking. Equally important is their discussion of Mariátegui's analysis of the class struggle in Peru. There is nothing novel about their review of the early years, though their economic characterization of Peru is suggestive. Toward the end of their essay they tend to downgrade Mariátegui's nationalism at the expense of stressing his internationalism. That is slightly rectified by the article of V. Kuteishchikova, "The Role of José Carlos Mariátegui in the Development of Peruvian National Culture," *Revue d'Histoire de la Civilization Mondiale*, 6 (1960). This is a very bland recopilation of commonplaces. Professor Von Manfred Kossok's, "José Carlos Mariátegui und die Entwicklung des Marxistischen Denkens in Perú," *Wissenschaftliche*

238 BIBLIOGRAPHICAL ESSAY

Zeitschrift der Karl-Marx Universitat Leipzig, 12 (1963), is a
superior work, not as original as Semionov's and Shulgovski's but
written from a solid scholarly standpoint. Moreover Kossok
brings to his essay his considerable historical knowledge of Latin
America, giving it a broader and fuller setting. The essay is available in several Spanish language sources, including an anthology published in Lima by the Empresa Editora Amauta. Gianni
Toti's "Mariátegui armò di una teoria il proletariado peruviano,"
Il Calendario del Popolo, 20 (1964), is less scholarly and more
activist oriented. It is not at all surprising to find that it is written from the theory of praxis perspective, and decidedly Gramscian.

At this point I am breaking the chronological order to deal
with seven citations before closing the essay with several references from Robert Paris. The first, "1968: El Amauta en varios
idiomas," *Caretas,* 371 (1968), is a brief informative reference to
works in progress to be published, on Mariátegui in Europe, the
United States and Latin America. This article points to, and
rightfully so, an awakening interest in Mariátegui of international
magnitude. The article by Antonio Melis, "Mariátegui, primer
marxista de América," *Casa de las Américas,* 8 (1968), reflects
that awakening interest. Melis gives us a very sophisticated
treatment of Mariátegui's significance, but he does not produce
any new data or suggest new interpretive directions. Melis calls
attention to the possibility of a direct Gramscian influence on
Mariátegui, without offering any new evidence for his assertion.
His is a significant contribution because of the well-ordered posing of certain questions and the suggestive implications he draws
from known sources. More original is his "Estética, crítica
literaria y política cultural en la obra de José Carlos Mariátegui,
apuntes," *Textual* (1973). Also important is his, "El debate sobre
Mariátegui—resultados y problemas," *Revista de crítica literaria
latinoamericana,* 4 (1976): 123–32. Melis, Meseguer, and Paris
figure among the most perceptive representatives of that tendency viewing Mariátegui essentially from a European standpoint.
César Lévano's " ' . . . la vida que me diste,' Anna, viuda de
Mariátegui," *Caretas,* 393 (1969), provides some significant remembrances by Mariátegui's widow of their times in Italy and
Europe. She reveals, for example, that Mariátegui met both
Gramsci and Togliatti at Livorno. Also interesting is Daniel R.

Reedy's "The Cohesive Influence of José Carlos Mariátegui on Peruvian Art and Politics," in *Artists and Writers in the Evolution of Latin America* (University, 1969), pp. 137–49, which includes comments by Ray F. Broussard, pp. 149–53.

Finally Renato Sandri has written a provocative essay entitled: "Mariátegui: via nazionale e internazionalismo nel 'terzo mundo'," *Critica Marxista* (1972). This is mostly an interpretive essay, written with considerable sophistication, and related to contemporary problems such as the theses of Andre Gunder Frank and references to the government of General Velasco Alvarado. Sandri finds Mariátegui's analysis of the Peruvian national situation and its structural connection to the international economy, highly relevant to contemporary problems and discussions.

The last seven references are all works of Robert Paris: "José Carlos Mariátegui; une bibliographie; quelques problèmes," *Annales*, 21 (1966); "José Carlos Mariátegui et le modèle du 'communisme' Inca," *Annales*, 21 (1966); Préface to *7 essais d'interprétation de la réalité péruvienne*, (Paris, 1968); "El marxismo de Mariátegui," *Aportes*, 17 (1970); "Mariátegui: un 'sorelismo' ambiguo," *Aportes*, 22 (1971); "Para una lectura de los *Siete ensayos*," *Textual* (1972); and Saggio introdutivo to *Sette saggi sulla realtá peruviana* (Torino, 1972). In the first piece, Paris comments on Rouillón's *Bio-Bibliografía*, finding numerous omissions and minor errors, and refers to translations and publication of some of Mariátegui's works devoted to revolutionary Russia and its literature in Soviet magazines of the inter-war period. Paris's first publication on Mariátegui, this brief essay already displayed his highly disciplined and scholarly style. The second article essentially interprets Mariátegui's conception of an Inca communismasanahistoricalpropositiondictatedbypoliticaland
ideological necessity. Paris therefore concludes in seeing Mariátegui's indigenista nationalist proposals as a "profession of faith," expressed by a "heretical Marxist." After reading this article one expects Mariátegui's excommunication to follow swiftly, and for him to be cast out of the temple by the High Priests of "the text." Here we have the fundamental problem with Paris's writings, his constant insistence on measuring Mariátegui's ideas according to sacred and scientific norms which are never clearly stated. There would also appear to be a contradiction between

Paris's ultra suggestive *Annales* style with its half-stated conclusions and his implied emphasis on scientific accuracy. Paris's own Marxism, in other words, is antagonistic to Mariátegui's; one is scientific, philosophic, subtly rigid, while the other is spontaneous, intuitive, and open. One can hardly deny, however, that Paris's criticism of Mariátegui's writings establish. a high standard indeed of scholarly performance.

Although in the preface to the French edition of the *Seven Essays*, he attributes originality to Haya de la Torre's indigenista formulations, suggests that Mariátegui came to his indigenismo via the APRA, and portrays Mariátegui as a "founder" of the APRA, it remains an important source because of the context he constructs for discussing Mariátegui's differences with Haya de la Torre, and later with the South American Bureau of the International.

"El marxismo de Mariátegui" deals with Paris's intellectual forte, the Italian milieu of the 1920s. His knowledge of the period, of its problems and personalities, is vast and impressive and he gives us a marvelous discussion, permeated with his usual reservations, of the philosophic sources from which Mariátegui created his own Marxist synthesis. Paris virtually ignores the influence of Barbusse, though he does more than justice to that of Sorel as evident in his, "Mariátegui: un 'sorelismo' ambiguo." The essay in the Italian edition of the *Seven essays*, and in *Textual* run in the same vein.

Index

241

246 *Index*